Health Governance in Europe

Health constitutes a core element of welfare states and a vital nerve in the trust relation between citizens and their governments. Focusing on the health sector, this book analyses the closely interwoven relationship between the European Union and its member states.

The authors explore the dynamic and multi-faceted process of denationalizing health policies and illustrate how European policies develop in a sector that still appears to be under exclusively national competence. They describe the multiple forms and paths the Europeanization process takes, driven by market integration, public health crises and politics of consumer protection. The authors also provide a detailed analysis of key topics: the pharmaceutical sector, market regulation of medical goods and devices, food safety, the blood provision and plasma industry, European politics on bioethics, and risk reduction in the field of drug abuse.

Providing a comprehensive and informed assessment of the Europeanization process in the field of health policies, this book will be of interest to students and scholars of health, European integration and policy-making.

Monika Steffen is Research Director at the Centre National de la Recherche Scientifique (CNRS) and is affiliated to the Institut d'Études Politiques de Grenoble, University Pierre Mendès-France in Grenoble, France.

Routledge/ECPR studies in European political science

Edited by Thomas Poguntke
Keele University, UK
and
Jan W. van Deth
University of Mannheim, Germany on behalf of the European Consortium for Political Research

ecpr

The Routledge/ECPR Studies in European Political Science series is published in association with the European Consortium for Political Research – the leading organization concerned with the growth and development of political science in Europe. The series presents high-quality edited volumes on topics at the leading edge of current interest in political science and related fields, with contributions from European scholars and others who have presented work at ECPR workshops or research groups.

Health Governance in Europe

Issues, challenges and theories

Edited by Monika Steffen

Routledge
Taylor & Francis Group

LONDON AND NEW YORK

First published 2005
by Routledge
2 Park Square, Milton Park, Abingdon, Oxfordshire OX14 4RN

Simultaneously published in the USA and Canada
by Routledge
711 Third Avenue, New York, NY 10017

Routledge is an imprint of the Taylor and Francis Group, an informa business

First issued in paperback 2015

Typeset in Times by Wearset Ltd, Boldon, Tyne and Wear

British Library Cataloguing in Publication Data
A catalogue record for this book is available from the British Library

Library of Congress Cataloging in Publication Data
Health governance in Europe : issues, challenges, and theories /
edited by Monika Steffen.
        p. cm.
    Includes bibliographical references and index.
  1. Medical policy–Europe.   I. Steffen, Monika.
    RA395.E85H35 2005
    362.1′094–dc22

ISBN 978-0-415-36452-2 (hbk)
ISBN 978-1-138-97588-0 (pbk)

Contents

Tables

Contributors

Christa Altenstetter is Professor of Political Science in the PhD Program in Political Science at the Graduate Center and Queens College of the City University of New York, and Visiting Professor at the Institute of Health Economics and Health Care Management at the GSF – National Research Center for Environment and Health, Neuherberg, Germany. She has published extensively on the German healthcare system and the impact of European integration on the healthcare system in member states. Recently, she co-authored (with R. Busse) 'Health Care Reform in Germany: Patchwork Change within Established Governance Structures', *Journal of Health Politics, Policy and Law*, 2003. CAltenstetter@gc.cuny.edu

Henri Bergeron, who has a PhD in Sociology, is a Research Fellow at the French National Centre for Scientific Research (CNRS). He has been seconded for five years to the European Monitoring Centre for Drugs and Drug Addiction as Scientific Coordinator of a programme for monitoring and analysing drug policies in Europe and contributing to the evaluation of the EU Action Plan on Drugs. He has published, *inter alia*, *L'État et la toxicomanie. Histoire d'une singularité française* (PUF, Paris, 1999) and 'When describing is explaining', in R. Boudon, M. Cherkaoui and P. Demeulenaere (eds) *The European Tradition of Qualitative Research* (Sage, London, 2003). Henri.Bergeron@emcdda.eu.int

Christophe Clergeau, formerly a member of the French Agriculture Minister's advisory team, is currently working on the final stages of his PhD thesis, 'Changes in Public Policies on Food Safety in France and the European Union', under the joint supervision of the École Nationale Supérieure d'Agronomie de Rennes, also known as 'Agrocampus Rennes', and the Institut d'Études Politiques of Paris. His main fields of research interest are food policies and the Europeanization of public policies, with a particular focus on risk governance. christophe@clergeau.net

Anne-Maree Farrell is currently a lecturer at the Law School, University of Manchester, United Kingdom. Her research interests broadly cover law, science and public policy-making with a particular focus on risk management, regulatory policies, and the role of scientific expertise. She recently obtained her PhD, which involved a comparative study of public policy-making arising out of HIV contamination of the blood supply in France, the United Kingdom and Ireland. amfarrell@ manchester.ac.uk

François D. Lafond is Deputy Director of the London-based Policy Network, an international think tank, and Associate Professor at the Institut d'Études Politiques of Paris. Previously, he was Deputy Secretary-General of the Research and Policy Unit at 'Notre Europe' in Paris (1999–2003). He has conducted comparative research on biomedical ethics in Europe at the European University Institute (EUI) in Florence, where he was a research associate at the Robert Schuman Centre from 1995 to 1999. He has published several articles and book chapters in this particular area of risk regulation. flafond@policy-network.net

Wolfram Lamping is Assistant Professor at the Centre for Social and Public Policy, Institute for Political Science, University of Hanover, Germany. He lectures, *inter alia*, in governance and public policy, especially social policy, from a national, comparative and European perspective. His main research interests are welfare state reform in European countries and the impact of European integration on national welfare states. He is co-editor of *Demokratien in Europa. Der Einfluss der europäischen Integration auf Institutionenwandel und neue Konturen des demokratischen Verfassungsstaates* (Leske and Budrich, Opladen, 2003). lamping@ipw.uni-hannover.de

Juhani Lehto is Professor of Social and Health Policy and Director of the Social and Health Policy Unit in the Department of Public Health, Tampere University, Finland. He has written, from an international comparative perspective, on healthcare and social care systems and their reform, in particular alcohol and drug policies, and national prevention and health promotion programmes. He is Scientific Director of the Health Services research programme of the Academy of Finland. juhani.lehto@uta.fi

Elias Mossialos is Brian Abel-Smith Professor of Health Policy in the Department of Social Policy, London School of Economics and Political Science. His research interests are in health policy relating to healthcare systems. Currently, his particular focus is comparative health policy, addressing questions related to funding healthcare, pharmaceutical policies and private health insurance. His most recent books include *Funding Health Care: Options for Europe* (Open University Press, Buckingham, 2002); *EU Law and the Social Character of Health Care*

Systems (Peter Lang, 2002); and (as editor, with M. Mrazek and T. Walley) *Regulating Pharmaceuticals in Europe: Striving for Efficiency, Quality and Equity* (European Observatory on Health Care Systems, Open University Press, Buckingham, 2004). E.A.Mossialos@lse.ac.uk

Govin Permanand is a Research Officer in health and pharmaceutical policy at LSE Health and Social Care, a research centre at the London School of Economics and Political Science. He is employed on projects for the World Health Organization and the European Commission, and is a part-time lecturer in international relations. Current research interests include theories of European integration and policy-making, and the impacts of globalization on healthcare issues. His most recent publication is 'The Politics of the EU Pharmaceutical Industry', co-authored with Christa Altensetter, in E. Mossialos, M. Mrazek and T. Walley (eds) *Regulating Pharmaceuticals in Europe: Striving for Efficiency, Quality and Equity* (European Observatory on Health Care Systems, Open University Press, Buckingham, 2004). g.permanand@lse.ac.uk

Monika Steffen is Research Director at the Centre National de la Recherche Scientifique (CNRS) and is affiliated to the Institut d'Études Politiques de Grenoble, University Pierre Mendès-France in Grenoble, France. She has specialized in health policy and the methodology of comparative policy analysis, and has published on the medical profession, the organization of medical services, AIDS policies in France and in Europe, and the 'contaminated blood scandal'. She also contributed to the *Dictionnaire de la Pensée Médicale* (Presses Universitaires de France, Paris, 2003). Her most recent article is 'AIDS and health-policy responses in European welfare states', *Journal of European Social Policy* 14 (2): 159–175. Monika.Steffen@upmf-grenoble.fr

Series editor's foreword

Since health is a fundamental and vital aspect of human life, the provision of healthcare and health policies are among the most important issues in every society. Hence, many countries have developed extensive programmes offering medical treatment on the one hand and measures to reduce to risk of sickness and disability on the other. Most of these programmes came into being within specific national frameworks and are still characterized by these national legacies. Especially in Europe, the development of a common market increasingly puts these national programmes under pressure. Besides, healthcare and health policies themselves are changing. The concentration of pharmaceutical industries, the rapid development of biomedical research (including work on embryonic stem cells, genetic selection and cloning) and the threats presented by AIDS and 'mad cow disease' are only a few factors to be mentioned. Health and healthcare are changing, and so health policies are changing too.

The contributions to this volume all deal with changes in the wide and diffuse policy domains related to health in Europe. At least since the appearance of 'mad cow disease' in 1996, it has been clear that health policies cannot be restricted to illness and medication: food safety and agricultural policies are highly relevant too. Similar arguments can be presented for drug policies or attempts to regulate the pharmaceutical sector. Yet the goal of this volume is much more ambitious than presenting an overview of the nature and scope of very different health-related policies in several countries. The authors all start from the presumption that health policies are increasingly influenced by decision-making processes in a European context. In spite of the absence of clear legal competences in this area especially the European Union initiated a number of interventions and proposals aiming at more coherence among the various national policies and at improvements in the protection of citizens.

Before changes in various health-related policies are discussed, Monika Steffen, Wolfram Lamping and Juhani Lehto offer an overview of the main aspects of these policies in their introduction to this volume. Furthermore, they present a synopsis of the ways a 'Europeanization' of health policies can be approached. The discussions on this last topic are continued by Wolfram Lamping in his extensive study of the rise of health policies in Europe and the crucial roles of the Commission and the European Court of Justice in this transformation (Chapter 1). Govin Permanand and Elias Mossialos demonstrate that a single pharmaceutical market is still precluded, mainly for political reasons (Chapter 2), while Christa Altenstetter examines the much less studied developments in the medical device sector in Europe (Chapter 3). The next three contributions focus on the clashes between free-market issues and (potentially) high risks for human health. Christophe Clergeau demonstrates the existence of close relationships between economic, food and health policies that have become particularly evident since the 'mad cow' crisis (Chapter 4). A rare example of direct intervention at the European level is presented by Anne-Maree Farrell in her study of the European Union-wide regulatory regime of blood and blood products (Chapter 5). Dealing with a very different area, François D. Lafond examines value conflicts and their consequences in the field of bioethics (Chapter 6). In the last contribution, Henri Bergeron discusses the ways increased medicalization has contributed to considerable changes in the field of drug policies in Europe (Chapter 7). Finally, Wolfram Lamping and Monika Steffen return to the central question of this volume – how does European integration affect policies that are exclusively placed under national competence? – in their extensive conclusion to the volume.

This book offers much more than a greatly needed overview of health policies in various countries and the ways they are affected by ongoing European integration. It shows that neither the absence of an unambiguous legal basis at the European level nor strong national traditions and interests have prevented the development of European health policies in specific areas. The differences between these policies are, however, immense. In this contribution to this volume, Wolfram Lamping nicely brings this to the point in his observation that 'European health policy integration is a process of path-dependency without anybody knowing the path'. The information presented in this volume certainly improves this situation. We still do not know exactly what the various 'paths' look like, but with this volume we have a unique collection of case studies available, each revealing the rapidly growing Europeanization of health policies.

Jan W. van Deth, *Series Editor*
Mannheim, July 2004

Preface

Like most publications on a new subject and unexplored issues, this book is the result of a collective enterprise. It benefited from fruitful collaboration between individuals and support from institutions, and drew on several research networks that specialize in comparative health policies, welfare state developments and European social policies. The decisive event in this process, leading from stimulating intellectual questioning to the book project itself and, finally, the actual job of writing and coordinating it, was the workshop 'Health Governance in Europe: Europeanization and New Challenges in Health Policies', organized by Juhani Lehto and myself at the Joint Sessions of the European Consortium of Political Research (ECPR) in April 2001 in Grenoble, France.

The long history of the book began by chance at the European University Institute (EUI) in Florence in 1999, at the Health Policy Seminar[1] where I met Juhani Lehto for the first time. We had an inspiring discussion on the role of 'Europe' in changing health policies, especially with regard to how the European Union and its politics, focused on the free market and public health issues, might relate to national health policies and reforms. These questions seemed so intriguing and sufficiently challenging to us that we decided to plan an ECPR workshop on the subject. An opportunity for initial collective discussion was provided in August 2000 at the congress of the International Political Science Association (IPSA) in Quebec, Canada. The topic was scheduled as part of the session that I convened for the Research Committee 25, 'Comparative Health Policies',[2] in which Juhani Lehto presented a first paper outlining the main Problems of the subject.

The decision to work towards the publication of a book was taken following the ECPR workshop in Grenoble, which proved to be a highly interesting and productive intellectual gathering. Attended by nearly twenty participants, the workshop involved contributions on a wide range of subjects which could be divided into two equal parts: half of them focused directly on European levels and competences in various health policy fields, while the other half concentrated on healthcare policies at national level and on the changes resulting from growing European pressure for reform and cost containment. We consequently designed a project for two possible publications, of which this book constitutes the first volume. The realization of the project comprised a number of stages. Several authors, especially those interested in European regulatory systems, participated in the inter-congress meeting of the IPSA Research Committee 25 in June 2002 in Paris,[3] which provided a platform for the discussion of manuscripts on ongoing research. In early 2003 two new authors were recruited to cover important issues. The aim was to provide a more informed assessment of the Europeanization process in the field of health policies.

I wish to acknowledge the contribution of two colleagues. The first is Juhani Lehto, whose collaboration was instrumental in getting the project off the ground. Although changed circumstances and heavy new responsibilities did not allow him to continue with what started off as a common project, this book would not have existed today without that initial support. I wish to thank him sincerely for his early engagement and lasting encouragement. The second is Wolfram Lamping, who was extremely helpful in the final stage when it came to drawing conclusions from the many different case studies and policy processes analysed in this book. Both of them offered invaluable support, for which I am profoundly grateful.

Sincere thanks too to my home institution, the Institut d'Études Politiques de Grenoble (IEPG), whose Scientific Committee generously agreed to support the book financially. The IEPG grant enabled us to cover the costs of translating those pieces written in French and of editing the others, a necessary task since few of the authors were writing in their mother tongue. This difficult job was entrusted to Liz Carey-Libbrecht, whom I would like to thank for her efficiency and dedication.

I also wish to express my gratitude to Jan W. van Deth, the Series Editor, for his patience and advice, and particularly for the anonymous reviews, which provided extremely valuable comments. Last but not least, special thanks to all the authors for their collaboration and for agreeing to rewrite and revise their manuscripts, some of them several times, as the subject progressed and the book took on its final shape.

Monika Steffen

Notes

1 Organized within the framework of the European Forum 'Recasting the European Welfare State' conducted by Professors Maurizio Ferrera, Milano University, and Martin Rhodes, Robert Schuman Center, EUI.
2 Session 'Globalisation and European Integration: What Impact on the Social Model of Medical Care?', IPSA Congress, 1–6 August 2000.
3 'Regulation of Health Care Industries and Patient Care', Paris, 20–22 June 2002. My special thanks to the Maison des Sciences de l'Homme and Hinnerk Bruhns, member of its Scientific Directorate, who kindly agreed to host the meeting and offered the excellent working environment.

Abbreviations

AFSSAPS	Agence Française de Sécurité Sanitaire et Produits de Santé (French Agency for Health and Product Safety)
AIDS	Acquired Immunodeficiency Syndrome
AIMD	active implantable medical device
AIMDD	Active Implantable Medical Devices Directive
BEUC	European Consumers' Organizations (Bureau Européen des Unions de Consommateurs)
BfArM	Bundesinstitut für Arzneimittel and Medizinprodukte (Federal Institute for Drugs and Medical Devices)
BIOMED	Biomedical and Health Research Programme
BSE	bovine spongiform encephalopathy (known in humans as variant Creutzfeldt–Jakob disease, or commonly referred to as 'mad cow disease')
CA	competent authority
CAHBI	Ad Hoc Committee of Experts on the Progress of Biomedical Science
CAHGE	Ad Hoc Committee of Experts on Genetic Engineering
CAP	Common Agricultural Policy
CDBI	Steering Committee on Bioethics
CEC	Commission of the European Communities
CECG	Consumers in the European Community Group
CECOS	Centres d'étude et de conservation des œufs et du sperme humains (Centres for the Study and Conservation of Human Embryos and Sperm)
CELAD	Comité Européen de Lutte Anti-drogue (European Committee to Combat Drugs)
CE mark	Conformité Européenne (i.e. conformity with EU regulations or directives)
CEN	Comité Européen de Normalisation (European Standardization Committee)
CEN/TC	Comité Européen de Normalisation/Technical Committee
CEU	Council of the European Union
CFSP	Common Foreign and Security Policy

CJEC	Court of Justice of the European Communities
CNRS	Centre National de la Recherche Scientifique
COREPER	Committee of Permanent Representatives
CPMP	Committee for Proprietary Medicinal Products
CTS	common technical specification
DG	Directorate-General
DNA	deoxyribonucleic acid
EAPPI	European Association of the Plasma Products Industry
EBA	European Blood Alliance
EC law	European Community law
ECJ	European Court of Justice
ECPR	European Consortium of Political Research
EES	European Employment Strategy
EFPIA	European Federation of Pharmaceutical Industries and Associations
EFSA	European Food Safety Authority
EFTA	European Free Trade Area
EGA	European Generics Association
EGE	European Group on Ethics in science and new technologies
EHC	European Haemophilia Consortium
EMCDDA	European Monitoring Centre for Drugs and Drug Addiction
EMEA	European Agency for the Evaluation of Medicinal Products
EMU	Economic and Monetary Union
EN	European Standard
ENVI	Committee for the Environment, Public Health and Consumer Protection
EP	European Parliament
EPC	European Patent Convention
EPFA	European Public Fractionation Association
ESLA	Ethical, Social and Legal Aspects of human genome analysis working group
ESLI	Ethical, Social and Legal Implications
EU	European Union
EUCOMED	European Confederation of Medical Devices Associations
EUDAMED	European Union Database for Medical Devices
EUI	European University Institute
FDA	Food and Drug Administration
GAEIB	Group of Advisors on the Ethical Implications of Biotechnology (1991–1997)
GDP	gross domestic product
GHTF	Global Health Task Force; Global Harmonization Task Force

GMMO	Genetically Modified Micro-Organism
GMO	Genetically Modified Organism
HACCP	Hazard Analysis Critical Control Points
HDG	Horizontal Drug Group
HEF	Human Embryo and Fetus working group
HER	Human Embryo Research working group
HIMA	Health Industry Manufacturers Association
HIV	Human Immunodeficiency Virus
HTA	healthcare technology assessment
HTLV	human T-cell lymphotrophic virus
IEC	International Electrical Committee
IEPG	Institut d'Études Politiques de Grenoble
IFBDO	International Federation of Blood Donor Organizations
IPSA	International Political Science Association
ISO	International Organization for Standardization
IVDD	In Vitro Diagnostic Directive
JHA	Justice and Home Affairs
LSE	London School of Economics and Political Science
MDA	Medical Device Agency [since 2002 merged with MHRA]
MDD	Medical Device Directive
MDEG	Medical Device Expert Group
MEP	Member of the European Parliament
MHRA	Medicines and Healthcare Product Regulatory Agency
NB	notified body
NGO	non-governmental organization
NHS	National Health Service
OECD	Organization for Economic Cooperation and Development
OJ/OJEC	*Official Journal of the European Communities*
OMC	open method of coordination
PCB	polychlorinated biphenyl
PPTA	Plasma Protein Therapeutics Association
PVC	polyvinyl chloride
R&D	research and development
SCF	Scientific Committee for Food
SEA	Single European Act
SEM	single European market
SHI	statutory health insurance
SOP	standard operating procedure
SPC	Supplementary Protection Certificate
StCF	Standing Committee on Foodstuffs
StVC	Standing Veterinary Committee
SVC	Scientific Veterinary Committee
TEC	Consolidated Version of the Treaty Establishing the European Community
TSE	transmissible spongiform encephalopathy

UNESCO	United Nations Educational, Scientific and Cultural Organization
WHO	World Health Organization
WTO	World Trade Organization

Introduction

The Europeanization of health policies

Monika Steffen, Wolfram Lamping and Juhani Lehto

Health policy, citizens and nation-states

For centuries, health policy and nation-states have been closely inter-linked. Very early on, mercantile states discovered the close relationship between their populations' health and the effectiveness and productivity of their economies (Rosen 1969). In many countries, health policy was a specific state-building or state-stabilizing resource, particularly in the context of industrialization and war. It has also been and still is an essential part of domestic politics regarding public security and internal social stability. Significantly, the development of modern healthcare and public health have formed a core element of the welfare state, which developed as an essential part of the nation-state (Therborn 1995). Health policy has therefore been a central concern of national politics since the very beginnings of national welfare statehood.

In European democracies, health policy has been a major instrument for shaping societies, not only increasing their productive capacity and economies, but also reducing individual risks and relieving people of existential fears: 'The health of the people is really the foundation upon which all their happiness and their powers as a state depend.'[1] Healthy populations are not only economically more productive, but also socially more cohesive. To ensure access to healthcare for people with little or no income was and still is a major confidence-building measure in OECD (Organization for Economic Cooperation and Development) countries. Health policy matters, because 'sickness' is different from other social risks. This may sound trite, but it is an important point: health is a valuable good for modern 'Homo hygienicus' (Labisch 1992). Not surprisingly, adequate healthcare, effective medical treatment and institutional protection against illness rank high on people's list of priorities. The individual wish to be and remain healthy comes first for the majority of citizens. Healthcare has thus been promoted to a fundamental human right and politically legitimized as such.[2] In democracies, and especially in welfare states, people expect their governments and public authorities to protect them against illness and disease, to guarantee safe and healthy food and environ-mental conditions, to reflect these expectations in national policies, and to be politically responsible for their achievement. Health policy touches a vital nerve in societies. If governments fail in this field, political trust and confidence are likely to be severely undermined. The French Socialists' experience of being voted out of power consequent to the 'contaminated blood' scandal clearly illustrates the point.[3] Healthcare has a considerable social-psychological dimension when it comes to establishing bonds of trust between citizens and states and maintaining strong state–society relations. Governments therefore feel particularly responsible for the medical care of 'their' patients, and are averse to 'Brussels' intervening in this privileged relationship between the nation-state and its citizens.

Healthcare and attitudes to medicine, illness and treatment have a strong cultural bias. They are deeply embedded in the respective societies and form part of nations' 'cultural heritage' (Payer 1988). Institutional infrastructures, actor networks and sectoral interests also result from long national histories, which makes convergent reform attempts a particularly difficult undertaking. European opinion polls attest to people's emotional attachment to their national health systems. In contrast to a large number of policy issues ranging from foreign relations to immigration and from unemployment to fishing, which have constantly received the support of the large majority of European Union (EU) citizens as a legitimate matter of European concern, and in which Europeans accept joint EU decision-making, policies in the fields of health and social security elicit a very dif-ferent response. Here a large majority accepts only policies and decisions made by their national governments.[4] The question is: how does and will the European Union deal with the politically tricky and technically complex health policy sector?

Health policy and European integration

European integration is necessarily challenging, if not incrementally abol-ishing, the traditionally established congruence of national citizenship and redistribution, on the one hand, and the exclusive socio-political compe-tences of national governments to shape state–economy–citizen relation-ships, on the other. With it, a borderless European market and social space is emerging. However, any step towards European social and health policy integration is a complex and conflict-loaded venture impacting on politically sensitive and traditionally national core domains with deep-rooted institutional configurations. Health systems have grown incremen-tally and therefore are unique institutional entities, each with a specific role distribution between the state, the medical professions and the various socio-economic partners, with specific internal logics, purchaser–provider relationships, financing and remuneration systems, and well-entrenched influential interest groups. Therefore, health systems in the EU member states differ substantially in their organization, regulation and financing, in the way they deliver services and mobilize and allocate resources, and, finally, in the role they play in the 'construction plan' of welfare states. Furthermore, the level of health expenditure varies considerably among EU countries, both per capita and as a percentage of Gross Domestic Product (GDP). European health systems thus differ markedly with regard to equity and efficiency. Unsurprisingly, there is no such thing as a European healthcare system, and as long as decisions on financing, organization and service delivery are taken at national level, there is little chance of one existing.

It would nevertheless be a mistake to conclude that the European integration process excludes the health policy sector. The authors of this book demonstrate two major findings. First, the legal absence of direct and substantial EU health policy competences does not mean that the Union's impact on member states' health systems and policies is negligible. Second, the 'Europeanization' of health policy is an ambivalent and extremely complex phenomenon operating on various levels, in different forms and with diverse effects. Different types of pressure result from the integration process and have varied impacts on national 'health care states' (Moran 1999). The latter form part of a scenario where health policy can no longer be discussed exclusively in terms of national autonomy and sovereignty. This book analyses the closely interwoven relationships between the EU and member state levels, from which a new European health policy regime has already emerged.

What are Europe and Europeanization?

Europe and consequently Europeanization have different meanings. In geographic terms, 'Europe' usually means the territory, including the islands, between the Atlantic Ocean and the Ural Mountains. In historical and cultural terms it is generally defined through the common inheritance from the Hellenic and Roman cultures, mediated through the Christian religion in its three major forms of institutionalization: the Orthodox, the Catholic and the Protestant Churches. In political terms, 'Europe' has more than one meaning. It may refer to the European Union, either with its fifteen well-established member states or in its enlarged version of twenty-five. It may refer to Western Europe, which also includes Norway and Switzerland, or to Western Europe plus Central Europe, which means the European Union plus potential future accession countries, or to Western Europe, Central Europe and Eastern Europe, including an undefined 'European' part of Russia. A number of international organizations apply even broader definitions. The World Health Organization (WHO) includes not only all the Asian countries of the former Soviet Union but also Israel in its 'European Region'. In economic terms, 'Europe' is perceived as one of the world's three rich competitors, the others being the

United States and Japan. In this perception, Europe normally refers to the European Union or the European Union plus a group of 'rich' countries around it.

This book concentrates mainly on processes within the European Union and between the Union and its member states. However, because of its close links with the few West European countries still outside the Union, most of the statements and conclusions are also valid for those countries. Similarly, with the growing impact of EU legislation and policies in the Central and Eastern European countries, many of the questions and issues also apply to them as they formally become members of the Union. 'Europe' covers a stretchable social and political reality, which inevitably reflects on an equally expandable concept of Europeanization. This is well illustrated by the contrast between the chapters focusing on single market regulations – for example, for pharmaceutical products or medical devices – on the one hand, and those on public health regulations – for instance, for food safety, blood safety or in respect of bioethics – on the other. The latter field in particular addresses issues that are clearly linked to the Europe of common cultural traditions and values, where 'Europe' is perceived not only through the European Union but also through the Council of Europe's striving to represent a larger European community of human rights and democratic values.

It is against this background that the concept of Europeanization, which has become an 'extremely fashionable term in the social science literature on Europe' (Olsen 2003: 334), has developed 'many faces' (Olsen 2002). There are various potential meanings of what can be described and analysed with such an open concept. It can be used to explain a 'confusing range of heterogeneous empirical phenomena and processes of change that may somehow have something to do with European integration and the penetration of the European dimension in national arenas of politics and policies' (Radaelli 2000: 3). The term 'Europeanization', inherently endangered by a tendency of 'conceptual stretching' (Sartori 1970) and ambiguity, is used in different ways to describe a variety of phenomena and processes of change. This is partly due to the fact that researchers are still not equipped to define the relatively new concept; consensus has yet to be achieved on the question of what 'Europeanization' is and what it is not, where it comes from and how it can best be grasped analytically. Consequently, the authors of this book do not try to propose a common definition of the processes of Europeanization. Rather, each of the chapters sheds light on the different facets of this process and on the ways it creeps into health policy. They illustrate and discuss at least five possible perspectives of Europeanization, all implying different modes, mechanisms and driving forces of change.

One – traditional – perspective is to conceptualize Europeanization as institution-building at supranational level and to focus on European Union-level policy-making, via formal institutions, established networks, guiding norms and shared ideas, and on its direct output in terms of collectively binding European policies. Health policy seems to be concerned very little by this perspective, if at all, since member state governments still perceive it as a genuinely national policy field and a state-consolidating resource.[5] This book shows that health policy has incrementally become a major EU policy field, and probably one of the most challenging concerns of future European activity. In fact – and this may explain the bias in perceptions – European health policy remains a divided policy field, because policy integration is marked by a traditional cleavage between *public health* (management of collective health risks) on the one hand and *healthcare* (treatment of individual illness) on the other. The chapters on medical devices (Altenstetter, Chapter 3), blood policy (Farrell, Chapter 5), food safety (Clergeau, Chapter 4), bioethics (Lafond, Chapter 6) and the pharmaceutical sector (Permanand and Mossialos, Chapter 2) document the ongoing process of establishing and extending public health as a genuine EU policy field, and of institutionalizing a robust EU mandate in this area. Though to a much lesser extent, this is also observed for the politically sensitive healthcare sector, in which a sustainable process of integration via case law can be witnessed. The European Court of Justice (ECJ), through its rulings, has established a set of new European social rights (see Lamping, Chapter 1).

This classical conceptualization of Europeanization as EU-level polity- and institution-building has been challenged by a complete change of perspective in which European integration impacts on all sectors and dimensions of domestic politics, polities and public policies. In this perspective (see Cowles, Caporaso and Risse 2001), Europeanization is conceptualized as an adaptive process at national level. This research agenda is best captured by the broad definition of Hix and Goetz (2000: 27), who define Europeanization as 'a process of change in national institutional and policy practices that can be attributed to European integration'. The perspective treats European-level developments 'as the explanatory factors, and changes in the domestic systems of governance as the dependent variable' (Olsen 2003: 343). This approach analyses changes that can be attributed to EU membership and European integration impacts, and that affect member states internally: their political systems, political routines, political parties and sectoral policies in fields that have become subject to European attention, such as poverty, equality and, last but not least, public health and healthcare. While some authors, like Börzel (1999), focus on the direct institutional effects of European integration on member states, others, like Radaelli (2003), draw attention to the more indirect manners in which 'Europe' affects domestic politics and policies, sometimes 'to the degree that EC political and economic dynamics become part of the organizational logic of national politics and policymaking' (Ladrech 1994: 69). The variable pressure to adapt to 'Europe', and with it varying institutional and strategic adjustments, has recently been discussed in terms of institutional 'fit' or 'misfit' – that is, the compatibility or incompatibility of national and European policies and institutional set-ups. Whatever one's perspective, the final research challenge is to explain the variations in European impacts, and the varying responses or non-responses of national actors and institutions to the European pressures. The health sector seems particularly fertile for this research question, as Lamping argues in his chapter and as the chapters by Altenstetter and Clergeau suggest when it comes to actually implementing EU regulatory policies.

From a third – that is, a political – perspective, Europeanization is a multi-causal phenomenon. It is the result of a complex and dynamic intertwining of top-down and bottom-up processes in a given policy area: EU-level activities and initiatives strongly affect domestic policies and politics (top down), while national actors interpret these 'impulses' and translate them into domestic political games (bottom up). At the same time, they tend to shift domestic issues to the supranational level and actively seek to influence these processes at the European level according to their economic interests and policy traditions (Héritier 1997; Putnam 1988). The process resembles a cycle rather than any linearity. This understanding of 'Europeanization' is restricted neither to the study of European institutions, institution-building and policies in the sense of EU output or the European Union as a source of constraints on member states, nor to the direct domestic impact of EU politics and policies in the sense of implementation, change of domestic policies, and intended or unintended policy outcomes. It analyses the various and confusing feedback loops, interactions, games and specific dynamics linking the two levels. In this perspective, Europeanization is a mutual process of influencing, negotiating and adjusting at both EU and member state level. The process is most obvious in the wake of public health catastrophes like AIDS (Steffen 2001, 2004): the epidemic was a catalyst for both an intensification of cross-national health management and cooperation, and the organization of public health capacities at EU level. In this book the chapters on the regulation of medical devices (Altenstetter) and the Europeanization of risk-reduction policies in the field of drug abuse policy (Bergeron) or blood safety policy (Farrell) exemplify these reciprocal processes of policy development, norm diffusion and policy adoption and reform, which at the end of the cycle may result in policy and organizational convergence.

A fourth perspective of Europeanization emerges as a soft variant, a transfer of ideas and of the way problems are perceived rather than European rules leading directly to structural or policy change at domestic level. European values, integration requirements and policy paradigms diffuse into national policy debates and arenas, shaping or influencing national policy formulation and strategic choices from within. This triggers a process of institutional and 'social learning' (Checkel 2001) and normative re-orientation. Most prominent examples are the Economic and Monetary

Union (EMU), the single European market (SEM) and the Stability and Growth Pact. Several chapters of this book demonstrate such processes of European 'policy-framing' (Liebert 2002: 6–7) in the health policy sector. The concept is understood as both the creation of shared frames of reference by framing common sets of beliefs and ideas, and the inducement of actors in member states to frame domestic structures and activities in ways that incorporate a European dimension. Both can have a major impact on domestic policy discourses (Schmidt 2000) in which national actors 'communicate Europe', and on the content of domestic politics in a growing number of policy issues. In the health sector the process is illustrated by 'cost containment', 'risk reduction' or 'equal access'. Europeanization, in this respect, is a process of convergence towards shared policy frameworks and beliefs. The effect is dependent on the intellectual influence of 'epistemic communities' (Haas 1992). In the health policy area such epistemic communities have been considerably reinforced through the establishment of stabilized networks of issue-interested groups and the direct institutionalization of problem-solving capacities, mainly through the creation of European agencies and 'observatories', comprehensive databases and comparative information systems, diffusion of best practice and incremental extension of regulatory competences. They encompass individual health policy experts, representatives of European and national research units, selected officials from member states and, most important in this sector, specific interest groups and non-governmental organizations (NGOs) such as patients' organizations. These groups work in close collaboration with the Commission and have often been strategically used by it to back its policy proposals and to lend them 'expertocratic' legitimacy. Although still an underestimated point of reference in national health policy, European integration and the European Union as an actor increasingly provide, as Knill and Lehmkuhl (2002: 263) sum up, 'a "focal point" for domestic developments, offering potential solutions or ideas to deal with domestic problems'. In this volume the chapters by Bergeron, Farrell, Clergeau, Lafond and Lamping each highlight different aspects of this phenomenon of 'incorporating' a European dimension into national health politics and policies.

The fifth perspective on Europeanization documented in this book is that of changing domestic opportunity structures. EU regulatory policy as well as the perceived or real European integration requirements affect the domestic distribution of power and resources and redefine the domestic rules of the game: new constellations of actors emerge while traditional veto players are weakened; new norms and challenges are formulated; and new opportunities open up for pushing previously marginal policies forward. European integration provides national actors – both governmental representatives and interest groups – with the opportunity to 'play the European card by shifting issues to the European level' (Vink 2003: 66) and/or to build up new strategic domestic and transnational coalitions.

In this case, domestic actors no longer rely exclusively on their national networks and resources, but participate in European policies and politics which may have major repercussions on domestic challenges. They use not only their national importance to gain European influence, but also their European capacities to reinforce their position in the national policy arena. Fairly regularly, European integration opens up a window of opportunity by using the European Union as a scapegoat for unpopular domestic reforms for which 'Brussels' can be blamed. The chapter by Permanand and Mossialos and the one by Lamping provide interesting empirical evidence for this effect of Europeanization in the health policy sector.

This book does not conceptualize convergence and Europeanization as synonyms. Yet policy convergence or the harmonization of regimes may often occur as the consequence of EU initiatives or European integration impacts. The challenge is to sort out those processes of policy convergence and policy harmonization that actually do have a 'European source', and to distinguish them from those policies or strategies that political actors pursue independently of European objectives. All the chapters of this book demonstrate that however one conceptualizes Europeanization, it is a complex issue that requires a precise analysis of cases, causes, causal mechanisms, and consequences responsible for and resulting in change. The chapters empirically reveal a twofold reality. First, the European influence 'is but one of several "drivers of change"' at national level, which also implies that European integration 'might matter in a rather less straightforward manner than the Europeanization literature tends to assume' (Goetz 2001: 225, 227). Second, European dynamics and impulses 'are interpreted and modified through domestic traditions, institutions, identities, and resources in ways that limit the degree of convergence and homogenisation' (Olsen 2003: 346). It is precisely these 'causal complexities' (Liebert 2002) characterizing the phenomenon of Europeanization and playing out differently in various policy areas that are addressed in this book.

What is health policy? What is Europeanized and how?

Like Europe and Europeanization, health and health policy can be understood and conceptualized in a number of different ways. Most often the term 'health policy' refers to policies that focus on the development of medical care and the organization of healthcare systems. Analyses concentrate on how people are provided with diagnosis, cure and care for disease. This part of the subject may be called *medical care policy*. In a broader context, the focus tends to be on the social security system and the regime of social protection in the case of sickness. In this frame, the question relates to how different systems of social protection cover the costs of buying medical care and temporarily remaining out of the labour market during a period of sickness. This may be called *social security policy covering sickness*.

Health policies may also be viewed from the perspective of health determinants such as work and living conditions, environment, traffic safety, nutrition, smoking and physical exercise, in addition to health education, vaccinations and screenings. Such analyses concentrate on prevention policies and health promotion. The term 'public health' refers in general to policies related to these foci of health policy developing at the margins or even outside the institutional borders of the healthcare sector. Epidemiological surveillance and expertise systems form part of this particular type of 'public' health policies. In some contexts the term 'public health', or the more recent concept 'health system', introduced and diffused by the WHO, is used for all the policies and institutions with health as their primary and main goal (WHO 2000). Both terms refer to a combination of healthcare and promotion, the sickness branch of social security, and prevention. Following the new WHO terminology, this global public health approach could be called *health system policy.*

The realm of health is also a significant arena for private enterprise, economic growth, employment and profit as well as industrial and commercial competition between the European Union, the United States and Japan. The pharmaceutical and the medical devices industries as well as the agrifood and other assumedly health consumer-product industries all seek to optimize their market and economic interests, particularly via the rapidly growing biotechnology industries. In this respect they are comparable to other public- or private-sector services, such as telecommunications or energy, and to more traditional economic sectors like the chemical or car industry, where safety issues constitute a major part of the business. From the perspective of the economic interests related to this arena, health policies may also be seen as *policies creating growth potential for health-related industries.*

While 'health system policy' refers to policies *primarily* aimed at health, it may sometimes be difficult to identify the primary goal of a given policy. For instance, do governments set high taxes on tobacco in order to protect citizens' health or to collect larger tax revenue? Concerning investments in biotechnological research, it would be tricky, if not impossible, to clearly distinguish the primary motive among the goals aimed at improving health opportunities and those intended to strengthen the national pharmaceutical industry's future position in global competition in the most promising economic growth sector. Quite often, policies with other primary goals may also promote health. The typical example is education. Improvements in the level of education are known to lead to better health and health conditions, although health is not the primary goal of education policies, at least not for most of the actors in education policy processes. These examples point out that there should be an even broader meaning for 'health policy' than the already extensive concept of 'health system policy'. In addition to policies, activities and institutions that have health as their primary goal, the concept could also cover those that have an impact on health, even if it is only a secondary or tertiary goal or no goal at all of the considered policy, activity or institution. This dimension of health policy should be recognized as *policies with health impact*.

These different aspects of health policy are related to Europeanization in different ways, which compounds the existing complexity of the processes. At first glance, the treaty on which the European Union is grounded explicitly defines the regulation, organization and financing of healthcare as a national core competence (Art. 152 no. 5 TEC, where TEC is the Consolidated Version of the Treaty Establishing the European Community).[6] National health authorities therefore perceive health policy as domestic policy and health systems as national 'property' which they jealously defend, and they still have great difficulty in perceiving health policy as a matter of Union concern. Formally, they are right: there is no strong legal Union competence for it, for direct influence of the European Union on national institutions has been widely excluded from the mandate of the Union[7] (Mossialos *et al.* 2001). To date, the various European treaties still remain somewhat reticent on healthcare issues. The 'Charter of Fundamental Rights of the European Union'[8] agreed by the Union in Nice in 2000, which set out for the first time a whole range of (not yet) legally binding civil, political, economic and social rights of European citizens and persons resident in the European Union, declares in Art. 35 that 'everyone has the right of access to preventive healthcare and the right to benefit from medical treatment under the conditions established by national laws and practices'. Even though the public health article (Art. 152 TEC), like so much that has to do with European integration, is open to different interpretations, it can be argued that healthcare systems as such are not the objective of the Union. The 'Draft Treaty establishing a Constitution for Europe' of July 2003 (CONV 850/03) is still unable to clear up this health policy ambiguity. It sticks to the rhetorically tricky path of conflict avoidance and competence-sharing, while simultaneously whenever possible implementing points of reference for future Europeanization and harmonization. The application of the 'open method of coordination' (OMC) to healthcare constitutes an example. Regarding the public health article Art. III-179 of the Draft, the Union is still restricted to 'complementing national policies' and to 'encouraging cooperation between the Member States'. All in all, the Treaty restricts the mandate of the European Union, differentiating it particularly clearly from the *medical care sector* and *social security covering sickness*. Yet the chapters of this book point out that there are many indirect ways in which the Union may have a considerable impact on the evolution of health policy in the member states, including in the medical care sector.

Article 3 of the TEC raises health protection to the rank of a Community objective. It provides the Union with a policy mandate for contributing actively 'to the attainment of a high level of health protection' (cf. also Art. 95 no. 3) including, *inter alia*, specific tasks formulated especially in

Art. 152 of the TEC. The latter article commits the European Union to encouraging cooperation and fostering coordination among member states and between governments and the Community. Unsurprisingly, it was the broad and vague area of *public health* (health system policy), a cross-cutting issue, that opened the back door to member states' health policies, and incrementally put health at the forefront of the European political agenda, as illustrated by the bovine spongiform encephalopathy (BSE) crisis. It was precisely in response to new challenges and political concerns related to public health issues and risks, all of an intrinsically cross-border dimension, that the limited resources of the Community in health policy were gradually expanded in the Treaty of Amsterdam through the addition of several new provisions. In terms of Art. 152 TEC, EU actions in the public health area should contribute towards ensuring the attainment of a high level of health protection, improve health, prevent human illness and disease, eliminate sources of danger to health, and ensure that all European policies are effectively compatible with health protection. In parallel, Art. 3 TEC commits the Community to a high level of health protection across the entire range of its policies and actions (see also Art. 95 no. 3 TEC). This robust EU public health mandate is in sharp contrast with the restriction of Union competence in medical care and coverage. The fact that the European Union is committed to public health action in cooperation with the member states is to be understood as a mandate for health system policy primarily, without intervention in the organization and financing of the social security policies concerning sickness. Finally, policies creating growth potential in health-related industries are included in most EU trade and industry regulations and in its research policies.

Plan and content of the book

The main purpose of this book is to point out the multiple ways in which health policy is Europeanized, and to gain a more complete picture of what might be called European health policy. The book includes chapters from selected aspects of health policy, with seven specific analyses of the development of a European dimension in different sections of this policy sector. While politicians and health professionals still think in terms of national health policy, specialists in this policy field are fully aware that European integration has definitely begun a new chapter in the history of health policy, shifting away from exclusively national competence and post-Second World War historical continuity. Several chapters shed empirical light on this ongoing process and propose elements for its theoretical understanding.

In the first chapter, Wolfram Lamping discusses why health policy may be one of the best possible examples for demonstrating how the European Union – specifically, the Commission and the European Court of Justice – has successfully made a non-topic issue one of the Community's most important and scientifically challenging future policy fields. Lamping systematically sorts out the issues when it comes to identifying the levels and dimensions of the new politics of health policy integration: its driving forces, its political nature, and the web of European policies and politics within which member states are increasingly involved when conducting their health policies. He concludes that even though European healthcare systems still formally appear to be national, European integration has steadily reduced the policy margin member states can effectively dispose of when regulating their healthcare sector. Both the supranational and the national level are slowly but surely on the way to becoming an institutional compound of health policy.

Although the EU's scope for 'positive' initiatives remains limited, the completion of the internal market as well as the consumer protection/public health mandate of the Commission allows for important Community regulations affecting even the medical care sector. A common regulatory framework for medicinal products and medical devices has thus been set up, covering manufacturing, safety and quality surveillance, market access authorization, and the free movement of pharmaceuticals and medical equipment within the single market. It is particularly this considerable market of pharmaceuticals and medical devices, tradable goods in the true sense, that is marked by a high level of integration and centralization of competence. Against this background, questions of national implementation of and institutional compliance with European policies are highly challenging for researchers in European integration and public policy analysis alike. What happens to EU directives after they have been transposed into national law? How and to what extent will national actors adapt the 'philosophy' of European impulses and adjust their practices to it? The following two chapters directly address these questions.

In the second chapter, Govin Permanand and Elias Mossialos demonstrate the clash between the subsidiarity claims of member state governments (national authority and self-interests to set prices and reimbursement rates and to pursue economic policy), and the free movement requirements of the internal market (medicines are tradable goods). Focusing on the disparate interests of the actors involved, they provide a political view and theoretical perspective on regulatory decision-making in the multi-level and multi-dimensional EU pharmaceutical sector. On the basis of three case studies they show that, on the one hand, specific parts of the European market for pharmaceuticals are highly harmonized and – from the point of view of competences – centralized, while on the other, the European market as such is still marked by a striking imbalance and deadlock that have precluded the completion of the single pharmaceutical market to date. Any further comprehensive Europeanization of this market, which would then concern crucial aspects of medical care policy, is difficult to conceive of since, as the authors demonstrate, the necessary widespread political will is still lacking.

In the third chapter, Christa Altenstetter discusses salient aspects of European regulatory integration in the field of medical devices. She examines the evolution of EU regulatory governance in this policy field and focuses on the theoretical and practical aspects that link EU regulation to domestic implementation, adaptation and change, taking a particularly close look at the conceptualization of the 'In Vitro Diagnostic Device' Directive and its domestic implications. Altenstetter provides *both* a theoretical framework for conceptualizing domestic implementation mechanisms and understanding different outcomes (implementation trajectories, causal mechanisms, etc.) *and* precise empirical analyses of the regulation of medical devices at EU level (policies and politics, comitology, regulatory principles, etc.) – a largely under-researched field. The chapter highlights an intrinsic regulatory dilemma of technology in general: progress in life-saving and life-enhancing medical devices and in tissue and cell engineering is most often advancing faster than solutions are found and agreed upon by national regulators, the Commission and the industry. Altenstetter concludes that European and national initiatives will continue to exist, that national variations in responses (implementation and outcome) will inevitably increase after the 2004 enlargement, and that regulatory harmonization of medical devices has not lowered quality standards. On the contrary, the common requirements of performance and the evaluation system have raised the safety threshold in the European Union and beyond. This finding suggests that a market-oriented Europeanization can also contribute to consumer and patient protection.

The broadly defined public health article of the Treaty as well as the explicit, cross-cutting consumer protection provision provide the European Union with a considerable policy mandate in a wide range of policy areas. The following three chapters analyse policies in which important free-market issues coincide with potentially high risks for human health. Not surprisingly, it was mainly outbreaks of communicable diseases or severe threats to public health that induced the Commission to push cooperation among member states and – a case in point – to institutionalize the surveillance and control of serious health threats at EU level, a process in which the Commission has demonstrated considerable political leadership.

In the fourth chapter, Christophe Clergeau demonstrates the long and thorny march on which food safety has progressively become a key component of EU health and consumer protection policy. The European Union not only has adopted comprehensive food laws in which the general principles, standards and procedures of food safety regulation are defined, but has also succeeded in institutionalizing a considerable administrative and scientific apparatus at EU level. Clergeau discusses both the crisis-driven history of EU food safety policy, marked by the complex relationship between agricultural politics and health protection in Community policies, and the gradual detachment of food policy from the narrow liberal single market perspective and the incorporation of food safety into the Union's health politics and policies. Clergeau concludes that, despite such important changes, Community action in the field of food safety is still neither coherent nor sufficiently coordinated and, to a certain extent, remains limited to support for national policies. Food policy in all its facets is still subject to incidental controversy between the European Union and member states, and will remain a politically salient issue in the enlarged Union.

The fifth chapter, by Anne-Maree Farrell, focuses on the catalysts of the European Union's gradual involvement in blood policy since the 1990s, in the aftermath of the political fallout from the HIV blood contamination crisis. The author analyses the use of burden-shifting from member states to the EU level, the development of a complex, diverse and politicized European blood policy community, and the important role of scientific experts on blood-related matters in EU policy formulation. In this policy area, EU-level activity is confronted with very different national traditions regarding blood collection systems and philosophical dogma on human blood, and with different public or private modes of organization of the plasma industry. The case shows how private actors, from the industry as well as from patients' organizations, initiated policy framing and actor networking at EU level. Farrell demonstrates that the establishment of a comprehensive EU-wide regulatory framework for the collection, manufacture and supply of blood and blood products is a significant part of the Union's growing competence and influence in public health governance.

The sixth chapter, by François Lafond, discusses how both the Council of Europe and the European Union have come under pressure from their representative bodies to address various politically and culturally sensitive issues: access to artificial insemination, cloning, research on the human embryo and, most importantly, patentability of the human genome, all of which symbolize the emergence of highly conflictual political responses that need to be considered in their European dimension. Lafond demonstrates that we are witnessing a process of Europeanization of bioethics politics. Both the European Union and the Council of Europe have taken a stand on biomedical ethical issues and are loci of permanent transnational discussions, learning processes and policy diffusion, although not to the same extent. While the European Union's intervention has been marginal and reactive to date, in the absence of robust competences in this policy field, the Council of Europe has gradually become an important political actor and point of reference for political initiatives. Lafond concludes that the different cultural and normative preferences of member states hinder *binding* European legal decision-making in the fragmented and disparate field of biomedical ethics, which encompasses important research and market issues.

Policy convergence constitutes the focal point in the seventh and last main chapter, by Henri Bergeron. This chapter, which analyses the Europeanization of policies to combat drug abuse, considers one of the most crucial questions in European integration research. Why, how and to what extent do national public policies converge in the wake of European integration, even though the Union has barely any competence and little if any experience in the policy field, and even though these public policies are politically salient and extremely sensitive issues in most member states? Bergeron provides empirical evidence for both a relative convergence of national policies and, simultaneously, the gradual extension of Community activities, although there still is no comprehensive or consistent EU drug policy. He demonstrates how the European Union establishes European problem-solving capacities and provides a forum for policy discussions between professional experts, scientists, governments and public administrations from member states. This has repercussions for national perceptions of problems and strategies to solve them. It produced a Europe-wide cognitive input and comparative assessment of national performances, for the use of the member states and the Commission. The chapter analyses the functioning and role of a European monitoring centre, a body in which 'good and bad practice' are defined and from which practical policy recipes are diffused.

The concluding chapter, by Wolfram Lamping and Monika Steffen, summarizes the results of the research presented in this book and relates them to general questions raised by the Europeanization of social policy in the context of a growing Union. 'Europe of health' is progressively taking shape, even though its contours are still confusing: core areas of health policy and health regulation have inevitably become subject to an incremental, though asynchronous, process of Europeanization and institutional harmonization. Obviously underdeveloped compared to economic integration and still far from having institutionalized a comprehensive and centralized regulatory regime, the process has nonetheless been on the way for many years. Given the adverse context, with the considerable liberal grammar of the European Union, the fact that political efforts to elaborate and adopt European rules are politically impeded by an assortment of substantial obstacles – not least the legitimate self-interest of member state governments – and the political sensitivity of health policy as a national domain, the progress of health policy integration deserves admiration. Against this background, European social and health policy integration has to be conceptualized as a parallel process of deregulation and liberalization on the one hand, and re-regulation and harmonization on the other. This book provides ample evidence of this intertwined process.

Notes

1 Benjamin Disraeli, 1877, quoted by Timmins (1995: 101).
2 Cf. the official declarations on healthcare and individual access to healthcare, such as the WHO declaration, the United Nations International Convenant on

Economic, Social and Cultural Rights, the General Comment on the right to health of the UN Committee on Social and Economic Rights, or the Ottawa Charter for Health Promotion.

3 For the French case as well as a European comparison of the national politics of medical crises, see part V, 'Managing Crisis: HIV and the Blood Supply', in Bovens, 't Hart and Peters (2001: 453–489).

4 See *Eurobarometer* no. 56 and *Standard Eurobarometer* 56 (2).

5 '[U]ntil now, the politics of health care have been regarded as too delicate, too influential in national elections, and too culturally diverse for the governments of member states to allow responsibility to pass into the hands of supranational authorities' (Redwood 2003: 52).

6 Consolidated Version of the Treaty Establishing the European Community (TEC), *Official Journal of the European Communities* C 325/35.

7 With the exception of cross-border social security rules, Art. 42 TEC; and some Council regulations.

8 *Official Journal of the European Communities* 2000/C 364/01.

References

Börzel, T. A. (1999) 'Towards Convergence in Europe? Institutional Adaptation to Europeanisation in Germany and Spain', *Journal of Common Market Studies* 37: 573–596.

Bovens, M., 't Hart, P. and Peters, B. G. (2001) *Success and Failure in Public Governance: A Comparative Analysis*, Cheltenham: Edward Elgar.

Checkel, J. T. (2001) 'Why Comply? Social Learning and European Identity Change', *International Organization* 55 (3): 553–588.

Cowles, M. G., Caporaso, J. A. and Risse, Th. (eds) (2001) *Transforming Europe: Europeanization and Domestic Change*, Ithaca, N.Y.: Cornell University Press.

Goetz, K. H. (2001) 'European Integration and National Executives: A Cause in Search of an Effect', in K. H. Goetz and S. Hix (eds) *Europeanised Politics: European Integration and National Political Systems*, London: Frank Cass, pp. 211–231.

Haas, P. M. (1992) 'Introduction: Epistemic Communities and International Policy Co-ordination', *International Organization* 49 (1): 1–35.

Héritier, A. (1997) 'Market-Making Policy in Europe: Its Impact on Member State Policies. The Case of Road Haulage in Britain, the Netherlands, Germany and Italy', *European Journal of Public Policy* 4 (4): 539–555.

Hix, S. and Goetz, K. (2000) 'Introduction: European Integration and National Political Systems', *West European Politics* 23 (4): 1–26.

Knill, C. and Lehmkuhl, D. (2002) 'The National Impact of European Union Regulatory Policy: Three Europeanization Mechanisms', *European Journal of Political Research* 41 (2): 255–280.

Labisch, A. (1992) *Homo hygienicus. Gesundheit und Medizin in der Neuzeit*, Frankfurt am Main: Campus Verlag.

Ladrech, R. (1994) 'Europeanization of Domestic Politics and Institutions: The Case of France', *Journal of Common Market Studies* 32 (1): 69–88.

Liebert, U. (2002) 'Causal Complexities: Explaining Europeanisation', CEuS Working Paper 2002/1, Centre for European Studies, University of Bremen, Bremen.

Moran, M. (1999) *Governing the Health Care State: A Comparative Study of the*

United States, United Kingdom and Germany, Manchester: Manchester University Press.

Mossialos, E., McKee, M., Palm, W., Karl, B. and Marhold, F. (2001) 'The influence of the EU law on the social character of health care systems in the European Union', Report submitted to the Belgian Presidency of the European Union, Brussels.

Olsen, J. P. (2002) 'The Many Faces of Europeanization', *Journal of Common Market Studies* 40 (5): 921–952.

—— (2003) 'Europeanization', in M. Cini (ed.) *European Union Politics*, Oxford: Oxford University Press, pp. 333–348.

Payer, L. (1988) *Medicine and Culture: Varieties of Treatment in the United States, England, West Germany, and France*, New York: Penguin.

Putnam, R. (1988) 'Diplomacy and Domestic Politics: The Logic of Two-level Games', *International Organization* 42 (3): 427–460.

Radaelli, C. M. (2000) 'Whither Europeanization? Concept Stretching and Substantive Change', *European Integration Online Papers* 4 (8).

—— (2003) 'The Europeanization of Public Policy', in K. Featherstone and C. Radaelli (eds) *The Politics of Europeanization*, Oxford: Oxford University Press, pp. 3–26.

Redwood, H. (2003) 'Towards a Mid-Atlantic Model of Health Care: A European Perspective', in Norbert Klusen (ed.) *Europäischer Binnenmarkt und Wettbewerb: Zukunftsszenarien für die GKV*, Baden-Baden: Nomos, pp. 52–69.

Rosen, G. (1969) 'The Evolution of Social Medicine', in H. E. Freeman, S. Levine and L. G. Reeder (eds) *Handbook of Medical Sociology*, Englewood Cliffs, N.J.: Prentice-Hall, pp. 17–61.

Sartori, G. (1970) 'Concept Misformation in Comparative Politics', *American Political Science Review* 64: 1033–1053.

Schmidt, V. A. (2000) 'Values and Discourse in the Politics of Adjustment', in Fritz W. Scharpf and Vivien A. Schmidt (eds) *Welfare and Work*, vol. 1, Oxford: Oxford University Press, pp. 229–310.

Steffen, M. (2001) *Les États face au Sida en Europe*, Grenoble: PUG – Presses Universitaires de Grenoble.

—— (2004) 'AIDS and Health Policy Responses in European Welfare States', *Journal of European Social Policy* 14 (2): 159–175.

Therborn, G. (1995) *European Modernity and Beyond*, London: Sage.

Timmins, N. (1995) *The Five Giants: A Biography of the Welfare State*, London: Fontana Press.

Vink, M. (2003) 'What Is Europeanisation? And Other Questions on a New Research Agenda', *European Political Science* 3: 63–74.

World Health Organization (2000) *World Health Report 2000*, Geneva: WHO.

1 European integration and health policy

A peculiar relationship

Wolfram Lamping

Europe matters. But why, and how, and to what extent? The impact of European integration on member states and the way they adjust to Europe continue to raise challenging questions for researchers. At the same time, a great number of empirical studies point out the varied impact of European integration on national polities, policy-making patterns and (public) policies. However, welfare state policies somehow seem to be different and apparently marginalized in European integration politics. Except for some market-building and compatibility policies, the welfare state and especially health policy actually appear to be an *enclave* within the integration process, and consequently one of the last key realms – and one of the last retreats – of national policy competence. It may be for this reason that most of the studies available on national health policy and healthcare reform still leave out the 'European dimension', instead focusing mainly on domestic challenges.

Is health policy an appropriate example for exploring the impact of European integration, considering that member states have explicitly declared in the Treaty that the organization and delivery of health services and medical care shall remain a matter of national competence? The argument of this chapter is that it is one of the best examples possible for demonstrating how the European Union (EU) and its institutions have successfully made a non-topic one of the Community's most important future policy fields. Core areas of health systems and health regulation have inevitably become subject to an incremental and irresistible process of harmonization and Europeanization. Moreover, health policy is a challenging policy field for examining the tensions and contradictions between economic and social integration within the new EU social policy governance system. Finally, it was foreseeable that social policy core competences would become Community targets, given the strong institutional self-interests of the European Commission, keen on enhancing its scope of action, clever in inventing new justifications for initiatives, persistent when claiming the transfer of new competences to the supranational level, and able to strategically raise citizens' expectations of a somehow 'Social Europe'.

Meanwhile, it is a truism among scholars of this specialized field that European integration has begun a new chapter in the history of health and social policy. The extent of the European Union's penetration into the national health policy arena has continually increased, while certainty, calculability and the capacity to act seem to have decreased proportionally in member states. The underlying assumption of this chapter is that the new politics of European health policy integration have rather effectively and sustainably changed the institutional and political environment in which future national health politics will take place. Therefore, the first section discusses the main aspects of health policy integration, its driving forces and its political nature, and will provide a more systematic approach in order to understand the various levels and actors of the new politics of European health policy integration. The second section analyses the impact of free movement and the internal market (SEM) competition regime on national health policy and provision. The wider issues of this perspective are discussed in the third section, which identifies six major challenges confronting national health policy. The final section goes back to the initial question. It concludes that the process of Europeanizing health policy can be characterized as a discontinuous, incoherent, unsystematic and sometimes fairly accidental one. However, the creeping Europeanization and institutional harmonization of health policy has become a self-dynamic, *political* (rather than simply technocratic) process that can best be understood as an inspired muddling through.

The impact of European integration on health policy: systematizing the jigsaw puzzle

One of the publications on the Europeanization of health policies starts with an apparently surprising statement. In their book *The Impact of EU Law on Healthcare Systems*, McKee, Mossialos and Baeten (2002: 13) observe that in 'a Europe that is becoming ever more integrated, the place of healthcare in European law is increasingly unclear'. This statement is surprising for two reasons.

Beyond the Treaty: the underestimated role of EU health policy

First, health policy is generally not considered as a policy area of the EU, basically because there is no legal Union competence for it. Even though the Treaty of 1957 included a chapter on social policy (Part III, Title III, Chapter I) as well as one on the free movement of workers (Part II, Title III, Chapter I), national governments have jealously and successfully tried to prevent the transfer of substantial health policy competences to the supranational level. In fact, they still have great difficulty in accepting health policy as a matter of concern to the Union. Consequently, direct influence of the EU on national institutions (with the exception of cross-border social security rules; Art. 42 TEC[1]) has been widely excluded from the mandate of the Union. To date, the Treaties have been rather modest on healthcare issues, formally conceding to member states exclusive health policy rights. Regarding Art. 3 TEC, which raises health protection to the rank of a Community objective, the European Union certainly has a policy mandate in contributing actively 'to the attainment of a high level of health protection', including specific tasks formulated primarily in Art. 152 TEC. The latter article encourages cooperation and coordination between member states and between governments and the Community (see also Art. 140 TEC). As a legal *sedative* for member states, the Treaty concedes that 'Community action in the field of public health shall fully respect the responsibilities of the Member States for the organization and delivery of health services and medical care' (Art. 152 no. 5).[2] Following prevailing interpretations of Art. 152 TEC (Wismar and Busse 1999; see also Busse 2001), healthcare systems *as such* are not the objective of the Union. Furthermore, despite the Treaty's impressive rhetoric and the Commission's ambitious blueprints, the notion of EU social policy and related areas of Community competence are still significantly limited. This is because the strong pillars of 'intergovernmentalism' and 'unanimity' do not allow social policy core areas really to catch up with economic integration. Decision-making in social policy remains highly political, as may be seen from the Treaty of Nice (Art. 137, 1) which has extended qualified majority voting with the exception of, *inter alia*, 'social security and social protection'. The latter are formally still well protected by unanimity (and governments' legitimate self-interests) in the Council. In these areas, national policies are coordinated or standardized by agreements at the European level, but 'national governments remain in full control of the decision process, none of them can be bound without its own consent' (Scharpf 2000: 13). Apparently it is not only governments that want this. The Union's restricted role also seems to be in accordance with citizens' expectations, particularly as regards health policy and social security.[3] National sovereignty still seems to be intact in health politics and policies. Formally speaking, health policy is a supranational *non-topic*, so there seems to be much ado about nothing.

Second – and this makes the above-mentioned statement by McKee, Mossialos and Baeten understandable – 'Social Europe' is continually taking shape, even though it still has bewildering and confusing contours. 'Social Europe' is on its way, but, rather than driving on the main highway, it is taking detours. However, the 'spirit' of European integration and European union is not confined to the various solemn political addresses made on the European stage. Regarding social policy, it is very often marked by vagueness and empty clichés; this is particularly apparent in the manner in which integration is going its own way. What is fuelling this process? To a certain extent it is political ideas and ideals; to a greater extent it is something else: it is the combination of extensive political leadership by the Commission, the (self-)interests of actors within institutions at EU level and national/transnational interest groups, and the accumulation of logical consistencies. In this respect, European health policy integration is a process of path dependency without anybody knowing the path. Moreover, health policy is an interesting example of a very successful process of stepwise denationalization of a core public policy. It is therefore misleading to conclude from the legal absence of direct and substantial EU competences that the extent of European integration's impact on member states' health systems and health policies must be negligible. Health policy is a challenging example of how to make a formal non-topic one of the Union's major future policy fields – despite the Treaty.

It is indisputable that for most of the Union's history, the European Community/European Union has necessarily concentrated on creating a single market, perceiving social policy solely as market enabling and market completing ('politics for markets'; van Kersbergen 2000b: 27), rather than defining it as an intrinsic element of the integration process ('politics against markets'; Esping-Andersen 1985). Furthermore, efforts to adopt more elaborate European rules are politically impeded by an assortment of substantial obstacles. Examples include the multiple institutional veto powers and the strong and legitimate national self-interests within the EU polity (Falkner 2000a, b; Scharpf 1997, 1999); the institutional, structural, normative and cultural diversity and complexity of European welfare states; the embeddedness of social policy in national historical, cultural and economic contexts, serving as a major source of political legitimacy, support and popularity for governments (Tsoukalis 1997; van Kersbergen 2000a); the lack of legitimacy, acceptance and identification still felt by most EU citizens regarding 'Brussels' as a welfare state agency; and, finally, the European Union's very limited fiscal resources, which do not allow it to take over substantial and powerful welfare state functions (Sykes 1998; Leibfried and Pierson 2000; Trubek and Mosher 2001). But though member states' political actors officially still claim to have full control and responsibility over their national sociopolitical 'closed shops', they have realized that the relationship between European integration and national health policy is more ambivalent, and that the integration process already has a wide-ranging and considerable impact on health systems. Governments' sovereignty and autonomy concerning social policy have been substantially affected and reduced, and the Union uses its entire toolbox skilfully. Meanwhile, European and member states' social laws are increasingly interwoven, while supranational law more and more is dominating national legal competences and authority.

Pressures of integration, levels of action and modes of governance: sorting out the impact

The 'Europeanization' of health policy is a complex phenomenon that takes place on various levels, in different forms and with different effects. In general, there are at least four major levels on which policy-making is carried out within the EU:[4]

- *within the single member states*, each with its own specific health policy regimes, functional requirements, and political/cultural priorities to which governments respond independently (national sovereignty);
- *between the member states*, strategically responding to or anticipating the policy choices of other governments, but still adapting nationally (mutual adjustment);
- *between the member states and the EU* within a more or less fragmented multi-level and multi-actor interaction system (intergovernmental negotiations);
- *within the EU* itself between its various institutions, on the basis of genuine competences (supranational sovereignty).

These levels of action are also found in the framework of Leibfried and Pierson (2000: 269), who identify three distinct ways or, rather, ideal types through which European integration impinges on domestic welfare states: 'positive' pressures for integration, 'negative' pressures for integration and the indirect pressures for integration. A fourth category should be added, one that will become increasingly important in the future: the *open method of coordination* (OMC), which functions through self-reflection and collective control. By applying the classification of Leibfried and Pierson and the fourth category to health policy, we can summarize the situation as follows.

The *first* mode of Europeanization concerns the *direct positive pressures* of integration resulting from political decision-making at supranational level, mainly via regulatory policies. It refers to direct social policy initiatives of the Union which member states have to adopt and implement. Even though at first glance these supranational initiatives have clear social purposes explicitly designed to limit or correct market effects, the rationale for intervening in these areas is at least as much an economic one. According to this 'mechanism of *Europeanisation by institutional compliance*' (Knill and Lehmkuhl 2002: 258; original emphasis), 'Member States have only limited institutional discretion when deciding the specific arrangements for compliance with European requirements', since 'community policies are explicitly directed at replacing existing domestic regulatory arrangements' (ibid.). Some of the 'supranationalized' social policies, in the form of either regulations or directives, are anything but substantial innovations created by 'Brussels'. Yet sometimes European regulation goes beyond existing policies in member states and forces them to implement higher social or consumer protection standards. The areas of gender discrimination, health and safety at work, product safety policy, and guidelines on parental leave or part-time work all provide examples. Some of these European standards on social and employment rights have been adopted through agreements reached in the 'Social Dialogue' of the leading organizations of capital and labour (see Falkner 1998; Roberts and Springer 2001). Additionally, the European Court of Justice (ECJ) plays an important role in defining and developing uniform EU standards. Although the European Union's scope for positive initiatives is basically restricted to specific policy areas, in healthcare the completion of the internal market as well as the robust *consumer protection – and public health – mandate* of the Commission have allowed for some important Community regulations. The most visible examples concern the common regulatory framework for medicinal products in the area of market entry, marketing, and the free movement of pharmaceuticals within the single market (see Feick 2002; Keck 1999); the certification and registration of medical devices (Altenstetter 2002; see also Altenstetter, this book, Chapter 3); and the mutual recognition of *professional (medical) qualifications* within the single market. In the past the European Union had already developed a system of coordination of national social security systems and health insurance coverage within the Community governed, among others, by Council Regulations 1612/68, 1408/71, 574/72, 3095/95 and 118/97. These binding regulations have their roots in the initial need to adopt social security measures in order to technically facilitate the mobility of migrant workers and their families within the European Economic Community (see Art. 42 TEC).[5] Even though, in general, this system of coordination is underestimated in scientific studies of EU social policy, one should bear in mind that for the first time this body of rules specified the conditions under which entitlements that had matured in a given national system could deliberately be exported or converted into the system of another member state: 'The regime made sure ... that the new exit options opened by the common market were actually matched by corresponding entry opportunities' (Ferrera 2003: 630). Council Regulation 1408/71 can without any doubt be judged a watershed not only in the relationship between the nation-state and its citizens (membership, portability of entitlements, inclusion of non-nationals), but also in that between the European Community and its member states, in that the Community forced governments to institutionalize a higher 'mobility compatibility' of their welfare regimes. Finally, without going into details here, it was especially the broad and vague area of *public health*, a cross-cutting issue, that incrementally put health at the forefront of the European political agenda. In the wake of new challenges and new concerns related to public health and cross-border public health risks, the limited resources of the Community in health policy (in Art. 129 of the 1993 Treaty of Maastricht) were expanded in the Treaties of Amsterdam and Nice (now renumbered Art. 152) through the addition of several new provisions. With hindsight, this expansion of powers and provisions has often been a crisis-driven and inadvertent process of competence accumulation at Community level – although it has been a process in which the Commission has demonstrated creativity and considerable strategic abilities.

The *second* mode of Europeanization concerns the *indirect pressures* of integration – that is, the implicit and functional spillover originating from market-building and intergovernmental self-bindings and the responses of national actors to these challenges. The (inherently political) pressures to adjust domestically to the common market and to the explicit economic self-bindings are a multi-dimensional and therefore complex phenomenon. It is essentially the combination of the Economic and Monetary Union (EMU), the 1996 Dublin Stability and Growth Pact, and internal market competition that challenges political scientists because its potential economic and political consequences are so diverse and difficult to measure. The joint constraints produced by them are in general regarded as considerable (see, for example, Jones 2003), leading to reductions in social expenditure, the implementation of austerity measures, increasing social inequalities across and within member states, and difficulties for national governments to maintain country-specific levels of social protection. The new economic and monetary framework places governments under pressure to bring macro-economic policies in line with the – perceived or real – functional demands of the euro zone. At the same time, it gives them an external justification for doing so. Growing public budget deficits, especially those resulting from state subsidies to social security or from the deficits of social security institutions, interfere with obligations derived from the Maastricht criteria and the Stability and Growth Pact. In this respect, European economic integration and monetary union have deprived national policy-makers of many of the policy options that they could and did employ in earlier decades in order to achieve and defend full employment and high levels of social protection (Scharpf 2000: 23; Wildasin 2002) – and in particular to manage the conflicting demands of contending groups in the struggle for redistributive transfers. A further crucial point is that, in the wake of enhanced intra-EU competition, high taxes and, above all, high social security contributions are regarded as weakening the economic and competitive position of states and firms alike. The dynamics of *regulatory competition* within a liberalized market, so this popular arguments goes (see Scharpf 1999), forces member states into a downward spiral with regard to social standards and in order to attract investment.

The challenging question is which domestic policies can actually be attributed to the indirect impact of European integration and which cannot. On a strategic level it might provide the legitimizing basis for domestic policy change, by making the SEM and EMU the scapegoats for governments' unpopular decisions in order to push domestically block-aded reforms and to overcome deadlock. In some countries, European integration, and especially meeting the EMU criteria, 'was portrayed as a force that imposes welfare cutbacks and restructuring, and was used as a justification for social policy restructuring by domestic actors' (Timonen 1999: 259f). This was the case in France, Italy and Austria. By contrast, in other countries such as Finland or Germany, such adaptation pressures played only a minor role in social policy reform debates. However, for many reasons, welfare states – at least their overall institutional archi-tecture – have proved to be fairly stable with regard to their respective core principles and institutional arrangements. A race to the bottom and a policy convergence towards retrenchment are far from becoming political reality in Europe. But there is empirical evidence that the price for rela-tive institutional stability might be new internal divisions, a larger differentiation among transfer recipients, cost-shifting to economically weak social groups, new risk privatizations, and a greater individualization in most countries. It may therefore be that the EMU, which limits deficit spending strategies and calls for sound public budgets, tends to lead to a partial dismantling of the welfare state *to the detriment of the poor*. Never-theless, challenged by economic globalization and internal pressures on the one hand and the run-up to the EMU on the other, many European countries successfully tried to find ways to achieve or maintain economic competitiveness without abandoning the normative foundation of their welfare states (see also Kittel 2002). In most member states, 'the politics of social policy centres on the renegotiating and restructuring of the terms of the post-war social contract rather than its dismantling' (Pierson 2001: 14; see also Rhodes 2001: 171), not least via tripartite concertation and 'social pacts' (see, for example, Ebbinghaus and Hassel 2000; Fajertag and Pochet 1997). At national level, most of these processes take place irrespective of European integration effects, as a reaction to economic crises, public-sector deficits, governance failures, and especially the inappropriateness and dysfunctioning of 'old' social security institutions *vis-à-vis* persistent 'new' challenges. This is also true for health policy and health systems.

Kanavos and McKee (1998: 48f) argue that health systems in Europe are facing considerable macro-economic constraints that

> may impact on the ability of publicly funded health systems to keep pace with rising healthcare costs in the near future. The need to meet an ever-increasing demand for health services from a total pool of resources which does not grow at the same time contributes to the national economies' budget deficits and indebtedness.

The 'relative importance of health within the state budgets', as Kanavos and McKee (1998: 30) put it, has proportionally increased the temptation to reduce public-sector deficits, mainly through various cost containment policies and, unfortunately, less often through intelligent policies that could increase the efficiency and effectiveness of institutional arrangements. Probably, cost containment policy has been or will become more intensive in healthcare reforms than would have been the case in the absence of EMU constraints. However, it is conceivable that most of the health policy reforms would have emerged anyway, independently of EU membership. European integration often further strengthens an already existing initiative or consensus for reform. It is not necessarily the economic and monetary self-bindings that force member states to recast the welfare state; it is still a matter of *political* decisions.

The *third* mode of Europeanization consists of the *negative integration policies* that, via the fundamental 'four freedoms' (freedom of movement of persons, goods, services and capital) and the SEM competition law, can be denoted as *explicit* spillover effects – that is, externalities associated with economic integration. They *directly* have an '*indirect*' impact on member states' systems and policies. Negative regulatory policies define conditions for market access and market functioning, and aim at containing legal prohibitions against national regulations that otherwise might function as obstacles and barriers to free movement, or as distortions of competition between member states within the Community. The four freedoms regime allows for cross-border market transactions irrespective of domestic regulations, while the competition law, directed at private actors and member states, likewise basically aims at liberalizing the single market. Regarding this hierarchical mode of Europeanization (Scharpf 2000: 14f), European legislation or jurisdiction affects domestic arrangements by altering the domestic rules of the game, and thus challenges traditional institutional equilibria at the level of member states. However, 'while European policies contribute to these potential challenges, they do not prescribe any distinctive institutional model to be introduced at the national level' (Knill and Lehmkuhl 2002: 258). They define 'negatively' the circumstances under which national institutions and policies do not correspond to the SEM regime. Analogous to the indirect pressures of integration, these direct pressures of negative integration sometimes generate consequences that either have been unintentional or could not have been foreseen.

There is yet another category, one that is fundamentally different from the three previous ones. The *fourth* mode of Europeanization results from the OMC[6] and could be understood as the institutionalization of self-reflection and self-control. The OMC is again an *indirect pressure of integration* which, once effectively institutionalized, will substantially alter the political environment in which domestic social politics take place. The OMC indicates once again that member states have increasingly become part of complex, multiple and dense networks of interaction and cooperation embedded in the grey area of European supranationality. As a complement to the traditional Community regulation through legislation, new modes of soft policy coordination have gained salience in debates on reforms of EU governance and in an increasing number of policy fields. For example, the Prodi Commission launched the debate on the reform of European governance with a White Paper on European Governance in July 2001 (Commission 2001e: 21f). It outlined the OMC as 'one specific but representative component of new governance [which] contrasts most clearly with old-style governance (regulatory, top-down, uniform), and it best captures the promise and potential of new governance (procedural, heterarchical, flexible)' (Eberlein and Kerwer 2002: 1). The OMC can thus be described as the 'third way' in EU governance, to be used when direct harmonization would prove unworkable and the politics of mutual adjustment via regulatory competition within the internal market would be too risky (ibid.: 2). In contrast to the *legal* coordination of member states' social security policies in the wake of workers' mobility, the OMC is a *political* form of coordination based on the concept of 'management by objectives'. Voluntariness and '"gentlemen's agreements" instead of directives' (Begg and Berghman 2002: 191) are the price the Commission has to pay in order to motivate member states to take part in these new procedures. But the Commission is well aware of the fact that once the OMC has proved to be an effective instrument, voluntariness will turn into moral obligation. Non-participation, failure to implement the fixed guidelines in national action plans, and ignorance of the recommendations will then have to be publicly justified in what may turn into an awkward situation for reluctant member states.

This new method can be seen as part of the Commission's new and strategic experimentalism in social politics. The OMC has strengthened the Commission's position while smoothly coaxing national governments into action – and into self-doubt. It involves member states in a complex procedure of external and self-evaluation in the wake of which strengths and weaknesses ought to become transparent and comparable (monitoring, benchmarking, peer-reviews, rankings, self-commitment, implementation of best practices, etc.). Whatever the 'qualitative' effect of the OMC will be, at this stage this new instrument, which bypasses European, national and regional parliaments and allows for the building up of parallel quasi-legislative structures, satisfies the strategic expectations of all the main actors involved. Even though the Commission carefully avoids use of the term 'harmonization', the OMC could be both an effective functional equivalent for the lack of EU competences in social policy core areas, and an effective catalyst for the smooth institutional harmonization of the harder cores of national social security systems in the case of consensual agreements. It consists of a complex procedure that originated in the framework of the 'European Employment Strategy' (EES) (see, for example, Bertozzi and Bonoli 2002; Goetschy 1999). Since the 2000 European Council in Lisbon, it has been extended stepwise from – *inter alia* – *social exclusion* and *pension policy* to *healthcare* and *health and safety at work.* Furthermore, in its Communication on 'streamlining open coordination in the field of social protection', the Commission (2003) outlined its ambitious project of integrating the current disparate actions and various strands of work on social protection into a coherent framework within the OMC.

The following section outlines the most spectacular area of the Europeanization of health policy: the complex relationship between the Community's internal market imperatives and national health policy regimes.

From closed shops to Europeanized healthcare systems?

Compared with other core areas of social security, and irrespective of the heterogeneity of member states' institutional arrangements, healthcare is one of the most regulated policy fields in all EU countries. Traditionally it has more 'market traces' (pharmaceuticals, remedies, medical equipment, private suppliers, etc.) than other social policy fields. Since the European Union systematically focuses on issues related to the functioning of the single market, arguments that the liberal EU single market regime has increasingly constrained governments' social policy activities and limited the sphere in which the nation-state primarily remains competent may be supported by empirical evidence, especially in the healthcare sector. The reasoning is that EU initiatives have made the 'tidy separation between market issues, belonging to the supranational sphere, and social issues, belonging to the national spheres' (Leibfried and Pierson 2000: 268), fictitious and unsustainable.

The 'four freedoms' regime

To guarantee fundamental freedoms is 'the *condition sine qua non* of the economic integration of Europe' (Fuchs 2002: 536; original emphasis). Health policy is both a key policy field for enabling personal mobility and a touchstone to verify the promises made by the Treaty. If the term 'European citizenship' is to have any real meaning, health policy is certainly one of the essential considerations with regard to social rights and geographic mobility. It was especially the delivery of health services and medical care to patients that was previously thought to be largely unaffected by European integration politics. National governments were in no way prepared for the ECJ rulings that have challenged them in the past decade. The Court, which was the only actor able and authorized to take the politically risky offensive, made it perfectly clear that market freedoms are *basically* also applicable to those areas of public policy that most national governments have explicitly excluded from the market *and from the Treaty.* In addition to the fact that the ECJ triggered a political earthquake among national health authorities, it is amazing how a few – albeit famous – ECJ decisions swept away both traditional social policy beliefs of political actors and restrictive legal regulations of member states. It is no longer possible to ignore the fact that healthcare is an essential part of SEM and that the influence of the 'four fundamental freedoms' is especially significant: the *freedom of movement for persons* (labour market for professionals; mutual automatic recognition of national qualifications and diplomas, especially in the health professions; Union-wide access of EU citizens to medical care), *goods* (the market for pharmaceutical products and medical technology) and *services* (cross-border delivery of services and the choices available to patients; freedom of establishment). Several ECJ decisions have pointed the way ahead for healthcare systems and future health policy:[7]

- In *Molenaar* (C-160/96) the Court ruled against hindrances to exporting and consuming German care-insurance cash benefits out of state (free movement of persons).
- In *Kohll* (C-158/96) the Court ruled against hindrances to obtaining dental care out of state (free movement of services).
- In *Decker* (C-120/95) the Court ruled against hindrances to obtaining spectacles on a prescription out of state (free movement of goods).
- In *Vanbraekel* (C-368/98) and *Geraets-Smits/Peerbooms* (C-157/99) the Court decided to rule against hindrances to out-of-state medical services, including hospital treatment. In principle, patients are now allowed to receive out- and in-patient treatment in other member states; normal and necessary treatment can only be refused on the basis of specifically defined objectives and non-discriminatory criteria.[8]
- In *Müller-Fauré/van Riet* (C-385/99) the Court stated that the principle of prior national authorization is basically not in accordance with the unrestricted freedom of services within the European Union. Consequently, the Court ruled that insured persons are basically entitled to receive ambulatory (non-hospital) treatment wherever and whenever they wish (being reimbursed within the limits of the cover provided by the health insurance scheme of the member state of affiliation).
- In *Ioannidis* (C-326/00) the Court clarified the entitlements of pensioners during a stay in another member state for a limited period: pensioners are allowed to claim medical treatment even in cases of chronic disease – again without prior authorization.

These Court decisions, particularly those on patient mobility, which were a step forward in the rights of European citizens (wider choice), set in motion a dynamic that governments and health policy actors cannot escape and with which they have to grapple. These ECJ rulings were internal market rulings and by no means health or social policy rulings, though they made Art. 152 (5) TEC largely redundant. Since these rulings,

Community involvement has moved beyond the traditional limits of the EU public health and social security coordination mandate. The ECJ did not interpret the fundamental freedoms extensively; rather, it interpreted them systematically, even though an interpretation more welcome to member states would undoubtedly have been possible. The ECJ made it clear to member state governments that it would be paradoxical to assume that full economic union could be created without further consequences being accepted. The ECJ explicitly stated that in- and out-patient care are services within the meaning of the Treaty – that is, by no means different from pure economic services even though, in national contexts, social services in general are usually part of public services which are regulated by social law. To be more precise, even though the Court variously confirmed member states' ability and responsibility to freely organize their health-care systems, it recalled at the same time that whatever member state governments do, they have to comply with Community law. This is not a paradox but the logical consequence of the Treaty's *political* imprecision and *legal* uncertainty concerning social policy. The *Kohll* and *Decker* decisions (1998) have been a nightmare for national health authorities. To them, and especially to the German government, which had explicitly agreed during the Maastricht negotiations to a deepening of the social dimension, 'these rulings represented an attack on their right to organize their health and social security systems in their own way under *subsidiarity*' (Commission 2001c: 11; original emphasis).

As Wismar (2001: 6) stresses, EU citizens are now entitled to 'travel *intentionally* to receive medical goods and services' (my emphasis). The patient's freedom goes far beyond the traditional 'E111 procedure': citizens are legally allowed to leave the exclusive institutional arrangements of their home welfare states in which they are embedded by social law. In this respect, one can observe the introduction of a new linkage between citizenship and social benefits on a larger (i.e. Community) level and across member states' borders. European legislation and jurisdiction have started spectacularly to break the tight social-law bonds that tie citizens to their country. Although EU citizenship is still a nebulous concept, it closely connects social rights and market freedoms. It thus constantly weakens – irrespective of Art. 18 III TEC – the normative basic assumptions of national social policy. What, however, in neo-functional terms seems to be an unspectacular, mere technical and functionally unavoidable spillover emerges as a highly political issue touching a sore spot in member states' self-perception: via the 'four freedom' regime, the European Union can, as Ferrera (2003: 640) notes, 'legitimately encroach into national social citizenships'. This constitutes without any doubt a soft revolution in the history of social policy: according to the famous sequence of Marshall (1950), the Union is incrementally constructing a supranational social citizenship.

Three major consequences are evident. The Court rulings imply a significant loss of member states' *sovereignty* in the key policy area of social security, and considerably weaken *territorial* and – which is crucial for social policy – *nationality* principles in healthcare. When one considers the consequences, a number of key implications emerge from the 'mobility judiciary' and the Council Regulations on coordinating social security systems:[9]

- *Declining control over external boundaries:* member states' healthcare systems are systematically separated from former congruency with national state borders, and are gradually shifting towards a Europeanized, 'borderless' and virtual healthcare market (free access and mobility of patients and professionals, regulations on medical goods, competition among providers, etc.).
- *Declining control over beneficiaries:* member states may no longer restrict welfare state access to their own citizens and may no longer limit most social benefits solely to their citizens. Benefits must be granted to all or withheld from all (equality of treatment between nationals and non-nationals).
- *Declining control over consumption:* member states may no longer insist that their benefits apply only to their territory and must therefore be consumed only there (export of benefits). Member states can in fact exercise their power to determine the territory of consumption (and to set the requirements non-nationals have to meet for having access) only when providing universal means-tested benefits. Additionally, member states can no longer prevent their (insured) citizens from consuming services of other EU systems, which they have to reimburse.
- *Declining control over administrative case adjudication:* member states have to accept that the beneficiary status (e.g. the status of being ill and thus entitled to treatment or sick pay) is determined by the 'agencies' of other member states.
- *Declining control over market access of foreign providers:* professionals such as doctors, dentists, nurses and pharmacists have free access to member states' labour markets and contractual systems (based on a set of specific directives and domestic legislation); health service providers are basically allowed to offer their services in other member states without being arbitrarily discriminated against in favour of national providers (freedom of services, free establishment, non-discrimination).

While member states were willing in the past to accept Community legislation confined to health services 'input' (such as pharmaceuticals and medical devices), they now have to accept that Art. 152 (5) TEC, which explicitly rules out Community involvement in member states' health systems, is a fairly 'blunt' instrument (comparable, in fact, to the whole doctrine of 'subsidiarity'). This article seems to be one of the most ambivalent ones of the Treaty since there are many ways of bypassing it, especially in combination with the European competition regime.

The European competition regime

While the financial, structural and practical consequences of the SEM 'four freedoms' are undoubtedly significant – but still seem to be in inverse proportion to the 'crisis scenarios' in national health policy debates – the effects of the single market competition regime remain an underestimated dimension. In a ruling of 1977 (C-13/77), the ECJ declared that 'any abuse of a dominant position within the market is prohibited ... even if such abuse is encouraged by a national legislative provision'. More specifically: 'in case of public undertaking and undertakings to which Member States grant special or exclusive rights, Member States shall neither enact nor maintain in force any measure contrary inter alia to the rules provided for in Articles 85 to 94' (i.e. the articles on the EU competition regime, now renumbered). In the event of incompatibility, EU competition law might effectively pressurize member states' institutional, regulatory and normative frameworks. Meanwhile, the rules of the game are slowly becoming clearer.

Article 81 TEC prohibits all agreements between undertakings, decisions by associations of undertakings and concerted practices that may negatively affect trade between member states. Analogously, Art. 82 TEC prohibits any abuse of a dominant position within the common market or in a substantial part of it as being incompatible with the common market. Very logically in its jurisdiction, the ECJ clearly holds that 'according to settled case-law, an undertaking which has a legal monopoly in a substantial part of the common market may be regarded as occupying a dominant position within the meaning of Article 82 of the Treaty' (C-219/97, paragraph 81; C-41/90, paragraph 29). While the articles concerning the 'ban on cartels' and the 'abuse of a dominant market position' refer to undertakings in general (but do not define what an 'undertaking' is or is not), Art. 86 (1) TEC directly targets national governments. In the case of *public* undertakings or undertakings to which member states grant *special* or *exclusive rights*, governments are prohibited from enacting or maintaining in force any measure contrary to the Union's competition regime. Finally, Art. 87 (1) TEC prohibits all kinds of direct or indirect financial support or allocation of funds by the state that distort or threaten to distort competition by favouring certain undertakings or the production of certain goods. Against this background, European competition law distinguishes between (i) the *function* of an organization, and (ii) its real *activity* on a specific market.

(i) Public health insurance funds seem to have a problematical 'double nature' in the sense that they are both service *suppliers* and service *demanders* in the private healthcare market. Health provision is based on a twofold public law relationship: between insurance funds and insured on the one hand, and between insurance funds and the state on the other. They operate in a regulated market based on contracts and relations with third-party providers. Although these two roles cannot be separated (they are complementary), it would be realistic to argue that public health insurance funds, from a *functional* perspective, are undertakings in the sense of the Treaty. The Court has held that in the context of competition law, every activity consisting of offering goods and services on a given market is an economic activity (see, for example, C-118/85). Whenever an entity acts economically it is legally treated as an undertaking, regardless of its legal status or the way in which it is financed or the profit/non-profit issue (see C-41/90, C-160/91 and others). The basic question in fact is whether or to what extent public health insurance funds really are *economic* entities.

ECJ case law provides clear lines of argument suggesting that offering social protection via social insurance is *basically not* an economic activity. National legislation attributing an exclusive and dominant position to organizations acting as suppliers of the specific public good 'healthcare provision' within a statutory social security system is – *when these organizations fulfil a clear social function* – in accordance with EU law. The Court explained in three of its decisions – *Poucet/Pistre* (C-159/91 and 160/91) and *García* (C-238/94) – that one cannot assume an economic activity if the overall aim of a social security system can only be achieved by applying the solidarity principle. Referring to the Treaty, the Court stated that

> the concept of an undertaking ... does not include organizations involved in the management of the public social security system, which fulfil an exclusively social function and perform an activity based on the principle of national solidarity which is entirely non-profit-making.
> (C-159/91 and C-160/91)

More explicitly, according to a judgment of 2000, the Treaty's concept of economic undertakings does 'not include bodies entrusted with the management of certain compulsory social security schemes, based on the principle of solidarity' (C-180/98 to C-184/98; paragraph 109). A social insurance institution therefore does not act economically when it exclusively pursues social objectives, and in doing so differs substantially from one offering private insurance.

Finally, in its judgment regarding the Italian National Institute for Insurance (C-218/00; see also C-41/90 and C-244/94), the ECJ took a further step towards clarifying the fragile border between an organization that has to be treated as an economic undertaking, according to/in the sense of the Treaty, and an organization entrusted by law with the fulfilment of a social function. A list of elements making a substantial difference can be drawn up:

- delegation by law of a task of general interest;
- non-profit-making status of social policy institutions;
- the state as overall (legitimizing and financial) guarantor of the scheme;
- compulsory affiliation necessary to fulfil its social function and purpose;
- social protection for nearly all workers or citizens;
- amount of contributions approved by the state;
- clear social objectives and clear elements of solidarity;
- contribution rate not systematically proportionate to the risk insured;
- contributions calculated according to the insured persons' income;
- benefits laid down by law and not dependent on the individual contributions (absence of a direct link between contributions paid and benefits granted);
- granting of exemption from payment of contributions for specific social reasons;
- compensation for financial risk among public insurance bodies.

From these elements, one can conclude, at least on a general level, that the likelihood is increasing that the European competition regime will have to be taken into account whenever the following conditions are fulfilled:

- Public social security institutions are substantially shorn of their redistributive elements (less solidarity, equity and equality).
- Governments extend private insurance analogies (less income protection).
- Competition for insured persons among public funds and between public and private funds increases (less compulsory affiliation; more risk selection).
- Specific tasks or activities can also be produced in the private market, and not exclusively via specific public agencies, without socially disadvantaging the beneficiaries.

Even though the overall tendency is clear, the basic message of the Court is still that 'the social aim of an insurance scheme is not in itself sufficient to preclude the activity ... from being classified as an economic activity' (C-218/00). That is the starting point of the more complex following issue.

(ii) The Court made it perfectly clear that it is wrong to argue that the *activities* of (public) social policy institutions do not fall within the scope of the competition rules simply because they are carried out by public undertakings granted special rights by the state and fulfilling a social function (see C 123/83; C-41/90; C-35/96; C-180/94 to C-184/98). Thus, looking at the demand side, the question again is: can public health insurance funds be judged as economic entities when they *act* as 'service enterprises' in the highly regulated market organizing health provision? If so, many core steering instruments in many healthcare systems would have to be altered because they privilege specific actors, produce exclusive effects, explicitly limit or exclude competition, and restrict access to the healthcare market. The simple answer is: it depends. The application of the *ban on cartels* and the *abuse of a dominant market position* cannot be judged on a general level but has to be investigated in each and every case.

While the ECJ and European Commission primarily focus on the economic context and the sometimes complex underlying economic rationale, Articles 16 and 86 (2) TEC open up a 'back door' for political decisions – that is, these articles have a more programmatic character and require a *political* assessment. These articles explicitly aim at protecting areas or practices from the European antitrust law. If the EU competition regime is to be constrained for political reasons, these articles are the normative basis for resolving the tension between a high degree of market liberalization and integration on the one hand, and the institutional organization of non-market activity via public agencies or undertakings that enjoy exclusive rights, on the other. The coverage and interpretation of Art. 86 (2) TEC and the limits it imposes on Art. 82 TEC have recently been widened. In 1999 and 2000 the ECJ passed important judgments on the relationship between EU competition/cartel law and specific social security institutions in the Netherlands.[10] On the occasion of these decisions, the ECJ continued its efforts to specify the function and role of public undertakings and undertakings to which member states may grant special or exclusive rights because they are entrusted with the management of services of general economic or social interest. The Court came to the conclusion that the restrictions on competition on account of a dominant position and exclusive rights granted by the state can be in accordance with EU competition law. It once again underlined the importance of Art. 86 (2) TEC in the sense that undertakings entrusted with the operation of services of general interest are subject to the rules on competition 'only in so far as the application of such rules does not obstruct the performance, in law or in fact, of the particular task(s) assigned to them' (C-219/97; see also C-41/90 and C-155/73). In this respect, the ECJ variously outlined the legitimate interests of member states in using certain undertakings, in particular in the public sector, as an instrument of economic, fiscal or social policy. In addition to that, the ECJ clarified in Case C-359/95 that Articles 81 and 82 TEC apply only to anti-competitive conduct engaged in by undertakings on their own initiative. In fact, public sickness funds in most countries are forced to comply with public law while carrying out an essential public policy. They act in place of the state as indirect public administration bodies and – according to the ECJ ruling in *Poucet/Pistre*

(C-159/91 and C-160/91) – are obliged to comply with the law and the political obligations and constraints imposed on them. It is the state that delegates legal competences and duties to public bodies, which act as quasi-state, norm-fulfilling and norm-implementing agencies within the jurisdiction of the state. Their decisions are considered to be functionally equivalent to state decisions. It is thus plausible to argue that most member states' public health insurance funds act neither autonomously nor economically according to Art. 81 TEC.

National policy choices: between formal sovereignty and the single market

In coming years, European integration – other things being equal (that is, given that national governments are neither willing nor able to change EU law fundamentally[11]) – will lead to a *regulatory dichotomy* and differentiation in the regulation of healthcare. While the national level is basically responsible for, and free to regulate, healthcare protection (i.e. to decide on eligibility criteria, entitlements to benefits, access to benefits, the catalogue of benefits, and organization of the demand side), coverage (personal scope; right or duty to be insured) and funding (income redistribution, financing) within the country and through its own legislation,[12] EU competition law will increase its impact mainly on the 'production of health' – that is, on domestic supply and delivery structures of health services and respective institutional frameworks. This will entail a situation in which providers and patients circumvent the state, and governments have a limited capacity to control the allocation of resources and exclusively to determine the healthcare coverage of their citizens. Additionally, governments are challenged both by a continuing qualitative increase in EU citizens' social rights *and* by the establishment of a European healthcare market that is increasingly governed by EU competition law but at the same time re-regulated and tamed, especially by the Commission's initiatives. Furthermore, we should expect to observe fierce conflicts about the uncertain and contentious borderline between supranational and national law. EU institutions, national governments and interest groups are struggling for competences and influence, and trying to define their claims. In doubtful cases, it is the ECJ that controls the border and therefore the market.

An important aspect of European market integration is that governments have slowly become aware of potential incompatibilities between national and supranational legislation. Mossialos *et al.* (2001: 5f) correctly point out that 'it is easy to see how poorly considered healthcare reforms … might render organizations unexpectedly subject to competition law'. Meanwhile, however, governments perceive that it is especially the 'low politics' – that is, the 'quiet accumulation of EU constraints on social policy connected with market integration' (Leibfried and Pierson 2000:

276) – that has profoundly challenged their sovereignty and regulatory capacities. But three facts need to be kept in mind. First, regulatory capacities of national governments have not been abolished; they have changed. Second, European integration does not simply restrict national policy choices; it simultaneously enhances strategic health policy options of governments and private actors. Third, there is undoubtedly no *general* pressure to liberalize or privatize institutional healthcare arrangements, even though one can observe a strong tendency to adjust to greater market conformity in certain sectors, and even though competition has become a rationale of the emerging European healthcare market. A fourth finding is that the nation-state is to a large extent deprived of the capacity to restrict the operations of market providers (Hagen 1999) and sometimes even to protect public service monopolies – *for solely socio-political reasons*. It may also be that European integration will broaden the concept of public social policy to a larger public–private mix, separating traditional redistributive issues (state) from those perceived as 'competitive' according to the European market regime (private). A new welfare pluralism is emerging, but in these processes national governments are in no way forced into the role of a spectator. Yet whatever they do, they have to respect the Commission's and the ECJ's holy cows: the fundamental principles of *non-discrimination on grounds of nationality* and *the right to free movement and open competition across borders*. A final conclusion is that processes of 'privatization' and sometimes of deregulation are also processes of denationalization, shifting regulatory social policy competences to other than national levels. Conversely, there are empirical examples that 'nationalization' prevents supranationalization and protects specific normative aims. There are many roads on which the European Union can drive within the member states, but sometimes member states are still able to stop the Union by putting the traffic lights on red.

The 'four freedoms' regime and European competition law are certainly only the spectacular tip of the iceberg. In order to offer a more comprehensive insight into the 'push factors' that put a Europeanizing pressure on health policy, the following section discusses the most important aspects.

European dynamics: governments caught in the maelstrom of integration politics

Health policy is characterized by the fact that 'there is no clear dividing line between country and European arena' (Kenneth 2001: 31). It is a policy domain where 'neither the country arena nor the EU arena seems to have the capabilities to deliver coherent and consistent policy outcomes.... Policy responsibilities ... are not neatly divided between country and European arena, but rather they waver between the two' (Wallace 2000: 43). Meanwhile, one can nevertheless outline the contours of what might be the health policy dimension of European integration, and identify some of the driving forces that are smoothly Europeanizing health policy. The European Union is not taking the national 'welfare fortresses' by storm. Rather, it is an incremental process of Europeanizing the political, institutional and ideological framework of member states' health policies and health systems that is under way. In fact, national healthcare systems face a set of seven European challenges, with very varied impacts.

(i) The *social policy* and *public health programmes* of the Commission,[13] which set out long-term agendas listing explicit social policy objectives, targets, and procedures. The European Union has – especially since 1999 – strategically promoted a new dialogue on health issues. The various proposals and papers of the Commission, but especially the 'Programme of Community action in the field of public health' (2001–2006) and the new programme (2003–2008), which replace the fragmented eight European health action programmes within the framework put in place in 1993 with the Treaty of Maastricht, explicitly seek to work towards coordination and common European policies.

(ii) A simultaneously growing healthcare 'epistemic community' (Haas 1992) or, in a more exclusive sense, 'policy community' (Jordan 1990) of experts at European level is established and operating. These communities are composed of specialists who share an active interest in a given policy area, a sense of being on a mission, and an *esprit de corps*. Initiated by the Commission and working in close collaboration with it, these experts are becoming more and more influential in debates on healthcare developments in the European Union. The result is an indirect intellectual pressure on member states' health policy choices, through the inclusion of experts and the accumulation of comparative expertise. These epistemic communities construct and diffuse a common perception of problems and solutions. They 'organize a cognitive and normative harmonization of social security reforms in Europe' (Palier 2000: 9). This collection, exchange and diffusion of *knowledge* and ideas is comparable to the work of the OECD and the WHO and will have an increasing impact on domestic reform discourses, especially in combination with the OMC.

(iii) The *Commission* and the *ECJ* constitute two important players on the healthcare agenda, both brought in by the lack of consensus among member states, their political inaction at government level, a clear tendency among governments to ignore the effects, whether intended or not, of the single market, and the imprecision of the Treaty concerning the healthcare sector's activities. The *ECJ*, which has become an ersatz legislator and therefore a key player in health politics, has been put in the position of 'de facto making health policy by defining the influence of EU regulations on healthcare' (Commission 2001c: 23; see also Sieveking

1997), and by developing a path dependency which is sometimes at odds with that of the member states. Systematically interpreting the overriding market-oriented philosophy of the Treaties, 'the ECJ has gone way beyond what we are generally used to, even from activist supreme Courts in federal systems' (V. A. Schmidt 1997: 133), although an analogy between the ECJ and the US or German Supreme Court is 'highly imperfect' (Kleinman 2002: 123), as these institutions function in fully democratic political systems. At the same time, the *Commission*, a 'policy entrepreneur' (see, for example, Cram 1993, 1994) *par excellence*, has rung in a new round in harmonizing member states' health policies and in redefining responsibilities. Health policy is a striking example for demonstrating how the Commission has become a master in intelligent 'soft governance'. Via different routes, it strategically coaxes member states into action, making extensive use of its genuine agenda-setting powers. The OMC is by no means the only illustration of the fact that the Commission has become 'subtly activist' (Wendon 1998) and a 'purposeful opportunist' (Cram 1993: 143) – that is, an institution which has a notion of its overall objectives and aims but is quite flexible about the way it achieves them. Additionally, as S. K. Schmidt (2000) exemplifies in other policy fields but as is also true for health policy, it makes strategic use of the ECJ and its decision competences for its own ends and in order to put pressure on the Council and national governments

(iv) The increasing *mobility of health professionals, health services and patients* has had and will have major repercussions on national systems, their 'permeability' and traditional steering instruments because of the impact of Europe-wide competition among providers, the free flow of goods and services, and EU citizens' right of access to healthcare irrespective of national borders. A complex problem will be to bring the following – *de facto* and *de jure* – into line with the new European healthcare market requirements: domestic *capacity planning policies* (hospital planning, restrictions on approval for doctors or dentists to practise, etc.) that have a restricting, excluding and privileging effect and thus serve as barriers to market entry in favour of insiders and expenditure control; and explicit *cost containment policies* (such as the setting of global expenditure ceilings or sectoral budgets for providers; restrictive and selective contracting; concepts regarding managed care; positive lists for drugs; and reductions in the supply of medical care, like waiting list or rationing policies). These national measures often have an excluding and privileging effect and thus serve as barriers to market entry in favour of insiders as well as barriers to expenditure control on purely national scales. Member governments, for example, fear that these measures can be bypassed by using foreign services. Though patient mobility is still fairly low outside, within border regions restrictions on the supply of healthcare and health services (for financial or other reasons) can be thwarted by access to supply (providers) abroad which, unlike domestic providers, governments cannot effectively control (in terms of costs, quality, efficiency, etc.). It is above all the individual right of patients, as citizens and consumers, to quasi-unconditional access to healthcare abroad that constitutes the new challenge to member states' systems. In this respect, European citizens have carefully started to compare healthcare and healthcare systems and to demand equal treatment and protection. Differences in health status, health outcomes and even in financial burdens for equal or similar treatment will increasingly become an important topic on the national and European agendas, and will at the same time trigger new processes of non-institutional harmonization (benefits, prices, etc.) geared at effective outcomes, via policy learning and policy transfers.

(v) This is most important with regard to *the open method of coordination*. By its very nature, the OMC aims at converging by naming and shaming: the shadow of hierarchy, effective in terms of sanctions, has been replaced by 'the shadow of mutual control', resulting from group pressure which might serve as an antidote against the pursuit of mere symbolic politics. There is reason to assume that in the medium term the OMC will turn into the old Community method in disguise – that is, into an expertocratic top-down instrument with a quasi-deliberative embellishment. Furthermore, it is not unrealistic to argue that the OMC is a strategically and politically necessary intermediate step from nationally rooted policy-making towards more collective regimes. Its purpose is, as Hodson and Maher (2001) argue, to be a smooth and unsuspicious transitional mechanism serving to reconfigure the boundaries of competence between member states and the Union. Following this line of argument, the OMC probably is, as Eberlein and Kerwer (2002: 11) point out, 'a prelude to regulatory harmonization', leading, eventually, to a 'hidden Europeanization' (Behning and Feigl-Heihs 2001: 474) of welfare state core areas: starting with benchmarks of EU quality for health goods and/or services and going on to define levels of protection, minimum standards of care provision and optimal ways of financing, and of achieving sustainability and equality. However, in health policy the OMC is still in the preparatory stage, and current politics are still far from this scenario. Given the institutional and policy differences between employment and pension policy on the one hand and healthcare on the other, it is not surprising that the application of the OMC to healthcare is still contentious. Nevertheless, the first steps towards the application of the OMC have already been taken. Following the explicit mandate of the European Council of Gothenburg in 2001, which called for the 'modernization' of social protection systems in the European Union, the Commission presented a first report on new orientations in the area of healthcare and care for the elderly in December 2001 (Commission 2001a). In order to find new responses to challenging problems encountered all over Europe, the Commission was assigned the task, at the 2002

European Council meeting in Barcelona, of discussing and examining aspects of cross-border healthcare and service arrangements, and questions of 'access' (guarantee of general access to health provision), 'quality' (guarantee of a high quality of provision) and the 'financial stability' (guarantee of long-term financial sustainability of healthcare systems) of member states' healthcare systems on the basis of performance indicators and benchmarking. Given the sensitivity of healthcare, most member states' health authorities still resist attempts to evaluate and rate their systems, to improve transparency and to make them comparable, and are afraid of coming off badly: 'member states do not want to be given grades. They do not agree on qualitative and quantitative indicators because their results might be used against them' (Stein 2003: 24). Similarly, interest groups in health systems often perceive the OMC as a threat to their own role and privileges. Against this background, it remains an open question whether the OMC will effectively facilitate convergence in health policies along the Commission's lines of argument.

(vi) In combination with the 'four freedoms' regulation, the *European competition regime* tackles member states' capacity to regulate, organize and finance their healthcare systems. At this level, it is the ECJ in particular that is 'in the driving seat on health policy' (Wismar 2001). For patients and professionals, the ECJ is a veritable source of hope, while for member state governments it is a daunting antagonist. The paradox is clear: national governments still play first fiddle in the European orchestra, but whatever they do, they have to take into consideration the fact that social policy has become rather vulnerable to EU market principles. The point is that differences make a difference. Whether or not the European competition regime may alter the regulatory structure of healthcare systems depends upon the specific features and institutional configurations of each and every system. It is thus still national policy choices that open the door for European single market law: the more national policies shift from (re)distributive to regulatory, the more public insurance systems are separated from income redistribution, the more health policy reforms adopt market mechanisms or market analogies, the more they remove social protection elements through private insurance analogies, the more member states' health systems become exposed to the Union's competition rules, and the more the European Union becomes involved in replacing or changing public-sector regulation. The interdependences between EU competition law and national health politics can be described as a game of chess: national governments are still able to move the main pieces and to move them wherever they want, but the SEM legislation has redefined the chequered board.

(vii) The impacts of *European Economic and Monetary Union* are usually stressed by those who use and abuse 'Brussels' in domestic political conflicts. However, for political scientists it is empirical scrupulousness rather than theoretical plausibility that is at play in ascertaining which policy developments can reasonably be attributed to the internal market and monetary union, and in distinguishing them from those policies for which the supranational level is not causally responsible. EMU and SEM alone do not seem to challenge European welfare states to an extent that might endanger their normative and institutional substance. Yet the implications of the Economic and Monetary Union might be more crucial for specific countries such as Germany. Given the heavily indebted national and social security budgets and the relatively high social security contribution rates, German governments – as if in a reflex reaction – set the (still generous) social security insurance provisions in their sights when they debated how to cut benefits, reduce entitlements and privatize risks. Even though social policy retrenchment has been fairly smooth to date, there is some reason to expect that current EU initiatives to make Germany consolidate its public budgets might have a more substantial impact on the statutory health insurance, which accounts for a part of the German budget deficit. In its '2002 Broad Economic Policy Guidelines', the Commission called on the German government to meet its obligations to respect the Treaty's criterion of keeping the general budget deficit below 3 per cent of GDP, and to implement 'the necessary reform of the healthcare system in order to reduce expenditure pressures' (Commission 2002a: 32). Since that time, health authorities have become more and more aware of the fact that the pressure to reduce deficits is real and inescapable, and that the costs of statutory health insurance is part of the public deficit.

Health policy stumbling towards Europeanization

Even though European healthcare systems still appear to be national, with member states formally still their guardians, European integration has steadily reduced the policy margin member states have in autonomously regulating healthcare. The painful experience that member governments have had in health policy has been the realization that the field of application of Community law is larger than the competences of the Community. Although health policy is widely seen as an area with firm member state control and a minimal EU role, there is clear evidence of the growing significance of European policy, the influence of actors other than member states, the increasing constraints on member state initiatives, and a new sharing of competences and joining of responsibilities between member state and European level. There is evidence that EU level and member states are, slowly but surely, on the way to becoming a more systematic and reflected institutional *compound* of health policy. The term 'compound' is used here to stress both the new quality of European health policy and the dispersion of competences between member states and Community institutions within a new entity formed by conjoining various parts, institutions and competences. While the EU level increasingly provides the 'software' of future European welfare statehood – that is, defining the (normative) principles governing future developments (such as non-discrimination on grounds of nationality, or definition of uniform social rights that guarantee new entry – and exit – options), and regulating the very essentials of European integration (cross-border mobility and economic transactions; competition, and restrictions on competition, within the internal market; transparency; uniform product standards and mutual recognition; and the like) – member states are providing the 'hardware'. It is the member states that are and will in years to come remain responsible for organizing, funding and regulating the demand side of healthcare, for ensuring citizens' access to adequate provision, and for implementing (and thus bearing the cost of) EU policies. Against this background, the notion of a dichotomy of national and European level is misleading and an obstacle to perceiving the two levels as part of a new whole. In this perspective, 'the happy, post-war marriage between the nation-state and the welfare state' (Hagen 1999: 661) is not simply coming to an end; rather, we are witnessing the amalgamation of the national and the European levels into a new compound European healthcare state.

In this context, it is fruitful to apply the concept of 'single social areas', which Threlfall (2003) introduces to identify areas where boundaries between member states have fallen to the extent that citizens can experience the European Union as if it were a single country – as in healthcare. In this 'single healthcare area', national (welfare state) frontiers are increasingly becoming (legally) insignificant for national citizens and making way to new European social citizenship boundaries. Regarding medical treatment, patients have the opportunity to experience Europe as if it were one country; it has become one 'Europe of Patients' (DGV 1999: 1) or, more emphatically, one 'Europe of Health'[14] – although one created mainly via case law, not politically.

Leibfried and Pierson (2000: 267) therefore appear to be right when claiming that Europeanizing healthcare policy is a process that is 'largely law- and Court-driven, marked by policy immobilism at the centre and by negative market integration'. But this is only half the story, since this argumentation seriously underestimates the role of the Commission as an increasingly *political* actor. The Commission can be described as a *laboratory* with, typically, a double assignment: control (adherence to the Treaties) and creativity (proposals for new policies and the advancement of the Community). In operating in this way, the Commission involves member states in processes of interaction, self-reflection and mutual evaluation, which is a new experience for European healthcare states. The European Union has created a web of policies and politics within which the member states are interwoven. Political scientists in search of logical, clear-cut strategies and rational choices may have some problems in understanding the logic and rationality of these processes because

European health policy has been developed in an extremely patchy and accidental manner. Much of European health policy can be understood as the 'intersection' between health policy and other policy fields in which the European Union has genuine competences. Yet in the end, the paradox may be that health policy, which is still officially a national core domain, will be nudged into Europeanization, even though most member states' health authorities still oppose it.

Notes

1 Consolidated version of the Treaty establishing the European Community (TEC), *Official Journal of the European Communities* C 325/33.
2 With regard to European public health policy, see, for example, Bellach and Stein (1999); Busse, Wismar and Berman (2002); Commission (1998); Holland *et al.* (1999).
3 See *Eurobarometer* no. 56, published in April 2002.
4 I partly owe this differentiation to Sykes (1998: 253), but I have broadened his perspective.
5 See also Commission (2001d, 2002b) for further details, as well as C-9/74 and C-20/85.
6 For more details on the OMC, see De La Porte and Pochet (2002); Göbel (2002); Hodson and Maher (2001); Jorens (2003); Regent (2003).
7 For details, see also Leibfried and Pierson (2000); Mossialos and Palm (2003); Fuchs (2002); Pitschas (1999).
8 Even though the 'freedom-of-service regime' is applicable to in-patient care, the Court conceded that it is – according to *specifically defined criteria* – still up to national health agencies to individually approve hospital treatment abroad. With respect to prior administrative authorization (see also C-205/99, paragraph 38), which is *eo ipso* suspected of constituting a barrier to free movement, a rejection of patients' applications for hospital treatment in other member states is limited to 'objective' and 'non-discriminatory' criteria (see C-157/99, paragraph 90, and C-205/99, paragraph 38) – that is, prior authorization can be invoked only in cases of a serious threat to the financial balance of the domestic scheme, or for reasons related to public health, and 'only if the same or equally effective treatment can be obtained without undue delay from an establishment with which the insured person's sickness insurance fund has contractual arrangements' (C-157/99, paragraph 103).
9 For some points, see also Leibfried and Pierson (2000: 279, 283); Leibfried and Pierson (1999: 22f, 28); Commission (2002b: 10); Ferrera (2003: 632).
10 See C-67/96, C-219/97, C-115/97 to C-117/97 and C-180/98 to C-184/98.
11 Fundamental change seems unlikely because on the one hand governments still perceive the present impact of EU law on national healthcare systems as marginal and not threatening their specific healthcare regulation setting. On the other hand, EU law and ECJ rulings 'affect member states differently, so there is no coalition of support to change disputed legislation' (Mossialos *et al.* 2001: 6).
12 See, for example, the interpretations of the Court in C-110/79, C-349/87, C-4/95 and C-5/95, in which it explained that member states are free to define and amend both the conditions for the granting of social security benefits, and who is to be insured under its legislation – provided that the respective legislation does not entail overt or disguised discrimination on grounds of nationality. Moreover (as mentioned above), in C-159/91, C-160/91 and C-238/94, the ECJ

clarified that member states retain their powers to make membership compulsory in social security schemes based on the principle of solidarity.
13 See, for example, Commission (2000; 2001a; 2001b), or the proposals listed in Commission (2001c: 22–26). See also Decision no. 521/2001/EC of the European Parliament and of the Council of 26 February 2001, and the Decision no. 1786/2002/EC of the European Parliament and of the Council of 23 September 2002.
14 David Byrne, Commissioner for Health and Consumer Protection, at the European Health Forum, Bad Gastein, 3 October 2003 (SPEECH/03/443).

References

Altenstetter, C. (2002) 'Regulation of Medical Devices in the EU', in Martin McKee, Elias Mossialos and Rita Baeten (eds) *The Impact of EU Law on Healthcare Systems*, Brussels: Peter Lang, pp. 77–304.

Begg, I. and Berghman, J. (2002) 'EU Social (Exclusion) Policy Revisited', *Journal of European Social Policy* 12 (3): 179–194.

Behning, U. and Feigl-Heihs, M. (2001) 'Europäisierung von Wohlfahrtspolitik: Ihre Genese und ableitbare Entwicklungstrends', *SWS-Rundschau* 4: 459–478.

Bellach, B.-M. and Stein, H. (eds) (1999) *The New Public Health Policy of the European Union: Past Experience, Present Needs, Future Perspectives*, Munich: Urban und Vogel Medien und Medizin.

Busse, R. (2001) 'A Single European Market in Healthcare?', *Issues in European Health Policy* 3 (4): 4–6.

Busse, R., Wismar, M. and Berman, P. C. (eds) (2002) 'Biomedical and Health Research. vol. 50', *The Impact of the Single European Market on Member States*, Dublin: EHMA.

Bertozzi, F. and Bonoli, G. (2002) 'Europeanisation and the Convergence of National Social and Employment Policies: What Can the Open Method of Co-ordination achieve?', Paper presented for the workshop 'Europeanisation of National Political Institutions' at the ECPR joint session, 22–27 March 2002, Turin.

Commission of the European Communities (1998) *Communication on the Development of Public Health Policy in the European Community*, Brussels.

—— (2000) *Social Policy Agenda*, Brussels.

—— (2001a) *The Future of Healthcare and Care for the Elderly: Guaranteeing Accessibility, Quality and Financial Viability*, Brussels.

—— (2001b) *Proposal for a Decision of the European Parliament and of the Council Adopting a Programme of Community Action*, Brussels.

—— (2001c) 'Health and Consumer Protection Directorate-General: The Internal Market and Health Services', Report of the High Level Committee on Health, Brussels.

—— (2001d) *High Level Task Force on 'Skills and Mobility'*, Brussels.

—— (2001e) *European Governance: A White Paper*, Brussels.

—— (2002a) '2002 Broad Economic Policy Guidelines', *European Economy* no. 4, Brussels.

—— (2002b) *Proposal for a Directive of the European Parliament and of the Council in the Recognition of Professional Qualifications*, Brussels.

—— (2003) *Strengthening the Social Dimension on the Lisbon Strategy: Streamlining Open Coordination in the Field of Social Protection*, Brussels.

Cram, L. (1993) 'Calling the Tune without Paying the Piper? Social Policy Regulation:

The Role of the Commission in European Community Social Policy', *Policy and Politics* 21 (2): 135–146.

—— (1994) 'The European Commission as a Multi-organisation: Social Policy and IT Policy in the EU', *Journal of European Public Policy* 1 (2): 195–217.

De La Porte, C. and Pochet, P. (eds) (2002) *Building Social Europe through the Open Method of Co-ordination*, Brussels: Peter Lang.

DGV (Directorate General V – Employment and Social Affairs) (1999) 'Free Movement and Social Security: Citizens' Rights when Moving within the EU', Bulletin no. 2, Brussels.

Ebbinghaus, B. and Hassel, A. (2000) 'Striking Deals: Concertation in the Reform of Continental European Welfare States', *Journal of European Public Policy* 7 (1): 44–62.

Eberlein, B. and Kerwer, D. (2002) 'Theorising the New Modes of European Union Governance', *European Integration Online Papers* 6 (5).

Esping-Andersen, G. (1985) *States against Markets*, Princeton, N.J.: Princeton University Press.

Fajertag, G. and Pochet, P. (eds) (1997) *Social Pacts in Europe*, Brussels: European Trade Union Institute.

Falkner, G. (1998) *EU Social Policy in the 1990s: Towards a Corporatist Policy Community*, London: Routledge.

—— (2000a) 'EG-Sozialpolitik nach Verflechtungsfalle und Entscheidungslücke: Bewertungsmassstäbe und Entwicklungstrends', *Politische Vierteljahresschrift* 41: 279–301.

—— (2000b) 'The Treaty on European Union and Its Revision. Sea Change or Empty Shell for European Social Policies?', in S. Kuhnle and J. van Deth (eds) *The Survival of the European Welfare State*, London: Routledge, pp. 185–201.

Feick, J. (2002) *Regulatory Europeanisation, National Autonomy and Regulatory Effectiveness: Marketing Authorization for Pharmaceuticals*, Max-Planck-Institut für Gesellschaftforschung Discussion Paper 02/6, Cologne.

Ferrera, M. (2003) 'European Integration and National Social Citizenship: Changing Boundaries, New Structuring?', *Comparative Political Studies* 36 (6): 611–652.

Fuchs, M. (2002) 'Free Movement of Services and Social Security – Quo Vadis?', *European Law Journal* 8 (4): 536–555.

Göbel, M. (2002) *Von der Konvergenzstrategie zur offenen Methode der Koordinierung*, Baden-Baden: Nomos.

Goetschy, J. (1999) 'The European Employment Strategy: Genesis and Development', *European Journal of Industrial Relations* 5 (2): 117–137.

Haas, P. M. (1992) 'Introduction: Epistemic Communities and International Policy Co-ordination', *International Organization* 49 (1): 1–35.

Hagen, K. (1999) 'Towards Europeanisation of Social Policies? A Scandinavian Perspective', in Mission Interministérielle Recherche Expérimentation du Ministère des Affaires Sociales (MIRE) (ed.) *Comparing Social Welfare Systems in Nordic Europe and France*, vol. 4, *Copenhagen Conference: France – Nordic Europe*, Paris: Ministère de l'Emploi et de la Solidarité, pp. 661–690.

Hodson, D. and Maher, I. (2001) 'The Open Method as a New Mode of Governance: The Case of Soft Economic Policy Co-ordination', *Journal of Common Market Studies* 39 (4): 719–746.

Holland, W., Mossialos, E., Belcher, P. and Merkel, B. (eds) (1999) *Public Health Policies in the European Union*, Aldershot, UK: Ashgate.

Jones, E. (2003) 'Liberalized Capital Markets, State Autonomy, and European Monetary Union', *European Journal of Political Research* 42 (2): 197–222.

Jordan, G. (1990) 'Sub-governments, Policy Communities and Networks: Refilling the Old Bottles?', *Journal of Theoretical Politics* 2 (3): 319–338.

Jorens, Y. (ed.) (2003) *Open Method of Coordination: Objectives of European Healthcare Policy*, Baden-Baden: Nomos.

Kanavos, P. and McKee, M. (1998) 'Macroeconomic Constraints and Health Challenges Facing European Health Systems', in R. B. Salman, J. Figueras and C. Sakellarides (eds) *Critical Challenges for Healthcare Reform in Europe*, Buckingham: Open University Press, pp. 23–52.

Keck, J. (1999) 'The European Union Single Market in Pharmaceuticals', *Eurohealth* 5 (1): 23–25.

Kenneth, P. (2001) *Comparative Social Policy: Theory and Research*, Buckingham, UK: Open University Press.

Kersbergen, K. van (2000a) 'Political Allegiance and European Integration', *European Journal of Political Research* 37: 1–17.

—— (2000b) 'The Declining Resistance of Welfare States to Change?', in S. Kuhnle and J. van Deth (eds) *Survival of the European Welfare State*, London: Routledge, pp. 19–36.

Kittel, B. (2002) *EMU, EU Enlargement, and the European Social Model: Trends, Challenges, and Questions*, Max-Planck-Institut für Gesellschaftforschung Working Paper 02/1, Cologne.

Kleinman, M. (2002) *A European Welfare State? European Union Social Policy in Context*, Basingstoke, UK: Palgrave Macmillan.

Knill, C. and Lehmkuhl, D. (2002) 'The National Impact of European Union Regulatory Policy: Three Europeanization Mechanisms', *European Journal of Political Research* 41 (2): 255–280.

Leibfried, S. and Pierson, P. (1999) 'European Social Policy', ZeS Working Paper 15/99, Bremen University, Bremen.

—— (2000) 'Social Policy: Left to Courts and Markets?', in H. Wallace and W. Wallace (eds) *Policy-Making in the European Union*, 4th edn, Oxford: Oxford University Press, pp. 267–292.

McKee, M., Mossialos, E. and Baeten, R. (2002) 'The Implications of European Law for Healthcare', in Martin McKee, Elias Mossialos and Rita Baeten (eds) *The Impact of EU Law on Healthcare Systems*, Brussels: Peter Lang, pp. 13–22.

Marshall, T. H. (1950) *Citizenship and Social Class and Other Essays*, Cambridge: Cambridge University Press.

Mossialos, E., McKee, M., Palm, W. *et al.* (2001) *The Influence of EU Law on the Social Character of Healthcare Systems in the European Union*, Report submitted to the Belgian Presidency of the European Union on 19 November 2001, Brussels.

Mossialos, E. and Palm, W. (2003) 'The European Court of Justice and the Free Movement of Patients in the European Union', *International Social Security Review* 56 (2): 3–29.

Palier, B. (2000) 'Does Europe Matter? Européanisation et réforme des politiques sociales des pays de l'Union Européenne', *Politique Européenne* 1 (2): 7–28.

Pierson, P. (2001) 'Investigating the Welfare State at Century's End', in P. Pierson (ed.) *The New Politics of the Welfare State*, Oxford: Oxford University Press, pp. 1–14.

Pitschas, R. (1999) 'Europäische Union und gesetzliche Krankenversicherung:

Entwicklungsperspektiven aus rechtlicher Sicht', *Zeitschrift für Sozialreform* 45 (8/9): 804–820.

Regent, S. (2003) 'The Open Method of Coordination: A New Supranational Form of Governance?', *European Law Journal* 9 (2): 190–214.

Rhodes, M. (2001) 'The Political Economy of Social Pacts: "Competitive Corporatism" and European Welfare Reform', in P. Pierson (ed.) *The New Politics of the Welfare State*, Oxford: Oxford University Press, pp. 165–194.

Roberts, I. and Springer, B. (2001) *Social Policy in the European Union: Between Harmonization and National Autonomy*, Boulder, Colo.: Lynne Rienner.

Scharpf, F. W. (1997) 'Economic Integration, Democracy and the Welfare State', *Journal of European Public Policy* 4: 18–36.

—— (1999) *Governing in Europe: Effective and Democratic?*, Oxford: Oxford University Press.

—— (2000) 'Notes toward a Theory of Multilevel Governing in Europe', Max-Planck-Institut für Gesellschaftforschung Discussion Paper 00/5, Cologne.

Schmidt, S. K. (2000) 'Only an Agenda Setter? The European Commission's Power over the Council of Ministers', *European Union Politics* 1 (1): 37–61.

Schmidt, V. A. (1997) 'European Integration and Democracy: The Differences among Member States', *European Journal of Public Policy* 4: 128–145.

Sieveking, K. (1997) 'Der Europäische Gerichtshof als Motor der sozialen Integration der Gemeinschaft', *Zeitschrift für Sozialreform* 3: 187–208.

Stein, H. (2003) 'The Open Method of Coordination in the Field of EU Healthcare Policy', in Y. Jorens (ed.) *Open Method of Coordination: Objectives of European Healthcare Policy*, Baden-Baden: Nomos, pp. 21–25.

Sykes, R. (1998) 'The Future for Social Policy in Europe?', in Rob Sykes and Pete Alcock (eds) *Developments in European Social Policy: Convergence and Diversity*, Bristol: Policy Press, pp. 251–264.

Threlfall, M. (2003) 'European Social Integration: Harmonization, Convergence and Single Social Areas', *Journal of European Social Policy* 13 (2): 121–139.

Timonen, V. (1999) 'A Threat to Social Security? The Impact of EU Membership on the Finnish Welfare State', *Journal of European Social Policy* 9 (3): 253–260.

Trubek, D. M. and Mosher, J. S. (2001) 'New Governance, EU Employment, and European Social Model', Harvard Law School, Jean Monnet Working Paper 06/01.

Tsoukalis, L. (1997) *The New European Economy Revisited*, Oxford: Oxford University Press.

Wallace, H. (2000) 'The Policy Process: A Moving Pendulum', in H. Wallace and W. Wallace (eds) *Policy-Making in the European Union*, 4th edn, Oxford: Oxford University Press, pp. 39–64.

Wendon, B. (1998) 'The Commission and European Union Social Policy', in Rob Sykes and Pete Alcock (eds) *Developments in European Social Policy: Convergence and Diversity*, Bristol: Policy Press, pp. 55–73.

Wildasin, D. E. (2002) 'Fiscal Policy in Post-EMU Europe', *European Union Politics* 3 (2): 251–260.

Wismar, M. (2001) 'ECJ in the Driving Seat on Health Policy: But What's the Destination?', *Eurohealth* 7 (4): 5–6.

Wismar, M. and Busse, R. (1999) 'Effects of the European Single Market Integration on the German Public Health System', in B.-M. Bellach and H. Stein (eds) *The New Public Health Policy of the European Union: Past Experience, Present Needs, Future Perspectives*, Munich: Urban und Vogel Medien und Medizin, pp. 83–98.

2 The Europeanization of regulatory policy in the EU pharmaceutical sector

Govin Permanand and Elias Mossialos

Introduction

Regulating the pharmaceutical sector is a particularly difficult challenge for policy-makers. While they seek to keep healthcare costs down and drugs affordable, along with ensuring their citizens the best possible access to the highest-quality medicines, they are equally interested in supporting a successful industry where one exists. These objectives are not always compatible, and the result is a perpetual balancing act between health policy and industrial policy – that is, between healthcare and public health interests on the one hand, and research and development as well as employment interests on the other. To reconcile these interests, the fifteen member governments of the European Union (EU) have developed different strategies that reflect not only their industrial and public health priorities but also the specifics of their healthcare systems. Bringing these regimes together under a single supranational framework – towards a single medicines market – has been an expressed goal of the European Commission since its 1985 White Paper on the Internal Market (CEC 1985).[1] Even before that, in the mid-1960s and the aftermath of the Thalidomide tragedy, it was recognized that common Community legislation was necessary to ensure high safety standards throughout the emerging common market. Since publication of the White Paper there has been progress in harmonizing national policies and convergence of standards, and Community competences now range from guidelines on good manufacturing practice through to the approval and licensing of drugs. Although most of these competences have been achieved under the 1992 single European market programme, a single medicines market remains very much a distant goal.

The reason for this is that EU pharmaceutical policy has reached something of a deadlock, stemming primarily from a dissonance between the principle of subsidiarity – which enables national governments to determine healthcare policy – and the free movement goals of the single market – under which medicines are treated as an industrial good. We thus see a clash between the authority of the member states to set their own medicine prices and reimbursement rates, and that of the Community, which regards medicines as a tradable commodity and seeks their free circulation within the European Union. The result of this tension has been a Community focus on industrial policy concerns in order to push the harmonization agenda forwards.

This chapter looks at the development of the European Union's regulatory framework for medicines up to the deadlock that will preclude completion of the single pharmaceutical market. It aims to elucidate a predominantly theoretical perspective on the impasse and the resulting Community focus on industrial policy concerns. Rather than addressing the economic aspects of regulation in the sector, we provide a primarily political and theoretical view of regulatory decision-making. More specifically, we look at the interests of the sector's main stakeholders and examine how, despite the dissonance, policies have been taken forward. We apply James Q. Wilson's (1980) cost–benefit typology of regulatory policy, tying it into wider theoretical perspectives on European integration and policy-making, most notably the 'multi-level governance' view of the EU policy process (Marks, Hooghe and Blank 1996; Christiansen 1997) and the so-called regulatory state conception of the Union (Majone 1996; McGowan and Wallace 1996). This enables us to develop a broader policy-making setting for medicines, from within which we hope to understand how such supranational policies as currently exist came about. In employing such a framework, we aim to contextualize the positions of the various EU pharmaceutical stakeholders not simply within an interest maximization relationship, but more with regard to how the regulatory issue at hand can affect the type of politicking that results, and how this in turn characterizes the achievement of outcomes. By way of context, a review of the 'Europeanization' of pharmaceutical policy in the Community to date is provided in the following.

The Europeanization of pharmaceutical policy

In reviewing the Community's medicines history, we can discern four phases: (i) the establishment of Community rules beginning in 1965; (ii) multiple state market authorization commencing in 1975; (iii) international competition and the Single European Act of 1986; and (iv) an agency approach to facilitating market access since 1995.

The Thalidomide tragedy of the 1950s and 1960s saw many developed countries introduce new medicines laws regarding safety and efficacy testing. In addition to establishing stricter guidelines at home, the six members of the then European Economic Community also agreed common controls and standards in 1965. *Inter alia*, as the first piece of Community legislation in the pharmaceuticals field, Directive 65/65/EEC[2] set out the rules regarding the development and manufacture of medicines in the Community; guidelines for post-market monitoring of drug safety;

and safety, efficacy and therapeutic benefit as the sole grounds for market approval. The reason for the Community's initial step into pharmaceutical policy was therefore a common health threat, and industrial policy interests were to be balanced against national and transnational health policy concerns.

With progress on dismantling tariffs progressing across the board, the Commission's next move in 1975 was to facilitate and speed up the intra-Community movement of medicines. Directive 75/318/EEC[3] created the 'mutual recognition' procedure, whereby a product that had been granted market authorization by the regulatory authority of one member state could be granted multiple member state authorizations (until then, applications had had to be made separately to each national authority). Again in 1975, Directive 75/319/EEC[4] established the Committee for Proprietary Medicinal Products (CPMP). Comprising representatives from each of the member states, the CPMP represented a single authorization body for the Community market. It was also to arbitrate, should a member state object to a product being granted automatic access to its market via the new procedure. However, the sensitivity of healthcare concerns for national governments, and resulting derogation to the free movement rules under Article 36 of the Treaty – where products could have potential negative health effects – meant that the mutual recognition procedure did not speed up authorization as envisaged. It in fact caused delays as the member states regularly raised objections.

In 1983, Directive 83/570/EEC[5] introduced the 'multi-state' procedure, under which the minimum number of countries to which authorization would be extended was dropped from five to two. Although more successful than mutual recognition in terms of the number of applications submitted, it also proved cumbersome, and in 1994, its final year of operation, objections by one or more member states were registered for every product put before it (CPMP 1994). Although all the directives stressed that health matters were of primary concern, they were mainly aimed at progress towards a unified medicines market.

The 1986 Single European Act (SEA) set out to establish a single European market for the free movement of all goods, services and capital by 1992. This represented the Community's response to a growing need to compete more effectively in global markets, in particular with the United States, which was setting up a free trade area of its own. Around this time the Cecchini Report – which had investigated the 'costs of non-Europe' in order to underline the benefits of a single market – was released. Echoing the 1985 White Paper, it cited the pharmaceutical sector as a problem area in that medicines were 'irretrievably linked to public health' (Cecchini with Catinat and Jacquemin 1988). Thus, once again with a view to rationalizing the authorization process, in 1987 Directive 87/22/EEC[6] was agreed. It created the 'concertation' procedure, which applied only to biotechnologically developed and other high-technology products.

Manufacturers were obliged to simultaneously submit their applications to the CPMP and one member state, and once both had completed their evaluations, together they facilitated discussions between the applicant and the other national authorities.

Also important in the post-SEA period was the prevalence (and scope) of price differentials between the member states: anywhere up to five times on single products in 1988 (Chambers and Belcher 1994). In the light of this, the Commission introduced the so-called Transparency Directive in 1989 (Directive 89/105/EEC[7]) requiring the member states to adopt verifiable and transparent criteria in setting pharmaceutical prices and their inclusion in national health insurance systems. Further legislation pertaining to labelling and packaging, patent protection, advertising and sales promotion, and wholesale distribution[8] followed, all taken within the context of meeting the provisions of the single European market. Ultimately, however, the Commission's inability to take the pricing issue forward – in terms of reducing intra-EU differentials – led in 1996 to the publication of the Community's view for the development of an EU industrial policy for pharmaceuticals (Resolution 96/C136/04[9]). Although no legislative progress came of the document, it is clear that the drive towards the single market had a major influence on the direction of EU pharmaceutical policy.

In February 1995 the European Agency for the Evaluation of Medicinal Products (EMEA) officially began operations. Established under Regulation 2309/93 in 1993, the Agency was to decide on all applications for market authorization within the Community. Complementing EMEA came Directive 93/39/EEC,[10] under which mutual recognition was replaced by a new, 'decentralized' procedure, with applications made directly to the Agency. Importantly, the decisions made under the decentralized procedure are *binding*, and member states can only query them on the grounds that they can be shown to have a negative public health impact on their populations. As the EMEA is the only one of the fifteen supranational agencies to be granted a quasi-regulatory mandate – the others (e.g. the European Environment Agency or the European Office for Harmonisation in the Internal Market) are more information-disseminating bodies – it is perhaps the clearest indication of the Community's commitment to harmonization of the pharmaceuticals market.

The picture that emerges from this chronological overview of the development of EU medicines policy is one that reflects the lack of a singular policy strategy for medicines; although there are several major strands. The most notable of these is the single market and the need to bring pharmaceuticals in line. Yet policies have developed outside the influence of the programme, and the single market impetus has not been sufficient to empower the Community in all areas of pharmaceutical policy. Thus, despite the dissonance and apparent policy deadlock, it is clear that a wide-ranging Community regulatory framework does exist, even if it does not amount to a single medicines market.

As the scope of this chapter does not allow for an in-depth analysis of all policies comprising this framework, we lay out three case studies: the Community's 1992 decision to grant medicines exceptional patent protection via the Supplementary Protection Certificate regime; the background to the 1995 launch of the EMEA; and the continuing divisiveness of the pricing and reimbursement issue. These are crucial policy initiatives within the framework, and although they concern disparate issues, each has involved protracted and complex negotiation among the main stakeholders. This helps to strengthen the value of our theoretical approach, particularly with regard to any further 'Europeanization' of the sector.

Theoretical discussion

European integration and policy-making theories are helpful towards understanding where and why specific EU pharmaceutical policies have developed, even if they are not sufficient. For instance, the neo-functionalist premise of 'spillover', where Community authority evolves as a result of policy developments in related fields, helps to explain how the single market programme came to dominate the Commission's approach to pharmaceutical policy during the 1990s. Yet it cannot account for the lack of spillover into the question of pricing and reimbursing medicines at EU level. Central to the spillover premise is that integration would become a self-sustaining dynamic through the emergence of the supranational European institutions. Clearly, this has not been the case across the board, and pharmaceutical policy makes the point. Intergovernmentalist theory – as a response to the supranationalist dynamic of neo-functionalism – argues that the member states remain firmly in control of the integration process. The fact that they closely guard healthcare competences, which hampers initiatives to harmonize the pharmaceutical sector, would seem to support this. Nevertheless, while intergovernmentalism may help to account for member state behaviour, it cannot necessarily explain outcomes in terms of how and why they were reached. So, while both neo-functionalism and intergovernmentalism are relevant to understanding the development of EU pharmaceutical policies, neither is sufficient in explanatory terms.[11]

In recognizing this common failing, more recent work has focused on how agendas are shaped. Moravcsik's (1993) liberal intergovernmentalist perspective concentrates on interdependencies between national decision-making and international (European) cooperation. While national governments retain control over the integration process, they are motivated or even forced to pursue further integration because of particular external and internal circumstances or pressures, such as the General Agreement on Tariffs and Trade and World Trade Organization liberalization regimes, or global climate change. Here the member states are seen as willing to cooperate in order to consolidate their position relative to others. On the one hand, they agree to concede authority over issues where they feel the Community is more likely to be able to protect their interests, and this in a redistributive and equalizing manner *vis-à-vis* their European partners, such as through the single market (e.g. the industrial policy aspects of pharmaceutical regulation). But on the other hand, they remain steadfast over more sensitive issues, such as healthcare and the pricing of medicines.

As Armstrong and Bulmer (1998) note, the liberal intergovernmentalist assessment minimalizes the role played by the European institutions. It is also unable to account for member state interests, which, like pharmaceutical policy, may be multi-layered. All countries may agree on not conceding pricing and reimbursement to the Commission, but their reasons for not wanting a single market in medicines – and indeed, the variance in their support for specific initiatives – stem from individualistic concerns. Still, the approach does offer some insight into what motivates the integration process and, in turn, why certain aspects of pharmaceutical policy have been mandated to the Community and others not.

Bearing in mind the gaps found in the wider theories, we therefore find it useful to concentrate instead on how specific actors were involved in affecting policy outcomes. This endorses Hix's (1994) distinction between theories of European integration and the 'politics of the EU policy process'. Policy outcomes for medicines are thus viewed in terms of bargaining scenarios between actors in the policy process. We restrict ourselves to meso-level analysis and consider the political manoeuvrings behind specific policy developments in terms of the roles played by the major stakeholders: the industry, the member states, the European Commission, and the representatives of consumer/patient interests. Citing these as the main stakeholders does not mean that they are always unified actors representing a single position. The complexity of what market harmonization means for the sector creates clefts within these actor groups: between the member states, between the different Directorates-General of the European Commission, and between sub-sectors of the industry. This approach accommodates the fact that there is a plethora of inputs into European pharmaceutical policy, whether internal or external to the European Union, and is strengthened when combined with Wilson's (1980) earlier-mentioned 'politics of policy' framework. As with both neo-functionalism and (liberal) intergovernmentalism, it recognizes the role played by European institutions and member states. The next step in our discussion, therefore, is to develop our meso level of analysis in order to apply it to the case studies.

The politics of regulation

The nature of Community competences means that most EU policy can be regarded as regulatory (Héritier, Knill and Mingers 1996). This has led to the characterization of the EU's role as primarily concerned with regulation – what Majone (1996) has termed the 'regulatory state' view. As one dimension of this view holds that policy is made as a trade-off between the European Commission on the supply side and organized interests (including the member states) on the demand side, it is of especial relevance to the pharmaceutical sector. The Commission has often found itself at odds with both industry and the member states, not to mention with the host of interests in between, such as wholesalers and distributors, healthcare professionals, pharmacists, and consumers (patients). The case studies will elaborate on this, but we now turn to Wilson's framework in order to analyse how certain polices have been achieved.

Wilson's politics of regulation perspective was developed around the 'iron triangle' conception of 1970s and 1980s US politics – that is, the relationship of interdependence between the state or a bureaucratic agency, a Congressional committee or subcommittee, and an interest group. His conclusions helped to show how industry interests could come to dominate policy discussions and outcomes, and expanded on the earlier arguments of other American scholars such Gabriel Kolko (1963) and George Stigler (1971) regarding the private interest view of regulation. Although US focused, the ability of his framework to integrate business interests (and lobbying specifically) into the policy process, rather than treating it as an external influence, is perhaps the main reason that scholars have sought to apply it beyond the American context. Hood (1994) and Majone (1996), for instance, have employed Wilson's approach respectively to examine at what level business lobbying can prove most successful and to explain EU regulation in general. Indeed, it seems particularly relevant to the EU[12] in that traditional pluralist or even neo-corporatist configurations do not adequately capture the dynamics at play in the Community's so-called multi-level governance structure.

Wilson asserts that policy proposals, particularly where economic stakes are concerned, can be classified in terms of the perceived distribution of their costs and benefits (concentrated or diffuse). These can be either economic or non-economic, or both, and the value they represent is changeable according to the political climate. Apart from simply qualifying regulatory decision-making in this way, he argues that this cost–benefit perspective generates four types of politicking in pursuing and attaining policy outcomes. Wilson's approach goes some way towards supporting Theodore Lowi's (1969) earlier assertion that the policy arena often determines the nature of the political processes within it. Table 2.1 offers a matrix representation of Wilson's framework. The typology characterizes the manner in which different types of policy interest are resolved and the level at which this resolution takes place, based on each player's perception of potential gains (or losses) where a given policy scenario is at stake. As Wilson was concerned with economic regulation at the national level, his stakeholders were industry, the state and the general public (the 'common good'). The multi-level governance nature of the European

Union implies a host of further embedded actors, and policy-making in the pharmaceutical sector reflects this. As our interest is with supranational policy, we see the main stakeholders as the industry, the European Commission, the member states and consumer/patient interests.[13] There may be further inter-actor divisions where the policy issue at hand provokes disparate reactions. It should, however, be noted that Wilson's framework is not perfect. Intermediate cases are likely, and the concentrated–diffuse measurement is a relative one. However, this does not diminish the conceptual value of his approach, as some degree of generalization is usually necessary within any theoretical application. We can, therefore, discuss perceived costs and benefits, within reason, and this we do below.

Majoritarian politics occurs where there is little incentive for collaboration and where the costs and benefits of a proposed regulatory intervention are spread among the affected parties. The likelihood of policy outcome is slim. The question of who is willing to pay what for what share of the benefit means that resolution will only take place where there is sufficient political will and popular support. With unanimity required, a policy outcome will only be achievable via *majoritarian politics*. In the EU context, where the issue is about extending supranational regulatory authority in a particular area, this means that all the stakeholders will have to consent to bearing some of the costs of a policy that will also benefit the others. Social policy has been cited as one such example (Majone 1996). The sluggishness of some member states in implementing the 1993 Working Time Directive[14] perhaps bears witness to this. In the light of the wide distribution of both costs and benefits, matters involving member state healthcare systems and the provision of health also fall into this category. The Commission may favour an increased Community role – though this needs centralizing, as several Directorates-General affect health policy decisions (Mossialos and Permanand 2000) – but the member states remain strongly opposed in view of the potential economic costs and political consequences.

Over issues where costs may be diffuse but the benefits concentrated, only a small group stands to derive the most gain. As there is considerable incentive for groups to seek to influence the policy process in their favour,

Table 2.1 The 'politics of policy'

		Benefits	
		Diffuse	*Concentrated*
Costs	*Diffuse*	Majoritarian politics	Client politics
	Concentrated	Entrepreneurial politics	Interest-group politics

Source: Majone (1996), based on Wilson (1980)

client politics emerges. This is the classic business lobbying profile, where the potential dominance of industrial lobbies – because the costs are so widely distributed that the price per capita becomes negligible and the likelihood of widespread opposition diminished – is usually countered by the use of independent regulatory bodies. Where such agencies lack power, Wilson suggests that the 'producer-dominance model' results (regulatory capture). Industry may thus receive favourable treatment by government via subsidies or simply a laxer regulatory environment. Industry lobbying over specific EU policies has long characterized the pharmaceuticals market, even before the single market – first, because of the market's fragmentation, and second, owing to the structure of the supranational policy process, which is equally horizontal and vertical. Moreover, industry has generally been very successful. This is because the issues at stake tend to be similar across national boundaries, and the multinational nature of the sector has enabled the industry to gain significant lobbying experience in a host of environments (Greenwood and Ronit 1994).

Entrepreneurial politics characterizes policies involving a wide distribution of benefits through a more concentrated spread of costs. There is little support for the proposed policy, as the small group responsible for bearing the costs is opposed to it, while the gains to the potential beneficiaries are too diffuse to spur them into action. This lack of interest may be due to a lack of knowledge about the benefits, or may simply reflect a general apathy because the relative gain per capita is insufficient. With interest in such an intervention thus lacking, Wilson proposes that an actor able to galvanize public support, the 'policy entrepreneur', becomes necessary. To garner support, the entrepreneur often dramatizes an issue and associates the benefits of the proposed policy with values or the common good. For example, by revealing environmental mismanagement by companies or associating regulatory policies with things such as cleaner water, a skilled entrepreneur can provoke support for strict and costly environmental protection policies. At EU level the European Commission often fulfils the entrepreneurial role. It is able (and has a responsibility as instigator of policy) to amass support on a host of issues, primarily on the basis of potential widespread Community benefits. This it has done over environmental issues, where the benefits of stricter standards are to be enjoyed by the member states' populations, while private enterprise is generally responsible for financing and implementing them. It should be noted that the entrepreneur need not be a completely objective party. More often than not, it will have an agenda of its own, as will be shown here of the European Commission in the pharmaceutical arena.

Finally, a policy offering considerable benefits to only a small number of interests at the expense of a small number of others who will bear the costs gives rise to *interest-group politics*. In an industrial setting, government subsidies or other incentives will usually favour one segment of industry while disadvantaging one or more others (sometimes even with regard to single companies). Accordingly, the motivation for both sides to organize in order to influence the policy process becomes acute. The question of the 'public good' is not normally raised in this configuration as the costs and benefits are not seen to really affect the wider population. The result is a multitude of groups with specific interests, all actively campaigning to ensure their own welfare – the few on the basis of the benefit they stand to derive, and the majority on the basis of the costs they may have to bear. The potential gains and losses implied by such policies at European level, such as Structural Funds, where the emphasis is on the redistribution of, and competition for, financial support, leads to a variety of bargaining scenarios. These often result in disagreement between the European institutions and the member states, as well as among and within them.

Applying these four categorizations to selected policies that make up the EU pharmaceutical framework gives rise to the typology of Table 2.2. The following discussion seeks to explain this application, thereby showing how EU policy in this sector involves the main stakeholders and, by extension, the reasons for the deadlock over a single medicines market.

Type of politics

As space limitations do not permit an examination of all the policies that comprise the EU medicines framework, we limit ourselves to three. These reflect not simply the relevance of the framework, but more the fact that supranational policy-making for medicines is extremely complicated. That various EU competences and policies correspond to different configurations within the Wilson approach reflects this complexity. Regulatory policy in more traditional industries might apply to one or perhaps two of the scenarios, but certainly not all of them.

Table 2.2 The 'politics of policy' as applied to selected Community pharmaceutical policy

Costs versus benefits			
Diffuse–diffuse	*Diffuse–concentrated*	*Concentrated–diffuse*	*Concentrated–concentrated*
• Pricing	• Patent protection	• Packaging, inserts and leaflets	• A fully integrated single market for pharmaceuticals
• Reimbursement	• European Medicines Evaluation Agency		
Majoritarian	*Client*	*Entrepreneurial*	*Interest-group*

Case studies

Of the three case studies, the first looks at the successful industry lobby over intellectual property rights as an example of client politics. The industry's claims that the patent protection rights accorded to medicines were not sufficient to sustain the research and development (R&D) costs required to produce new and innovative medicines were upheld in a 1992 Regulation extending the protection period for pharmaceuticals. The second is the establishment of the EMEA. As the discussion will show, the reasons for its establishment appear to be a case of entrepreneurial politics by the Commission, though by the time the Regulation was approved, the grounds may have shifted towards client politicking. The third example is the pricing and reimbursement debate. Commission initiatives to overcome this deadlock are looked at, as are the reasons why this area remains such a sticky point; this is seen as majoritarian politics, given the continuing impasse. A fully integrated medicines market corresponds to the interest-group scenario, with the winner–loser division between member states lying at its heart. Some of the reasons for the deadlock have already been raised, and others will become clear throughout the remainder of the discussion. The next stage is to examine the policy process in each case and to demonstrate the relevance of the theoretical framework.

Supplementary patent protection for medicines

Intellectual property rights are seen as central to the research-intensive segment of the pharmaceutical industry and, following intensive lobbying by the European Federation of Pharmaceutical Industries and Associations (EFPIA), in 1992 the European Commission agreed Community legislation extending patent terms on new medicines. Regulation 1768/92 introduced the European Community's Supplementary Protection Certificate (SPC) scheme, despite the fact that pharmaceutical patents are covered by the 1973 European Patent Convention (EPC). Under the SPC, manufacturers were granted fifteen years' patent protection from the date of first *market authorization* of their product in the Community – as opposed to the twenty years from first *patent application* under the EPC.[15] This represented a clear benefit to the research-based industry in terms of the length of time its products would be covered under the patent term. The industry had in fact been seeking such a derogation from the EPC since the late 1980s. EFPIA's lobbying efforts were centred around the growing cost of bringing a new medicine to market[16] and the fact that the period from identification of the new molecule to the launching of the derived product represents a much longer R&D and market approval process than is found in other sectors. As patents are granted on the new molecule in the first instance, the duration of the approval process impacts on the length of time a drug is actually available on the market under patent protection. The industry argued that this period, the 'effective patent life', was decreasing, thereby damaging the prospects for further investment.

Intellectual property rights (patent protection) in the pharmaceutical industry represent a clear clash between industrial policy and healthcare expenditure concerns. During the SPC campaign, EFPIA lobbied over its concerns that as the number of new chemical entities being discovered was diminishing, the length of the discovery and approval processes (and hence their own costs) were increasing. The reasons for this were said to be stricter licensing procedures in the member states and growing pressures to look into as yet untreatable conditions such as HIV and cancer. On the other side, consumer groups such as the Consumers in the European Community Group (CECG) felt that (lengthy) medicine patents, which limit the speed of access to new therapies, were not in the interests of public health; patients were not being granted access to the best possible therapies. There are clearly merits to both positions, and the Commission ought to have been torn between its interest in promoting a strong industry (in production and employment terms) and its interest in safeguarding the health of its citizens. Thus, the question is how, in the SPC, the Commission could have ultimately delivered a proposal so clearly in favour of the industry.

In lobbying the Commission, EFPIA was initially turned away by the Competition Directorate-General (DG IV). With the single European market programme well under way, Berthold Schwab, the head of DG IV's Intellectual and Industrial Property Unit, did not see patent term extension on medicines as a Community concern, given the healthcare implications. The industry regrouped, abandoned its intellectual property approach, and refocused its arguments around the idea that current patent protection terms were starving innovation, which could potentially have negative effects *vis-à-vis* both the Community's industrial competitiveness and public health. It now targeted the Pharmaceuticals and Cosmetics Unit in the Industrial Affairs office (DG III), which, as Shechter (1998) notes, chose to see patent term extension as an industrial policy and therefore a Commission affair, and set about making the case to other Community institutions and actors on behalf of DG III.

To make its case, EFPIA drafted a data-intensive report on the European industry, including the economic costs associated with patent protection, and provided copies to selected officials and Members of the European Parliament (MEPs).[17] *Inter alia*, the report cited a six-year approval process in some member states, which, when subtracted from the twenty-year protection accorded by the EPC, in fact resulted in a diminished effective patent life compared to other industrial products (CEC 1993). EFPIA's members also pointed to revised medicines patent legislation in the United States (1984) and Japan (1987) to support their case. Closer to home, France and Italy had by 1991 themselves sought unilaterally to pursue patent restoration measures, though these were nullified when the SPC legislation took effect. In addition to the issue of declining competitiveness, the industry lobby strengthened its case by associating patents with better medicines, namely by claiming that improved patent protection periods would allow pharmaceutical companies to recoup their costs in order to then be able to reinvest in R&D. This line of argument proved a powerful foil against criticisms that the industry was simply driven by the profit motive.

Generics manufacturers were unhappy with the proposed legislation, as it sought to limit them to beginning their R&D only after the date of approval for the originator product. Prior to the SPC they had been able to do so from the submission date of the patent for the original product, and were in theory thus able to release their copy on the day the patent expired. EFPIA's members viewed this as an unfair advantage in view of their higher costs, but the generics industry saw the old arrangement as its only means of competing, as its costs were also rising. Not only was this limitation going to have repercussions in Europe, but it was also feared that, as much of the European generics industry's output was sold as bulk pharmaceuticals to US drug-makers, the SPC might negatively impact on the US industry as well. With patent extension having already been legislated on in the United States, the view of Lee Fensterer, the then president of the United States Generic Pharmaceutical Industry Association, was that 'It's the same crazy battle we had in the US in the early 80s, with the Pharmaceutical Manufacturers Association saying that US patent life was only eight or nine years. And, of course, that was a horrendous lie' (as quoted by Bahner 1993). Unlike the research-based companies, however, the generics manufacturers did not yet have a representative body at EU level to lobby the Commission.

The member state governments also had concerns with the proposals. Their primary interest was in controlling healthcare costs, and it was felt that patent extension could delay the introduction of cheaper generics, thereby keeping drug prices high. Generic substitution was developing as a popular cost-saving mechanism at the time. That said, not all governments had identical interests. The United Kingdom and Germany, with their major research-based industries, were initially reluctant because of the effects any changes might have had on pharmaceutical prices. Germany was in a particularly delicate position, as it also has a considerable generics industry. Other countries with mainly generics industries, such as Spain and Portugal, opposed the proposals outright. Patients and consumer groups were also unhappy, lobbying on health grounds. The European Consumers' Organization (BEUC) viewed the proposals as a 'blank cheque for industry' (BEUC 1991), while the CECG argued that 'increased protection should apply only to new molecular entities which represent a genuine therapeutic gain' (CECG 1993).

Given these divergent views, EFPIA had to ensure that the European

Parliament and the Council would accept the proposals, and here the Commission's support went a long way to convincing key individuals of the merits of the SPC. According to Shechter (1998), for instance, Berthold Schwab – who now supported the position – was consulted by Friedrich Merz, the *rapporteur* assigned the task of delivering the Parliament's views. And Mr Schwab set about advising Mr Merz on the best way to present the proposals so as to ensure Parliamentary support. In the end, both the Parliament (on second reading) and the Council voiced some initial reservations but gave their approval subject to minor amendments.[18]

As regulations are uniformly binding pieces of legislation, positing the SPC as a Regulation would pre-empt any further national measures, thereby giving the Community exclusive competence. Also noteworthy is the fact that opposition to the legislation by some member states, patient and healthcare interests, and the generics industry, not to mention dissenting voices from the United States, simply came too late and/or was not strong enough. Organized, collective opposition from the generics community was, for instance, heard only after the Council Common Position was issued. Moreover, prior to the single market there was no European representation for generics producers to counter EFPIA, which had been established in 1978. The European Generics Association (EGA) was formed only in 1992, the very year the SPC legislation was passed. The Commission was therefore able to remain firm in its resolve and, on the basis of EFPIA's claims, an SPC offering a fifteen-year protection period from the first authorization was agreed.

Invoking Wilson's typology, the diffuse costs but concentrated benefits 'client politics' scenario clearly characterized the SPC initiative. The costs of patent extension were to be spread among a host of actors: first, the national governments and insurance funds, which pay for medicines; next, the generics companies, which were comparatively hindered by the longer patent times; and third, consumers, who were arguably worse off in that their access to cheaper medicines had been diminished. The benefits were to be derived only by the research-intensive companies and, indirectly, a minority of national governments with innovative industries. And though this came about through heavy lobbying of the Commission, it was itself a willing party. For although it seemed to have simply sided with EFPIA, the Commission's main interest was in maintaining a strong European industry within the context of completing the single market. It played a major part in convincing the European Parliament and Council the merits of the EFPIA position. Moreover, the first draft of the SPC had called for a twenty-year period of protection,[19] which was considerably more generous than the fourteen years' protection under the 1984 Hatch–Waxman Act in the United States, or the eleven years that was being discussed in the United Kingdom prior to the SPC. Clearly, the Commission had its own agenda as well, and while this may suggest an entrepreneurial role, the impetus for patent term extension had come from the industry. It was the extensive lobbying campaign undertaken by EFPIA that persuaded the Commission to pursue such a favourable derogation.

The industry's success with the SPC thus shows three things. First, the sector is characterized by severe informational asymmetries. The Commission accepted the case put to it by EFPIA and the industry lobby even though, as mentioned earlier, there was evidence (also from the United States) indicating that drugs did not necessarily lose profitability as soon as the period of patent protection ran out. Second, understanding the Commission's industrial policy interests is central to understanding its priorities *vis-à-vis* pharmaceutical policy. And third, in part as a consequence, a relatively small number of organized interests can, as the client politics scenario suggests, come to dominate the EU (pharmaceutical) policy agenda, to their obvious gain.[20]

The European Agency for the Evaluation of Medicinal Products

Responsible for granting EU market approval to new medicinal preparations (for human and veterinary use), the European Agency for the Evaluation of Medicinal Products (EMEA) was created in 1993 under the terms of Regulation (EEC) 2309/93, and has been operational since February 1995. The agency was charged with fostering market access for medicines in the Community via the 'centralized' and 'decentralized' procedures, the latter being a revamped mutual recognition procedure. The first applies to products derived from biotechnology and the second to conventional products. Under the decentralized procedure, following the approval of a national application, other member state authorities are expected to recognize this authorization. The Committee for Proprietary Medicinal Products (CPMP), which prepares the agency's opinions on medicines for human consumption, simultaneously considers the original application and then delivers a binding verdict on extending market access to the other member states – the agency's decisions being based solely on the criteria of quality, safety and efficacy, in terms of the original 1965 Directive. However, the member states continue simultaneously to assess applications themselves. The point to be borne in mind from the outset, therefore, is that market approval of new medicines in the European Union remains a joint national–supranational competence, despite there being an EU licensing agency.

Not just replacing the previous market authorization procedures, the EMEA has a broader impact on pharmaceutical policy in the European Union. It has a role in pharmacovigilance and has committed itself to operational transparency *vis-à-vis* the drug approval process. Here the agency's website posts the Summary of Product Characteristics for new medicine applications, the European Public Assessment Reports, which detail the rationale behind positive marketing opinions, as well as a host of other relevant information. In bringing the expertise of some 2,300 experts together,[21] the agency also aids national authorities by filling gaps in knowledge. Furthermore, by streamlining the regulatory environment it helps to make the European Union a more attractive place to do pharmaceutical business generally. Its role thus serves a combination of public health and industrial policy goals.

This differentiates the EMEA from the fourteen other EU agencies, which are primarily information-disseminating offices and do not have as strong a remit or influence on the Commission. The EMEA is thus a quasi-regulatory body in that it operates a virtual informational monopoly over pharmaceutical applications, using this to take binding decisions on market authorization. Additionally, it has full authority over biotechnology via the centralized procedure. Still, the EMEA does not wield authority in the manner of the US Food and Drug Administration (FDA). Comprising a relatively small core staff, it issues recommendations rather than making policy. Indeed, it is not the agency itself but experts in the member states working on its behalf who carry out the assessments upon which the CPMP then bases its opinions. Although none of the EMEA's opinions has been rejected, it is officially the Commission that retains the final say. Moreover, healthcare concerns and pricing and reimbursement remain catered for at the national level by public regulatory agents.

It is therefore interesting that, in a statement made at the time of the agency's inauguration, the Commission claimed that the EMEA represented above all a benefit to the patient (CEC 1995). Quicker and more transparent approval procedures were cited as central to the discovery of new medicines and thus to citizens' health. Indeed, the agency's first Director has pointed to some 150 new approvals completed within the centralized procedure's 240-day time-frame as indication of this quicker and improved regime (Sauer 2000). Notwithstanding the member states' continued reassessment of applications, the industry too regards the agency as having delivered a more efficient approval process, reflected by 60 per cent of applicants declaring themselves satisfied or very satisfied with the work of the CPMP and 70 per cent satisfied or very satisfied with the 'transparency, dialogue and advice' they have received from the agency (EFPIA-EMEA 1999). But does this 'efficiency' really have a positive impact in public health terms? While there is a link between faster market access and improved consumer health, it depends entirely on what sort of drugs are being approved, and here the EMEA has been subject to considerable criticism in relation to concerns over its mandate and an apparent pro-industry leaning.

One of the fiercest critics comes from within the CPMP. Silvio Garattini, one of the two Italian members, has consistently questioned the agency's commitment to public health, as opposed to serving industry. He has argued that most of the drugs approved via the agency have been copies, or so-called me-too drugs (Garattini and Bertele' 2001). These tend to be drugs on which the companies anticipate good returns. And with the agency using a rather thin definition of innovation in terms of the therapeutic benefit of new drugs – in comparison to the FDA, for example – 'need' has not been a consideration in the drugs it authorizes. Another example of potential industry bias is that companies have access to the CPMP's initial consultation documents concerning their applications. This either enables them to withdraw their application before a final decision has been reached, or gives them forewarning of a negative decision so that they can immediately begin work on an appeal. By contrast, neither consumer nor patient interests are involved in the CPMP's work.

Further criticism stems from the fact that the companies are able to choose the national experts who undertake the evaluation of their applications on the EMEA's behalf. Companies obviously choose those most sympathetic to their own interests – in other words, those *rapporteurs* with the quickest approval procedures. As Abraham and Lewis (2000) note, this has led to the United Kingdom, Sweden, France and the Netherlands being either first- or second-choice *rapporteur* in the majority of cases. Again, speed of approval does not necessarily equate to improved public health, especially when the medicines being authorized are not necessarily those most needed. Indeed, we are not aware of any evidence to suggest that EMEA's quicker approvals have had a measurably positive impact on citizens' health. There are further criticisms of the manner in which the agency works and cooperates with individual companies – often in such a way as potentially to compromise public health[22] – but these are beyond the scope of this chapter.

The point to be made, therefore, is that the premise of a public health benefit is not really the EMEA's prime function, nor was it the basis on which the Commission launched its case for the agency. In initially discussing the need for a European medicines agency, the main rationale cited by the Commission, the industry and even the member states was the need to speed up market access (Permanand 2002). Industry saw mutual recognition as slow and inefficient, and member states were constantly raising objections to approvals granted under the procedure. During the first four years of the CPMP procedure, for example, each of the (only) four multiple applications submitted was sent back to the Committee by at least one member state (Hancher 1990), and the industry continued to express a distinct preference for single market applications.

The relative disuse of mutual recognition represented a major setback to the Commission's aims to promote the single market. With the 1992 deadline imminent, and clear signs that the pharmaceutical sector would not be ready, it was therefore the Commission that first sought to gauge interest in a European medicines office. In 1988 it circulated a document asking 'interested parties' (the other stakeholders) about the future 'definitive system' for the free movement of medicines, also making its own preference for a European-level answer clear. Although the member states, industry and consumer interests were initially reluctant, or at least had differing views on what role a pan-European medicines agency might play, the Commission went on to present an initial proposal document in 1990. This incorporated the industry's demand for a more efficient multiple market authorization procedure, and invoked Article 100a of the Treaty – designed to facilitate completion of the single market through harmonizing national laws – as the requisite legal basis. In the words of Fernand Sauer, then head of DG III's pharmaceuticals unit, 'The idea of creating a single European agency is to make evaluation more efficient' (as quoted by Koberstein (1993)). But the proposals led to criticism from consumer interests, such as the BEUC, which accused the Commission of being 'more concerned about promoting the recognition of other countries' medicines, despite differing safety standards.... Proposals for opening up the market take precedence over those which have to do with the quality of healthcare' (as quoted by Orzack (1996)).

The creation of the EMEA thus reflects the clash between health and industrial interests in the sector. The view is dependent on which camp one sits in. For instance, while one analyst, who had hitherto criticized the Community's authorization process as being too fragmented, proclaimed, 'At last, a real European milestone ... the importance of this step cannot be underestimated [*sic*]' (Albedo 1995), another feared that the agency mandate would lead to an 'uneasy' relationship with national regulatory authorities, in turn raising 'questions about public accountability, public protection, and health' (Orzack 1996). The reason was that while most national regulatory systems were designed to protect patients first, the EMEA (in its own words) instead aims to 'coordinate the existing scientific resources of the Member States in order to evaluate and supervise medicinal products ... throughout the whole of the European Union' (EMEA FAQs). This has led to the above-mentioned ongoing criticism over the lack of a policy dimension oriented more towards consumers and healthcare.

It is therefore as a result of early and continued criticism that the European policy-makers have sought to stress the agency's public health role. The Commission has even claimed that the agency was established 'partly in response to demands from consumers' organisations ... and the European Parliament' (CEC 2000), even though there is no evidence of this. As early as 1986, in fact, the BEUC had registered its dissatisfaction that consumer organizations were not formally included in consultations on drug approval under the CPMP procedure, while the views of industry were in fact actively solicited (Orzack 1996). The Commission's change of line reflects the pressure it subsequently came under from those who felt that the model the Commission was pursuing lacked transparency, and who were upset that no consumer or patient representation had been present during the policy-making process (Mossialos and Abel-Smith 1997). In reality, the agency's function reflects, to a considerable degree, the Commission's preoccupation with the single market. Again in the words of former Commissioner Bangemann, 'this decision [creating the agency] shows that we have taken an important step towards completion of the internal market, also for pharmaceutical products' (as quoted by Albedo (1995)) – namely, quicker approvals, a binding authorization system and a mandate that involves helping companies prepare their applications so as to ensure approval.

From this, it appears that the agency's design, the grounds on which it was established, and indeed its function are all decidedly leaning towards industrial policy. Moreover, the EMEA lies within the jurisdiction of the Enterprise DG, formerly DG III for industry and the single market. This may suggest that the EMEA resulted or evolved primarily as 'spillover' from the single market programme. But this is only a superficial conclusion, and one that fails to acknowledge the direct role played by the industry and the Commission respectively. For instance, the establishment of the decentralized and centralized procedures is said to have reflected the wishes of the industry to avoid a single authorization procedure along the lines of the FDA, which, it was felt, was unduly bureaucratic and excessively slow (Matthews and Wilson 1998). As regards the Commission's hand, in the EMEA's first annual report the Commission, and DG III in particular, is cited as primarily responsible for the preparatory work behind the agency's establishment (EMEA 1996). The Commission had actively canvassed advice not only from firms and industry associations, but also from relevant government departments and national authorities with regard to their interests in speeding up marketing approval. Both actively sought an industrial policy role for the new agency – the industry to facilitate its business, and the Commission to bring the market in line with the single market and to promote a strong industry – despite later pronouncements regarding European patients.

In viewing the creation of the agency from within Wilson's typology, the beneficiaries were clearly the Commission and the industry. The EMEA represented a major step in the Commission's search for (i) a level playing field for business and an integrated pharmaceuticals market; and (ii) competitive advantage for the European industry in terms of attracting and rewarding R&D, and strong global sales by domestic European industry. The quicker approval procedures have obviously also brought a concentrated benefit to industry.

In terms of those bearing the costs, the member states feared not only that their own regulatory authorities were slowly being squeezed out (although this has not really happened in practice), but also that a streamlined authorization procedure would mean rationalization of some industry operations, reducing the industrial contribution of the industry to national economies. Patients too have perhaps borne certain 'costs', in that there is no proof that they have benefited from the quicker approval times, least of all in terms of needed medicines.[23] This is in part because patient representation via consumer or patient groups was not of serious interest to the Commission, given its aim to free up market authorization.[24]

If one takes the view that the by no means inconsiderable influence of industry played a major role in actually setting the agency's mandate, the establishment of the EMEA may be regarded as a case of 'client politics' in the Wilson framework. However, as the discussion has shown, it was the Commission that instigated proceedings, and that managed to push its own agenda. This conforms with the 'entrepreneurial politics' scenario, especially as the benefits are so concentrated and the costs so widespread. The agency thus represented a cost–benefit ratio that decidedly favours the Commission's preoccupation with the single market aspect of the pharmaceutical sector. It ought not be surprising, therefore, that EMEA's mandate reflects this in practice.

Pricing and reimbursement of medicines

As the pricing and reimbursement of drugs is a healthcare competence, member states retain control over it in their national markets. Demographic differences, disparities in income, cultural factors and differing healthcare systems with their consequent approaches to financing have led to very different strategies among them. Despite the differences, however, pharmaceutical expenditure in most member states is reimbursed by social security systems, albeit at different rates. Detailing each of the very different national pricing regimes is not possible here; suffice it to say that the majority of countries employ either (or at times both) direct price controls or reference pricing mechanisms, the United Kingdom being an exception in operating a profit control system. This simplification belies a host of further variables, but the main point is that as medicines are paid for and delivered via national healthcare systems, none of the member states is prepared to renounce any autonomy in this regard. Within the context of the single market these varying regimes cause difficulties, the most troublesome of which is price variations between countries for the same product. This is unlike price differentials in other sectors, which are more the result of market forces, and has led to the controversial issue of parallel trade. The Commission has traditionally viewed this distortion as the major obstacle to establishing a single medicines market and has tried numerous strategies to address the issue. Most often it has done so in reference to the 'free movement' principles. Three successive initiatives warrant specific mention.

The first is the initial push for a 'European' dimension to member state pricing methodologies. Directive 89/105/EEC, which came into force in early 1990, was designed to ensure open and verifiable criteria in member state pricing and reimbursement decisions within their healthcare systems. This was to ensure that national policies did not represent a restriction on the import and export of medicines in the Community – in other words, to promote the single market. It was in part spurred by several Court rulings in favour of parallel trade in medicines within the Community.

The approved Directive was somewhat thinner than the first draft, issued in 1986, which itself had been subject to numerous revisions. The European Parliament had made major amendments, ultimately resulting in the removal of proposed measures to promote price harmonization. In discussing the final text, approved in April 1988, the Commission was forced to accept the fact that on the basis of different 'per capita income, healthcare systems and traditions of medical practice', price harmonization at this stage was 'not realistic' (Burstall 1992). The Directive's preamble thus refers simply to 'further progress towards convergence', and the Commission ultimately deemed it an initial move towards eventual price harmonization via a step-by-step approach.

The Commission did seek to launch a second Transparency Directive, but there was insufficient support among the other stakeholders to see it through. Consumers' interests, such as the BEUC, did not see price controls or harmonization as bringing 'substantial benefits' to consumers (Albedo 1991). The research industry was also unhappy with the Commission's renewed interest in price harmonization and, via EFPIA, voiced its concerns about direct Commission involvement in member state pricing policies as potentially harmful to business. Finally, the member states – at least those that responded to a Commission questionnaire in 1992 as a follow-up to the Transparency Directive – generally emphasized that they would not accept any Community infringement on their sovereignty where healthcare was concerned. Thus, in a speech to the United Kingdom's Institute of Economic Affairs, ex-Commission Vice-President Leon Brittan pointed specifically to the principle of subsidiarity as having limited the further development of Community competence in the area of pricing (Brittan 1992).

In the light of the stakeholders' divergent interests *vis-à-vis* price harmonization, the Commission's next step was to identify an area of common interest. This it tried to do in 1993 with the 'Communication on the Outlines of an Industrial Policy for the Pharmaceutical Sector in the European Community' (COM 1993). It sought to make the case that European-level policies were needed to sustain and promote the industry in the face of growing international competition, and that a successful industry was in everyone's interest, in both industrial and health policy terms. The Communication focused on comparative industrial statistics and provided an assessment of competition policy/legislation in other major industries and markets, mainly the United States and Japan. As the Commission's interest was to generate some movement on pricing (as necessary for a successful industry), the Communication sought to encompass the views of the other vested interests.

At least ten different drafts were prepared, with the final version being very different from initial attempts (Mossialos and Abel-Smith 1997). There are several reasons for this. One was that a split developed between the DGs for industry and social policy, as the latter sought to have proposals for deregulating drug prices removed (Anon. 1994). Another reason was that the member states disagreed with the Commission on several points but also disagreed among themselves. The stated intent of the Communication to 'monitor the impact on the functioning of the internal market of national pharmaceutical pricing and reimbursement measures ... to assess the need to adapt [the Transparency] Directive in light of experience' did not assuage member state concerns regarding their interests in cost containment (Furniss 1997). Despite shared concerns on the potential for job losses, they of course voiced different requirements where industrial policy was concerned.

The BEUC also registered its disapproval, most notably in a 1994 opinion paper criticizing the Commission for ignoring the lack of competition in the sector and choosing instead to persuade the industry to consolidate its position in Europe (BEUC 1994). By contrast, EFPIA warmly endorsed the Communication. After the document had been shot down by the Parliament and Council, and there being no legislative follow-up, the Commission claimed that it had in fact intended the Communication more as a means of facilitating dialogue than as a final policy statement (Deboyser 1995).

Building on this 'inclusive' approach, the Commission organized a series of 'Roundtable' discussions with the major stakeholders under the auspices of the Industry Directorate.[25] Chaired by Commissioner Bangemann and meeting twice in Frankfurt (in 1996 and 1997) and once in Paris (in 1998), the talks were intended to give all stakeholders a platform on which to express and eventually reconcile their concerns. These meetings developed out of informal consultations between Dr Bangemann and the industry through the Joint Task Force on Pharmaceutical Policy. Without detailing what took place during each meeting, we can identify some common threads.

First, the Commission seemed to accept the fact that price harmonization would not be likely, at least not via a top-down approach – hence the need for all parties to sit together. Next, the meetings had very restricted guest lists: Commission representatives, the industry (EFPIA and individual companies), national regulatory authorities, various professional organizations and the member state officials, along with selectively invited experts. Absent at the first meeting were patient or consumer interests, although they were present at the second and third rounds. The media were barred entry to those two later meetings, which led to accusations of secrecy and deal-making (Furniss 1997). Third, the underlying theme of all three meetings was the liberalization of the pharmaceutical market generally, and the specific question of how to pursue a single pricing regime that would meet the interests of industry, the member states and consumers in an equitable manner (Huttin 1999). Finally, the consequences of national price differentials in the European Union – that is, parallel trade – was a key topic at each gathering. It is one that clearly reveals the divisiveness of the pricing question where the stakeholders are concerned.

Because of differing health and industrial policy priorities, the position of the member states on parallel trade is nuanced. While they wish to keep their autonomy over pricing (and have different cost-containment strategies), they also seek to promote their local industry. Germany and the United Kingdom have sought to discourage the practice of parallel trade, as it impacts on their strong research-oriented sectors, while countries such as Denmark and the Netherlands have actively encouraged it as a manner of reducing costs. The other stakeholders are also divided. The research-based industry views parallel trade as anti-competitive, while generic manufacturers are strong supporters. This has resulted in a leading role for the European Court of Justice, and the Court has traditionally ruled in favour of the practice. Four days before the first Roundtable, it delivered a judgment in two joint cases, ruling that price distortions resulting from different pricing legislation in a member state were to be remedied by Community measures, rather than via national policies that might be incompatible with free movement rules (ECJ 1996). Although the Commission endorsed the Court's stance in its 1998 Communication on the single market in pharmaceuticals (COM 1998) by stressing the integrative force represented by parallel trade, it also noted the inefficiencies created. Such divergent views were also heard during the Roundtables. Consumer representatives and politicians tended to stress the importance of the practice as a manner of ensuring affordable medicines and sustainable healthcare financing, while industry, and to a degree the Commission, tended to point to the resultant distortions.

Apart from pricing and parallel trade, other points of discussion at the Roundtables were the role of over-the-counter and generic medicines; developing Europe as a strong base for pharmaceutical R&D; information systems and electronic commerce; and the potential effects of EU enlargement. Despite some common ground having been reached, no real policy decisions resulted from the meetings. The Commission perhaps became less dogmatic about price deregulation as the sole way to achieve further harmonization, endorsing a more gradual approach, but its remit remains bound by the free movement obligations of the Treaty. As for the other stakeholders, the continued divisiveness of the pricing issue does not suggest that any of them changed their views; in part because the Roundtables were characterized by defensive position-taking, where the invitees spent more time countering each other's statements than they did explaining their own concerns (Kanavos and Mossialos 1999). This reflects the fact that the interests at stake were, and remain, too sensitive to concede on. Despite meeting as a group on three occasions, the major stakeholders have been unable to agree on a way forward, and since Commissioner Bangemann's departure in 2000, no further Roundtables have been programmed.

The Wilson framework suggests that these disparate views and

reactions to the prospect of harmonizing pricing and reimbursement indicate that the passing of any regulatory policy is going to be a complicated
affair. The difficulties behind the three Commission initiatives highlighted
reflect this. The stakeholders are all affected by the costs and benefits
involved, but not sufficiently to force a change in the status quo. The
incentives for cooperation in pushing a single agenda are not there, given
the differences in interest, and the Commission lacks the necessary clout,
in legal and policy-making terms, to take the issue of price harmonization
forward.

All actors pursue individualistic lines, so that majoritarian politics
emerge. The Commission's lack of healthcare competence has seen it rely
on Articles 30–36 on promoting the internal market in order to make any
headway. The subsidiarity principle, Article 152 of the Treaty of Amsterdam, the need to control healthcare costs in each country, the differences
in member state pharmaceutical industries, markets and drug consumption
patterns, and the income redistribution implications potentially raised by
an EU pricing regime all preclude any willingness on the part of the
member states to rescind authority over medicine pricing.

Along with the costs, the benefits of a harmonized pricing and reimbursement regime would thus be widely spread. But as the benefits would
be thin in view of the diffuse costs, the incentive to pursue such a policy is
bound to remain weak and even absent. Given that it is not entirely clear
whether a single European pricing system would in fact prove beneficial to
begin with, there is no real motivation for any actor to try to secure widespread agreement on any front. Therefore, despite the Commission's best
efforts to galvanize support on the issue, not only do the member states
remain sceptical, but the other stakeholders remain for the most part
happier with the current situation. It may in part be put down to uncertainty over what a harmonized market might actually bring in practice, but
as (industrial and administrative) costs to governments and industry could
potentially be considerable, interest in following the Commission's lead
has been weak.

Conclusion: the politics of policy in the EU pharmaceutical sector

It is the issue of market harmonization and the divergent views of the
main stakeholders that ties our three case studies together. Since the 1985
White Paper, the Community's aim has been harmonization of member
states' pharmaceutical sectors, and considerable progress has been made.
Yet as the discussion has shown, any further Europeanization of the EU
pharmaceuticals market is a difficult prospect. The interests of the stakeholders are too disparate for agreement to be reached over the outstanding (healthcare) policy aspects of a comprehensive EU approach to
medicines. The clash between the legal and policy frameworks of the

Community in the area of health(care) means that the Commission is unable to force an agenda through.

As this is more observation than an analysis, we employed a theoretical framework in order to demonstrate that, as there are other factors which impede progress, there have also been other impetuses for policy beyond the single market programme. Through the application of Wilson's cost–benefit typology, the discussion has shown when and to what extent European medicines policies have been achievable. Policy outcomes were shown to be the result of at least three different policy-making styles, with the fourth corresponding to the wider issue of an integrated medicines market. This variation is the result of the different cost–benefit configurations in terms of perceived gain and loss to the stakeholders.

Beginning with the Supplementary Protection Certificate, the push for increased patent protection periods for new drugs was driven by interests standing to make major gains. Indeed, the content and passing of the legislation shows just how powerful the 'pharma-lobby' can be. At the same time, it also served the Commission's interest in fostering the single market and serving Europe's industrial aims. So, while the Community has been active in initiating legislation for trademarks, copyrights and patents, and the SPC may be seen in terms of a natural progression (spillover), it was more than that. The industry's arguments about rising costs and loss of competitive edge in what was one of the few high-technology industries in which Europe was at the time stronger than the United States or Japan appealed to the Commission's interest in maintaining a healthy European industry. DG III thus pointed to the potential distortions caused by (the then) twelve different national patent procedures and argued that a Community-wide patent policy would be the most effective and desirable approach to overcoming this. Article 100a, which requires the approximation of national provisions in order to facilitate the internal market, allowed the Commission grounds on which to make at least initial representations.

To a considerable extent, therefore, the industry's and the Commission's interests overlapped, and healthcare policy concerns were all but completely neglected. Deregulating pricing was viewed simply as a way of fostering the market. Consumer organizations were informed only at a very late stage. The fact that their agendas were, in a sense, complementary may go some way to explaining how the industry was able to engage in client politicking to convince the Commission to push through an SPC that afforded it such a favourable derogation. In fact, client politics appear particularly relevant to proposals to further harmonize the European pharmaceuticals market on several counts.

First, the market is dominated by a small number of multinational companies, but, more importantly perhaps, these companies represent a strong industrial lobby in terms of both financing and the ethical imperative associated with medicines. Additionally, members of the public have little knowledge about the market and costs, which reduces public opposition to proposals. Second, there exists deep-rooted disagreement between actors because of the divisiveness of the issues at stake. The nature of stakeholder relationships in the pharmaceutical sector is, moreover, unusually complex, given the health dimension, and consequently offers opportunities to cooperate and reasons to disagree. A third point is that Community policy-making is of a multi-level governance structure, which allows many conduits through which to influence the policy process. What finally matters is the cost–benefit relationship in which third-party payers (governments and insurance funds) bear the costs of medicines (diffuse) while the benefits promised by a uniform market are mainly simpler market access and the reduction of manufacturing as well as marketing costs, to the benefit of industry (concentrated).

Yet the development of the EU regulatory framework for medicines has not only been about client politicking and successful lobbying by major actors. This chapter has also shown that the Commission manages policies in an entrepreneurial way. Its efforts to speed authorization in the Community, thereby affording itself more say over the industrial aspects of the sector, were what galvanized interest in a medicines agency. The other stakeholders were initially reticent about the prospects of a Community regulatory body for medicines. Indeed, despite its own interests in rapid market approval, the industry was very sceptical about a pan-European agency; it was generally content with national regulatory arrangements. Now of course the industry is a strong supporter of the EMEA and wants even more of its products to qualify for centralized approval. Patient interests hold a different view, as their fears over a 'rubber stamp' approval process at the expense of more rigorous authorization criteria have in part been realized. Although the EMEA must take public health and safety into account, it does not exercise executive decision-making power over health and healthcare matters in a manner comparable to that of either national authorities or the US FDA. The Commission has been equally entrepreneurial with respect to issues of standardization (packing, leaflets, inserts and advertising), again towards facilitating the single market.[26]

Our use of the Wilson typology reveals the multi-dimensional nature of the EU pharmaceutical sector from a policy-making perspective. It shows what the Commission's role – limited by a lack of healthcare competence – has meant in practice, and what the other main stakeholders have done in response. Different aspects of the EU regulatory framework for medicines correspond to different configurations in Wilson's cost–benefit typology. This is unusual, because regulatory policy in other areas or industries would generally fit one scenario, perhaps two at most. EU pharmaceutical policies thus correspond to an industry in which the reaching of regulatory outcomes is characterized by numerous policy styles: when healthcare concerns are coupled with the interests of a strong and extremely profitable industry, the stakes involved are such that there are bound to be major winners and losers for each and every policy. Equally, the relative gains or losses per capita will vary. It is because of this that the regulatory issue under discussion can lead to particular types of policy-making and, ultimately, particular outcomes.

The peculiarity and sensitivity of the sector have ensured that harmonization would not be easy. Albeit incomplete, a strong regulatory framework does exist. Major steps were achieved in the run-up to the single market, as this gave the Commission the authority to pursue its harmonization aims. The Commission's obligation to the single market programme has in turn meant that it has essentially been forced into developing competences wherever and whenever it could, resulting in a host of disparate powers. These competences require consolidation under a comprehensive strategy that tackles the healthcare policy aspects as well. Not only will this require a major alteration to the Treaty, to overcome the subsidiarity versus free movement clash, it will also mean moderating the costs and benefits to the stakeholders to ensure their support. Regulatory policy towards the full establishment of a single market is in theory achievable via interest-group politics (Wilson's fourth policy scenario), but is dependent on widespread political will, the very factor that is currently lacking.

In conclusion, viewed within the overarching drive to establish a common European medicines market, the history of European Community pharmaceutical regulation up to the 1990s is one of political motivations and reactionism. It has been primarily about establishing a level playing field for business in Europe and the maintenance of a strong industry. Although this process has to a considerable extent been spurred by developments in other major markets, it has equally been restrained by the clash between the objectives of the single European market along with the principle of subsidiarity, and the different healthcare interests and needs of the member states. As it has always involved difficult relations between a relatively stable group of actors, characterized by consensus-building to effect policy outcomes, it is a process that lends itself to scrutiny through a political lens focusing on actor and institutional behaviour.

Notes

This chapter covers developments until late 2002.
1 The White Paper specifically cited pharmaceuticals as a problem area regarding the removal of barriers.
2 Directive 65/65/EEC of 26 January 1965 on the approximation of provisions laid down by law, regulation or administrative action relating to proprietary medicinal products. *Official Journal of the European Communities* L22, 09.02.65: 369.
3 Directive 75/318/EEC of 20 May 1975 on the approximation of the laws of member states relating to analytical, pharmacotoxicological and clinical

standards and protocols in respect of the testing of medicinal products. *Official Journal of the European Communities* L147, 09.06.75: 1.

4 Directive 75/319/EEC of 20 May 1975 on the approximation of provisions laid down by law, regulation or administrative action relating to medicinal products. *Official Journal of the European Communities* L147, 09.06.75: 13.

5 Directive 83/570/EEC amending 65/65/EEC. *Official Journal of the European Communities* L332, 28.11.83: 1.

6 Directive 87/22/EEC of 22 December 1986 on the approximation of national measures relating to the placing on the market of high-technology medicinal products, particularly those derived from biotechnology. *Official Journal of the European Communities* L15, 17.01.87: 38.

7 Directive 89/105/EEC of 21 December 1988 relating to the transparency of measures regulating the pricing of medicinal products for human use and their inclusion within the scope of national health insurance systems. *Official Journal of the European Communities* L40, 11.02.89: 8.

8 Directive 92/27/EEC of 31 March 1992 on the labelling of medicinal products for human use and on package leaflets, Regulation 1786/92 of 18 June 1992 concerning the creation of a supplementary protection certificate for medicinal products, Directive 92/26/EEC of 31 March 1992 concerning the classification for the supply of medicinal products for human use, and Directive 92/25/EEC of 31 March 1992 on the wholesale distribution of medicinal products for human use.

9 Resolution 96/C 136/04 of 23 April 1996, designed to implement the outlines of an industrial policy in the pharmaceutical sector in the European Union. *Official Journal of the European Communities* C136, 08.05.96: 4.

10 Directive 93/39/EEC of 14 June 1993 amending 65/65/EEC, 75/318/EEC and 75/319/EEC. *Official Journal of the European Communities* L214, 24.08.93: 22.

11 As macro theories that delineate the pattern and impetus for integration, neither neo-functionalism nor intergovernmentalism makes any claim to explain all elements of EU policy-making. In this vein, Hix (1994) points to the need to differentiate between the politics of the EU policy process and the process of European integration.

12 The authors have also applied the framework to the development of EU health policy; see Mossialos and Permanand (2000).

13 Other actors, most notably the European Parliament and Court of Justice, also have major roles. As they are not affected by policy, they are thus seen as secondary stakeholders for the purpose of our discussion.

14 Directive 93/104/EC of 23 November 1993 concerning certain aspects of the organization of working time. *Official Journal of the European Communities* L307, 13.12.93: 18.

15 According to the EPC, the period of patent protection coverage on a given product began from the date the seeker of the patent filed for their patent. The SPC was proposing that the period of protection for new medicines would begin once the medicine had actually been approved for sale throughout the Community.

16 Current estimates put this figure in the vicinity of €500–560 million (EFPIA 2001). These are the industry's own statistics and, among other things, do not acknowledge that there is a ceiling in innovation capacity.

17 Such information would have been impossible for Commission officials and MEPs to have sourced on their own. Shechter (1998) claims that those MEPs who did not appear sympathetic to the industry's stance were not given copies of the report.

18 These involved a transition period for Greece, Portugal and Spain (those coun-

tries that had officially opposed the proposals), allowing them until 1998 to implement the legislation.

19 The opposition of Greece, Portugal and Spain in the Council of Ministers saw the twenty-year proposal ultimately shortened to fifteen.

20 The most recent example of the industry's lobbying success is perhaps the recent Commission decision to allow companies to provide information on specific drugs in the cases of AIDS, cancer and asthma therapies. For many critics, this is at best an implicit endorsement of direct-of-consumer advertising for medicinal products (banned in Europe under Directive 92/26/EEC), and at worst a first step.

21 This represents the number of experts that the EMEA can in theory call upon, although most are not used.

22 For an in-depth discussion of how the EMEA's authorization processes do not sufficiently take public health requirements/interests into account, especially in comparison to national agencies, see Abraham and Lewis (2000).

23 In the Commission's 2000 review of the EU's market authorization procedures, interviews with consumer groups reflected their unhappiness with the types of drugs being approved (Cameron McKenna 2000).

24 Many patient groups are disease specific, and are often sponsored by the industry. Thus, when policy-makers (at both national and EU levels) seek to consult with these bodies, they are often faced with demands *vis-à-vis* specific courses of treatment.

25 Pharmaceutical policy was the remit of DG III (Industry) until the reform of the European Commission in 1999, and was shared with EMEA following its institution. DGV (Social Policy) had no competence over pharmaceuticals *per se*, though it was involved in health matters. Now the Enterprise DG is responsible for medicines policy.

26 More recent evidence of the Commission's entrepreneurial role was its suggestion for industry representation on the EMEA management board – a proposal approved with minor amendment by the European Parliament on first reading in late 2002.

References

Abraham, J. and Lewis, G. (2000) *Regulating Medicines in Europe: Competition, Expertise and Public Health*, London: Routledge.

Albedo (1991) 'Transparency Directive II: Sequel or Remake?', *Pharmaceutical Technology Europe* September: 12–20.

—— (1995) 'At Last, a Real European Milestone', *Pharmaceutical Technology Europe* December: 8–11.

Armstrong, K. and Bulmer, S. (1998) *The Governance of the Single European Market*, Manchester: Manchester University Press.

Bahner, B. (1993) 'Generic Drugs Threatened by New European Patent Law', *Chemical Marketing Reporter* 19 July: 3–5.

BEUC (1991) 'Longer Patent Protection Periods for Medicines: A Blank Cheque for the Pharmaceutical Industry?', BEUC press release, Brussels: Bureau Européen des Unions de Consommateurs.

—— (1994) *BEUC's Opinion on the Outlines of an Industrial Policy for the Pharmaceutical Sector in the EC*, Brussels: Bureau Européen des Unions de Consommateurs.

Brittan, L. (1992) 'Making a Reality of the Single Market: Pharmaceutical Pricing and the European Economic Community', paper presented to the Institute of

Economic Affairs Conference on Pharmaceutical Policies in Europe, London, December 1992.

Burstall, M. (1992) 'The Transparency Directive: Is it Working?', *Pharmacoeconomics* 1 (supplement 1): 1–8.

Cameron McKenna (2000) *Evaluation of the Operation of Community Procedures for the Authorisation of Medicinal Products*, Report to the European Commission, European Commission: Directorate-General Enterprise (Pharmaceuticals and Cosmetics), Brussels: Commission of the European Communities.

CEC (1985) *Completing the Internal Market: White Paper of the Commission to the European Council* COM 83(310), Brussels: Commission of the European Communities.

—— (1993) *Background Report: The European Medicines Evaluation Agency*, ISEC/B33/93.

—— (1995) 'Inauguration of the European Agency for the Evaluation of Medicinal Products', press release DN: IP/95/64, 1995–01–26, Brussels: Commission of the European Communities.

—— (2000) *Pharmaceuticals in the European Union*, Commission of the European Communities, Enterprise Directorate-General, Brussels: Commission of the European Communities.

Cecchini, P. with Catinat, M. and Jacquemin, A. (1988) *The European Challenge 1992: The Benefits of a Single Market*, Aldershot, UK: Wildwood House.

CECG (1993) *Pharmaceuticals in the Single Market*, Consumers in the European Community Group.

Chambers, G. and Belcher, P. (1994) 'The Consumption of Medicines in the European Union', in E. Mossialos, C. Ranos and B. Abel-Smith (eds) *Cost Containment, Pricing and Financing of Pharmaceuticals in the European Community: The Policy-Makers' View*, Athens: LSE Health and Pharmetrica.

Christiansen, T. (1997) 'Reconstructing European Space: From Territorial Politics to Multilevel Governance', in K.-E. Jorgensen (ed.) *Reflective Approaches to European Governance*, Basingstoke, UK: Macmillan.

COM (1993) 'Commission Communication to the Council and Parliament on the outlines of an industrial policy for the pharmaceutical sector in the European Community', COM (93) 718, 02.03.94.

—— (1998) 'Commission Communication on the Single Market in Pharmaceuticals', COM(98) 588 final, Brussels: Commission of the European Communities.

CPMP (1994) *Annual report 1993–1994*, Brussels: Committee for Proprietary Medicinal Products.

Deboyser, P. (1995) 'An Industrial Policy for the Pharmaceutical Industry', in N. Mattisen and E. Mossialos (eds) *Healthcare Reforms and the Role of the Pharmaceutical Industry*, Basel: Pharmaceutical Partners for Better Healthcare.

ECJ (1996) European Court of Justice. Judgement of 5 December 1996 in joint cases C-267/95 *Merck v. Primecrown* and C-268/95 *Beecham v. Europharm*, Luxembourg: European Court of Justice; 6285–6392.

EFPIA (2001) *The Pharmaceutical Industry in Figures – Key Data (2001 Update)*, Brussels: European Federation of Pharmaceutical Industries and Associations (EFPIA).

EFPIA–EMEA (1999) 'EFPIA INFO DAY 2000 MINUS 2: Performance Indicators of the Centralised Procedure', 1999 (http://www.eudra.org/gendocs/PDFs/GENERAL/infodayen.pdf).

EMEA (1996) First General Report on the Activities of the European Agency for the Evaluation of Medicinal Products 1995, EMEA/MB/065/95.

EMEA FAQs 'The European Agency for the Evaluation of Medicinal Products: Frequently Asked Questions' (http://www.eudra.org/gendocs/PDFs/ GENERAL/FAQs/FAQen.pdf).

Furniss, J. (1997) 'The Bangemann Round Table: A Beginning and Not an End', *Eurohealth* 3 (1): 27–28.

Garattini, S. and Bertele', V. (2001) 'Adjusting Europe's Drug Regulation to Public Health needs', *The Lancet* 358: 64–67.

Greenwood, J. and Ronit, K. (1994) 'Interest Groups in the European Community: Newly Emerging Dynamics and Forms', *West European Politics* 17: 31–52.

Hancher, L. (1990) 'The European Pharmaceutical Market: Problems of Partial Harmonisation', *European Law Review* 15: 9–33.

Héritier, A., Knill, C. and Mingers, S. (1996) *Ringing the Changes in Europe: Regulatory Competition and the Transformation of the State – Britain, France, Germany*, Berlin: Walter de Gruyter.

Hix, S. (1994) 'The Study of the European Community: The Challenge to Comparative Politics', *West European Politics* 17 (1): 1–30.

Hood, C. (1994) *Explaining Economic Policy Reversals*, Buckingham, UK: Open University Press.

Huttin, C. (1999) 'Drug Price Divergence in Europe: Regulatory Aspects', *Health Affairs* 18 (3), May/June: 245–249.

Kanavos, P. and Mossialos, E. (1999) 'Outstanding Regulatory Aspects in the European Pharmaceutical Market', *Pharmacoeconomics* 15 (6): 519–533.

Koberstein, W. (1993) 'EC: The Euro Revolution', *Pharmaceutical Executive* January: 28–30.

Kolko, G. (1963) *The Triumph of Conservatism: A Reinterpretation of American History, 1900–1916*, New York: Free Press.

Lowi, T. (1969) *The End of Liberalism*, New York: W.W. Norton.

McGowan, F. and Wallace, H. (1996) 'Towards a European Regulatory State', *Journal of European Public Policy* 3 (4): 560–576.

Majone, G. (ed.) (1996) *Regulating Europe*, London: Routledge.

Marks, G., Hooghe, L. and Blank, K. (1996) 'European Integration from the 1980s: State-centric v. Multi-level Governance', *Journal of Common Market Studies* 1996; 34 (3): 343–378.

Matthews, D. and Wilson, C. (1998) 'Pharmaceutical Regulation in the Single European Market', *Medicine and Law* 17: 401–427.

Moravcsik, A. (1993) 'Preferences and Power in the European Community: A Liberal Intergovernmentalist Approach', *Journal of Common Market Studies* 31 (4): 473–524.

Mossialos, E. and Abel-Smith, B. (1997) 'The Regulation of the European Pharmaceutical Industry', in S. Stavridis, E. Mossialos, R. Morgan and H. Machin (eds) *New Challenges to the European Union: Policies and Policy-Making*, Aldershot, UK: Dartmouth.

Mossialos, E. and Permanand, G. (2000) *Public Health in the European Union: Making It Relevant*, LSE Health Discussion Paper 17, London School of Economics and Political Science: LSE Health.

Orzack, L. (1996) 'Professionals, Consumers, and the European Medicines

Agency: Policy-Making in the European Union', *Current Research on Occupations and Professions* 9: 9–29.

Permanand, G. (2002) 'Regulating under Constraint: The Case of EU Pharmaceutical Policy', PhD dissertation, London School of Economics and Political Science.

Sauer, F. (2000) 'New Drugs in the Global Economy: Risk Assessment and Risk Management in the European Union and Co-operation with the USA', speech delivered to the Graduate School of Public Health, University of Pittsburgh, 13 November 2000.

Shechter, Y. (1998) 'Interests, Strategies, and Institutions: Lobbying in the Pharmaceutical Industry of the European Union', PhD dissertation, London School of Economics and Political Science.

Stigler, G. (1971) 'The Theory of Economic Regulation', *Bell Journal of Economics and Management Science* 2 (1): 3–21.

Wilson, J. (1980) 'The Politics of Regulation', in James Q. Wilson (ed.) *The Politics of Regulation*, New York: Basic Books.

3 Bridging European and member state implementation

The case of medical goods, in vitro diagnostics and equipment

Christa Altenstetter

Introduction and background

Everywhere, enormous changes in the health sector are under way. Some are driven by globalizing forces and regional integration, while others result from domestic healthcare reform. European regulatory integration and healthcare reform have combined to move medical supplies and patient-supporting and life-sustaining aids and heavy equipment closer to centre stage in policy-making and technology assessment. There is increasing concern for the quality of medical services, as well as for medical vigilance of accidents associated with the use of medical devices. There is a growing realization that medical, environmental and food risks to health need to be managed better than they have been in the past. Will the management of health risks – perceived or actual – become a vehicle for opening up currently closed channels of problem-solving, information, transparency and accountability at both the European and national levels?

This chapter grew out of an interest in European integration, as well as the discovery a few years ago of a dearth of information on the medical device sector, which is in striking contrast to the comprehensively researched pharmaceutical sector (Altenstetter 1994, 1998a, b). Yet medical devices are central to clinical practice and patient and home care. They are at the heart of diagnosis, treatment, prevention and rehabilitation, and are the engine that drives medical progress and innovation. The lack of attention paid to these devices was surprising, especially at a time when a debate about cost containment raged in every single member state of the European Union, and medical devices had begun to come under the scrutiny of public payers. In its resolution of 7 May 1985 the European Council had addressed the concerns of the medical device industry by developing the so-called *new-approach* legislation for product regulation, and by adopting the global approach to conformity assessment (Commission of the European Communities 1994, 1999), affecting seventeen industrial sectors including medical devices.

Medical devices actually are an ideal entry point for the exploration of the effects of European regulatory integration: varied outcomes affecting national regulators, products, manufacturers and distributors, purchasers/payers, users, patients, and the global medical device market itself can be observed. Although most device-related issues are primarily framed in terms of trade, medical device issues really concern public health. As such, they raise complex cross-cutting issues, internal and external to the healthcare system, which intersect with other debates involving scientific knowledge in several disciplines, as well as political judgements.

The international health policy community and European integration specialists share with policy-makers, patients and users the assumption that the products used in clinical practice and home care are safe and of good quality, and perform as intended by their manufacturers. However, this is not always the case. Whether patients are recipients of prescription drugs, medical devices or transplanted tissues does not make a difference; nor is it a concern whether devices incorporate drugs, whether drugs need a medical device for delivery to the patient (for example, an asthma inhaler), whether medical devices are transplants, or whether products incorporate human cells, biologically or pharmacologically active substances, or synthetic device-like structures, as long as they can be used safely and effectively. However, these differentiations matter a great deal for the development of a legally clear and fair regulatory regime, appropriate regulatory strategies, and feasible mechanisms for compliance, enforcement and implementation. Regulation is treated as a distinct type of policy-making (Majone 1996, 1997; Lowi 1964).

A 'right' theory of implementation?

To implement is to interpret and execute political decisions. Yet implementation involves more than simply translating intentions into decisions and action. In the European context it is also about collective and individual learning through trial and error over time (Commission of the European Communities 2003a) and adaptation of European regulatory requirements into national contexts. The debate about the 'right' theory of implementation and, in particular, between the proponents of 'bottom-up' versus 'top-down' perspectives has generated an abundance of literature. Similarly sterile academic debates about European integration continue between intergovernmentalism and neo-functionalism, and supranational governance (Sandholtz and Sweet 1998).

Theoretically, this research focuses instead on fairly standard questions raised in the tradition of domestic implementation research (Najam 1995; Goggin *et al.* 1990; Elmore 1979). In this research tradition, implementation means tracing the effects of policy on target groups and assessing final outcomes. This analytical focus is quite different from the unique, legalistic meaning it is given in the European Union–member state nexus (Mendrinou 1996), which has increasingly come under criticism recently (Börzel and Cichowski 2003; Stone Sweet 2003). Drawing a distinction between pre-decision and post-decision processes of bargaining over compliance with EU rules, Tallberg and Jönsson (2001: 2) identified three bodies of literature: public policy research on implementation; legal and political research on the European Commission's execution of its functions as 'guardian of the treaties'; and legal and political research on the interaction between the European Court of Justice (ECJ) and national courts in the decentralized enforcement of EC law. Each research school uses compliance, enforcement and implementation slightly differently; and the analytical focus rarely extends past the relations between EU institutions and member states.

The core issue for domestic implementation research is: what happens to EU directives after they are transposed into national law? What adaptations to national and local practices are made? Are additional national requirements added to EU regulations? Blueprints such as the transposed legislative texts specific to medical devices hardly provide answers to these questions. Nor does the literature on EU compliance, enforcement and implementation serve as a basis for plausible statements about potential outcomes, since this literature primarily addresses the nexus between the European Union and the member states. In order to find out more about adaptation and transformation processes, two steps should be taken. First, a more *problem-oriented* rather than legalistic perspective of implementation needs to be adopted; 'the facts' and 'reality' about implementation need to be discovered from those directly involved in the process. Second, the meaning that policy actors give to EU directives once they are transposed into national law needs to be revealed, along with the mixture of meanings and practices that emerge from shared policy arrangements over the regulation of medical devices and prior national practices (Yanow 1996). Moreover, as Scharpf noted nearly three decades ago:

> [i]t is unlikely, if not impossible, that public policy of any significance could result from the choice process of any single unified actor. Policy formation and policy implementation are inevitably the results of interactions among a plurality of separate actors with separate interests, goals, and strategies.
>
> (1978: 347)

After thirty years of research on domestic implementation, a scholarly consensus on a broad research design has emerged, despite disagreements on some fine points. Five clusters of factors are hypothesized as shaping, though not determining, the process of implementation and final outcomes. For this research project, the 'critical' components are:

* the *content* of policy before and after EU directives and the Community regulatory regime;

- the *context* (the degree of dominance of organizational actors);
- *commitment* in support of or in opposition to EU regulatory policy;
- *capacities* (manpower, skills, funds, information and communication);
- *clients and coalitions* (target groups affected by EU regulatory policy, which include regulators, notified bodies, manufactures, clinicians, nurses, patients, home caregivers, tissue banks, reimbursement bodies, etc.).

A discussion of regulatory policy *content* and *context* requires further explanation. The challenges for identifying content and context are huge. Not only are national officials 'setting' and 'shaping' EU regulatory policy (Peterson and Bomberg 1999), they also are key players in domestic enforcement, monitoring of compliance, and implementation. This dual role justifies examining EU policy-making at length in a study that primarily focuses on domestic implementation. The traditional paradigm of law and public administration, as well as an assumed hierarchy of commands and controls, is widely used in European integration studies. However, from a problem-oriented domestic implementation perspective, this framework can be misleading. If we recognize that pure hierarchies hardly exist, the concept of 'policy networks' of interacting actors operating at different levels of decision-making and action is more appropriate (Héritier *et al.* 2001; Ladeur 1999; Altenstetter 1994, 2001). Yet one should not overstate the importance of informal compared to formal provisions either. In regulatory policy, a formal-legalistic paradigm constitutes reality in the everyday life of a good many policy actors and relates to important systemic conditions (legal-administrative, professional, political). Centrally legitimized norms and rules, and standard operating procedures (SOPs), are ubiquitous and influence adaptation processes at both European and national levels (Altenstetter 2003a, 2005). Domestic central actors expect these mandates to be enforced in a fairly streamlined implementation process. Yet such rigid control and command mechanisms have never existed in the fifteen pre-2004 EU member states, nor in any democracy. Nor do they exist following the enlargement in 2004. On the contrary, national variations in implementation have significantly increased. Within their respective constitutional structure and legal and administrative traditions, France, Germany and the United Kingdom have placed a premium not only on centralization but also on decentralization, and have felt the need to strike a balance between European and national central mandates and their larger home environments. They all experience strong pressures for decentralization, regionalization, and devolution of government tasks.

EU regulatory policy on medical products is embedded in the creation of the single market and the *new approach* to regional integration and technical harmonization, thus launching a new era in regulatory policy. Historically, the regulation of medical devices in the member states prior to 1985 was connected with market correction rather than market creation. This novel element raises a number of salient issues about the goals and impact of EU regulatory policy on domestic implementation. In what follows, a brief overview of the regulation of medical devices in the European Union is presented. In order to situate EU decision-making on medical devices within the larger framework of EU governance, I draw on secondary literature by presenting the core characteristics of decision-making by EU institutions. I then examine medical device regulation by committees. Finally, I examine the highly unusual directive on diagnostic products and domestic implementation.

Regulating medical devices in the European Union and beyond

The general policy on the single market provides the basic framework for the three medical device-specific directives. The Council Directive on Active Implantable Medical Devices (AIMD, 90/385/EEC) of 20 June 1990 has been in force in the member states since 1 January 1993, and the Council Medical Device Directive (MDD, 93/42/42/EEC) since 1 January 1995. The MDD covers all products that are neither implants nor in vitro diagnostic products. After a delay of more than seven years, the In Vitro Diagnostic Directive (IVDD, 98/79/EC) for in vitro diagnostic devices was finally published on 7 December 1998 in the *Official Journal of the European Communities*. Not unexpectedly, the IVDD amended the two prior directives in important ways, as will be detailed below. The IVDD was supposed to come into force on 7 December 1999 but was postponed to 7 June of the following year because no member state had met the deadline. Variable transition periods for placing devices on the market applied until 2003, and for putting them into service until 2005. A series of amendments and additional directives have been put in place since then.[1] However, the focus in this contribution is on the three central directives, which roughly correspond to three very different industrial sectors, as documented in Table 3.1.

Medical devices are classified according to a fourfold scheme of risks understood in terms of duration of contact with the human body, degree of invasiveness, and parts of the anatomy affected. Risk levels are not identical with the three product categories shown in Table 3.1. Worldwide, there are about 100,000 low-risk devices (Class I) on the market, 10,000 medium-risk devices (Class IIa), 1,000 higher-risk devices (Class IIb) and about 100 of the highest-risk (Class III). The stricter the risk, the higher the regulatory requirements. Over the past ten years the most intense controversy has centred around Class IIb and Class III devices and medical devices that are at the borderline between medical devices and pharmaceuticals such as diagnostic products. Some argue that these should be treated like drugs and thus fall under drug regulation, while others insist that several items in these two classes should be subject to tougher

Table 3.1 The heterogeneity of medical devices

Anaesthetic and respiratory equipment: CEN/TC 215[a]		*Implants for surgery: CEN/TC 285*	
1	Tracheal and breathing tubes	9	Cardiac implants
2	Anaesthetic machines	10	Vascular implants
3	Medical breathing systems	11	Osteosynthesis implants
4	Medical gas supply systems	12	Reconstructive implants
5	Lung ventilators	13	Joint replacement tools
6	Pressure regulators	14	Mechanical contraceptives
7	Flow-metering devices		
8	Connectors		

Non-active medical devices: CEN/TC 205		*Electrical equipment*	
15	Urinary and drainage catheters	29	X-ray equipment
16	Hypodermic syringes and needles	30	Medical electron systems and accelerators
17	Plasma filters	31	Cardiac defibrillators and monitors
18	Condoms	32	Ultrasonic therapy equipment
19	Extra-corporeal circuits	33	Nerve and muscle stimulators
20	Blood gas exchangers	34	Lung ventilators
21	Transfusion and infusion sets	35	Electroconvulsive therapy equipment
22	Parenteral devices	36	Endoscopic equipment
23	Medical gloves	37	Baby incubators and radiant warmers
24	Clinical thermometers	38	Electrocardiography
25	Anti-embolism hosiery	39	Blood pressure monitoring equipment
26	Pen injectors	40	External cardiac pacemakers
27	Enteral feeding tubes	41	Magnetic resonance equipment
28	Surgical tapes and gowns	42	Heated pads, blankets and mattresses
		43	Electrically operated hospital beds

Source: Adcock, Sorrel and Watts (1998).

Note

a CEN is the European Standardization Committee (Comité Européen de Normalisation). TC translates into Technical Committee.

requirements. Some Class IIb products such as breast implants were recently reclassified as Class III,[2] and a proposal to bring all borderline high-risk products under the pharmaceutical regime has had its first reading in the European Parliament.

In July 2003 the Commission accepted the June 2002 report by the Medical Device Expert Group (MDEG). According to this report, the legal framework concerning safety aspects and technological evolution is appropriate. However, the report noted that there was ample room for improving domestic implementation through the coordination of post-market surveillance and vigilance, improving the European Union Database for Medical Devices (EUDAMED), more consistency in clinical investigations, better checks over conformity assessment, more transparency and mutual trust among the member states, improved market surveillance, and better cooperation between the Commission and member states (Commission of the European Communities 2003b). Finally, the MDEG proposed yet another High Level Committee for Medical Devices.[3]

A comparison of the different pathways to market authorization for medical devices and pharmaceuticals indicates the linkages between the two regulatory regimes, especially concerning the AIMD and the MDD. In prior research I found major differences in terms of the historical timing of regulation, principles of market authorization and strategies of European regulatory policy, including the strengthening of post-market surveillance and improvement of medical vigilance systems (Altenstetter 2002; Commission of the European Communities 2003a). A brief summary of the essential components of EU medical device regulation, as exemplified in the AIMD and MDD, follows. It shows how much leeway is left to the member states, despite regulatory harmonization at the EU level.[4]

Regulatory policy on medical devices is based on five principles implied in *new-approach* legislation. First, CE-marking[5] serves as a guarantee of conformity with particular EU regulations or directives. The mark is a kind of market authorization, but should not be confused with the pre-market approval or licensing of individual products or the strict product testing regime in the pharmaceutical sector, which is subject to *old-approach* legislation.[6] Second, EU directives, which need to be transposed in their entirety into national law, specify the essential requirements (technical-scientific and clinical) in highly detailed annexes. These requirements must be met as a precondition to market authorization. Third, these annexes reference harmonized European standards (EN) or international standards by the International Organization for Standardization (ISO), rather than national standards. Within this framework the member states have considerable discretion. As a fourth principle of the new approach, member states can invoke the safeguard clause – Article 36 of the Treaty of Rome – in the interest of public health. Such action should be based on reasonable doubt that essential requirements for products are in fact respected, or on evidence that product standards are applied inappropriately or do not exist. Member states can act within parameters set by the Commission when a risk is proportional to the actual or perceived risks, is product specific and is only temporary. France took action regarding condoms, breast implants and animal tissues, and had an open inquiry into electrical safety; the United Kingdom took action in regard to Class III implants. Fifth, and lastly, home-country control governs enforcement and implementation. Member states have ample discretion to organize implementation as they see fit, which means that in most cases they decide on the basis of a legacy of their pre-existing administrative and regulatory

Table 3.2 Medical device issues and member state sovereign powers

Clinical investigation/evaluation	Unregulated medical devices
Labelling	Advertisement/promotion
Medical institutions	Professional and lay users
Post-market controls and surveillance	Reimbursement (NHS or SHI)
Distribution	Price-setting (NHS or SHI)
Installation	Evaluation (NHS or SHI)
Vigilance	Notification/registration for placing on the market

ideas and practices. Table 3.2 provides a summary of policy issues over which the member states retain control.

EU ground rules are not tailor-made to fit each category of highly different product ranges as under the *old approach*. However, to allow for the unique characteristics of medical devices, exceptions to this five-step legislative format were made and extra – and largely medicalized – articles were added. The drafters of the EU directives incorporated clinical investigations and, after 2001, clinical evaluation into the essential requirements as follows: the utilization of medical devices must not compromise the clinical state of a patient; medical devices must achieve the performances indicated and stated by the manufacturer; and secondary and undesirable effects must constitute an acceptable risk based on the state of knowledge. Risk analysis should identify and anticipate the hazards of medical devices, and estimate likely risks. Whatever method is used to obtain the CE mark, the manufacturer is responsible for risk analysis and associated documentation.[7]

As already noted above, the IVDD was delayed by eight years (Altenstetter 2002). However, the European Parliament did not delay it simply as a show of political force. In recent years, European parliamentarians from a wide spectrum of political groupings have become increasingly concerned about health and consumer protection issues and health risks arising from unsafe food, including salmonella in eggs and poultry. The single most important crisis, which set off intense debate in all political arenas and particularly in the European Parliament, was the BSE, or variant Creutzfeldt–Jakob, disease scare. The risks associated with BSE and similar transmissible spongiform encephalopathies were of great concern to consumers, health advocates, scientists and policy-makers, as well as farmers, industry leaders and distributors. After heated debates, the European Union banned specific risk material derived from bovine, ovine and caprine sources in order to eliminate any risk associated with such material entering the human and animal food chains. The implications for the medical device industry were clear, since it uses such material in manufacturing. Stearic acid derivatives are used in the processing of PVC, polyamide, polyester and other plastics, which come in contact with a patient's body and organs through, for example, the use of surgeons' gloves.

For a decade now, controversy has raged in EU institutions over regulation of the use of human or animal tissues and derivatives in medical devices. The European Parliament favoured stiffer regulations in this area and supported pertinent amendments to the proposed IVDD in March 1996. However, failure to agree on the use of human tissue almost derailed adoption of the IVDD. In the meantime, France pushed for much stricter legislation in 1998. At a meeting in November 1997, the Commission and representatives of EU countries accepted the majority of France's requests, but refused the French call for a sixty- or ninety-day pre-market approval. The adoption of the IVDD was finally saved by separating the issue of human tissue from the IVD directive, providing a solution palatable to all policy-makers.

It took another five years before a draft version of a Human Tissues and Cell Products Directive, agreed upon by the European Parliament and Council, began to circulate. The consultation process was closed on 30 September 2002, and the European Parliament voted on it on 16 December 2003. National regulators from France and the United Kingdom on one side and Germany on the other, seem to have reconciled their differences; the industry, speaking through the European Confederation of Medical Devices Associations (EUCOMED 2001a, b, c), also sorted out its differences with the Scientific Committee on Medicinal Products and Medical Devices (European Commission 2001a). A major bone of contention between the member states and their opponents in industry and the Commission concerned the method of regulation. Should EU human tissue rules be developed under the regulatory guidelines for medicinal products or the medical devices regulatory regime? Alternatively, should a separate regulatory arrangement be made for human tissue products under the umbrella of the medical device regime, with a European-wide Tissue Engineering Regulatory Body (Kent *et al.* 2003)? The Scientific Committee's recommendations for further EU regulatory intervention was to end debates that had lingered on since the early 1990s.[8]

From a patient safety perspective, promising yet troubling technological advances in life-saving and life-enhancing medical devices in clinical practice and tissue engineering are appearing faster than regulators, the Commission and the industry can agree on solutions. These innovations have real potential for improving patient care. Synthetic skin and cartilage are already in use; in the next ten years these will be joined by replacement parts for the human body, such as heart muscles. Predictably, demand for access to these products will rise. Yet cost may not necessarily rise with it, provided old and obsolete technologies and surgical procedures are replaced by newer, more efficacious ones. As a result of cost concerns in the past ten years, scientific assessment (evaluation) and political appraisal of technologies not only provide a new toolbox for cost-containment policies in most European countries (*International Journal of Technology Assessment in Health Care* 2002, Special Issue) but are insisted upon by industry. The industry suggests that evaluation should provide 'timely access to up-to-date medical care, including medical devices and technologies', that healthcare professionals and the industry should play a key role, and that payers should not have 'a monopoly on the assessment process' (HIMA–EUCOMED 1999). Even when all the safeguards for technology assessment are secured, medical professionals are known to engage in 'off-label' use of high-risk procedures. 'Off-label' use, which may harm patients, primarily concerns the medical profession.

The deciding and managing of health risks is a growing agenda item of EU institutions. They are concerned with rare diseases; revising product liability issues (Hodges 1999b); handling health data through the EC Data Protection Directive (Hodges 1999c); reviews of patient consent forms for breast implants five years after France withdrew silicone gel breast implants from the market; amending the MDD (Directive 2001/104/EC) by including substances derived from human blood and blood plasma (as distinct from human tissues) – an amendment that came into force on 10 January 2002; and many other health-related issues. Finally, a new Commission Decision on medical devices with specific risk materials was adopted in 2001 and should put an end to feelings on the part of some regulators that the earlier definition was too lax (EUCOMED 1998).

A battle between the medical device and pharmaceutical regimes may also have been resolved. A five-year review of the MDD implied that advocates for trade inside the Commission, along with those who favour integration of the medical device regulatory regime under the pharmaceutical regulatory regime, would win out. This intra-Commission conflict between the medical device unit and the pharmaceutical unit inside Directorate-General Enterprise (previously DG III) influenced, if not dominated, the debates during 2000 and 2001. The conflict also mirrors the respective pressures of economic interests inside the Commission services. However, arguments based on the distinctive nature of medical devices as compared to pharmaceuticals carried the day at the EU level. The two regulatory regimes have not been merged, at least not for the moment. Almost everyone who influences final decision-making now seems to agree that those medical devices with the highest risks – for example, those derived from human and animal tissues – require stricter regulation, and that this should be achieved within the medical device regime. The umbrella MDD is considered to work well to the extent that when problems are encountered, they tend to lie in domestic implementation. As previously mentioned, stakeholders agree that implementation gaps must be resolved through better domestic implementation and better European guidelines.

Manufacturers are widely regarded by some as the only group with the necessary knowledge of medical devices. This has justified the building up of independent expertise both inside and outside national regulatory agencies. Yet both groups are reported to know less than is assumed, and considerable differences in interpretation and application by competent authorities, notified bodies and the industry have been found to exist (European Commission 2001c; Thompson 2000). When a shift was made from clinical investigations to clinical evaluation, and thus from a Clinical Investigation Task Force to a Clinical Evaluation Task Force following opposition from industry representatives, all three groups were found to be lacking in experience and knowledge.

Policy-making by EU institutions and rule-setting by committees

Regulatory policy on medical devices is subject to the same legislative processes and procedures as all EU action. The 1997 Treaty of Amsterdam added a new committee layer to an already highly complex multi-level system of governance by committees, also known as the 'comitology system'. Committees can be related to the Commission, the Council or the European Parliament (Maurer and Larsson 2001; Haibach, Schaefer and Türk 2001; Fouilleux, De Maillard and Smith 2001; Neuhold and Polster 2001). Decision-making by committees is nothing new: it has been at the heart of the EC's methods since as far back as Jean Monnet. Depending on the policy area, scientific advice in EU policy-making has been available through the Commission's 150 advisory committees, 60 management committees and 80 regulatory committees. Overall, the number of committees has grown at the micro, meso and macro levels of EU policy-making (van Schendelen 1998: 1–22, 277–293). The reasons for these committees' importance is that they not only shape policy, but also make, apply, interpret, evaluate and set new rules, as well as determining existing and new funding allocations (Haibach, Schaefer and Türk 2001: 11). In 1997, new scientific committees for medical products, medical devices and veterinary science were established (van Schendelen 1998; Joerges and Vos 1999; Vos 1999a, b; Joerges and Neyer 1997). The Commission now has to justify its decisions on all internal market proposals with scientific evidence (Art. 100(3)), and, given the variety of medical products, this evidence will be generated from a variety of highly differing scientific and technical fields and working groups within the multi-level committee system that exists in the medical device field.

Why bother with European committees in a study of domestic implementation? As a rule of thumb, 80 per cent of decisions on policy details are made by working groups; another 18 per cent reach the Committee of Permanent Representatives (COREPER), the diplomatic representation of the member states and, with the exception of 'historic decisions and policy-setting decisions' (Peterson and Bomberg 1999), very few end up on the agenda of the Council. Following Peterson and Bomberg's work, scholars have widely underestimated who 'shapes policy content', in contrast to who influences 'historic decisions' or who serves as 'policy-setting bodies', namely the Council and Parliament. In Rhinard's (2000) assessment, these committees are 'non-majoritarian bodies, non-transparent, unaccountable and secretive'. Wessels (1998: 211–218) proposes seven alternative explanations for these committees' political significance, in addition to their role as shapers of policy. Committees are:

- watchdogs of the masters of the Treaty;
- integral to blocking defence by moribund nation-states;
- indicators of spillover and the shifting of loyalty;
- home to smooth technocratic problem-solving;
- part of the mega-bureaucracy plot;
- indicators of a non-hierarchical system beyond the state;
- arenas for merging administrative and political systems.

Given these political roles, Wessels suggests, committees are a key variable explaining EU governance as a multi-level system, and should be part of the search for a dynamic and comprehensive middle-range theory.

In Community risk regulation, much is at stake when scientific decision-making has the last word. This was amply demonstrated in the BSE crisis, when the Scientific Committee on Veterinary Medicine delivered the scientific opinion as to whether trade sanctions on British beef should be lifted. The committee was chaired by a representative from the same country against which the product ban was first imposed and then to be lifted (Matthews 1998a, b). Under these circumstances, claims of scientific independence and objectivity are questionable. In any event, a risk-averse public is as disturbed by the presence of scientific evidence as by the absence thereof, as shown in the case of genetically modified micro-organisms (GMMOs) and novel food (Landfried 1999). I agree with Joerges and Vos (1999; see also Vos 1999a, b) and others that risk regulation is both a political and a technical issue, and that it requires some democratic legitimacy, accountability and transparency.

Decision-making by committees is justified because of the complexity of issues that need to be resolved. Problem-solving can best be done by insulating decision-makers from politics. Supposedly, network members are in a position to search for the 'best' solutions based on current know-how and benchmarking of good or 'best' regulatory practices. Empirical data confirm the existence and workings of a similar multi-level committee system with similar tasks, functions and composition in the medical device field, to which we now turn.

Medical device regulation by committees

The study of decision-making by medical device-specific committees is non-existent in European policy and integration studies. Yet these committees decide rules and standards for safety, quality, performance and clinical efficacy for all patients in Europe and beyond. Their influence has also been growing enormously, in part as a function of highly complex issues involved in this field and in part as a means of inter-administrative cooperation and coordination across the Brussels services and national services in the interest of public health.

The complexity of problems to be resolved relating to medical devices is immense. Defining borderline products or concepts such as the 'lifetime' of a medical device or the meaning of 'shelf life', 'service life', 'regulatory life' or 'unknown regulatory life' (enforcement action) (Bennetts 2001) is not at issue. In my view, what are at stake are the following issues: are standard-setting and rule-making committees neutral and independent of lobbies and economic interests? Where do public health interests come in? Do officials work for public health or, alternatively, unhampered trade? And which national officials from which departments or offices are represented in the EU-based committees when particular kinds of issues are decided and become binding on domestic implementers? Are the most appropriate spokespersons diplomats with an interest in pursuing national interests, generalists with an interest in rules for free trade, or specialists of the medical device field who are most likely to pursue public health interests? Answers to these questions require more in-depth research. What can be pieced together is the profile of decision-making and rule-setting bodies for medical devices from a variety of sources through triangulation. My research and field notes indicate that Wessels's explanations for committee significance fully apply to decision-making on medical devices. Accordingly, in the medical device field European and national political and administrative spaces are merging in highly complex ways, as in other policy domains (Organization for Economic Cooperation and Development 1998).

Decision-making by committees must distinguish between four (soon to be five) decision-making layers. The first layer consists of two standing committees: the Committee on Medical Devices, which routinely has served as the main regulatory committee, and the Committee on Standards and Technical Regulation. In 1997 an Article 7 Committee was created, which met for the second time only in the autumn of 2001, according to a Commission source. The regulatory committee is made up of representatives of national administrations and Commission services. The Commission chairs the meeting, sets the agenda and submits issues to the committee for decision-making (Art. 2(a)) and/or 'for information or a simple exchange of views, either on the Chairman's initiative, or at the written request of a committee' (Council Decision 1999/468/EC, *Official Journal of the European Communities* 2001/C38/03, 6.2.2001). If no agreement is reached, the next step will be a decision by the Council or, the ultimate step, a procedure before the Court of Justice (Hodges 1999a). Given the fact that the Article 7 Committee met for a second time only in the autumn of 2001, the question arises as to whether decision-makers were idle between 1997 and 2001. But in practice, EU procedures (Council Decision 1999/468/EC) allow for a formula by which MDEG meetings are conducted in two separate parts. In a general meeting, input from all parties of the MDEG group is solicited (Art. 2(b)); a second part of the meeting is declared a meeting of the regulatory committee and includes the Commission and national officials only (European Commission 2001b).

The second decision-making layer is the Medical Device Expert Group (MDEG), composed of representatives from the Commission, competent authorities, notified bodies and, recently, candidate countries. Industry is also represented through EUCOMED, the European trade association. 'Industry' in this case really refers to globally operating multinationals and their products. Although EUCOMED's membership includes small and medium-sized firms, their representatives are seldom found on the attendees list. Finally, a third layer includes seven working groups (plus several subcommittees) made up of a Commission official and representatives from industry and notified bodies. The working groups concern the following: accreditation and surveillance of notified bodies; device classification, with a subcommittee on BSE; vigilance with a subcommittee on data management/exchange; silicone gel breast implants, with a subcommittee on auditing; dental amalgam; drug/device issues, with a subcommittee on latex allergy; and, finally, meeting of notified bodies. Fourth, scientific advice on issues specific to medical devices is provided by the Scientific Committee on Medicinal Products and Medical Devices.[9] The Commission announced the creation of a new High Level Group for medical devices, 'allowing for consultation and mutual information between Commission and national authorities on issues in relation to medical devices' (Commission of the European Communities 2003b: 40).

Three additional features, which describe the nature of EU policy-making by committees – consensual decision-making between actors drawn from existing networks, low procedural formality and an underlying ethos of technocratic and managerial problem-solving (Rhinard 2000: 8–9) – apply to the multi-layered committee system for medical devices. First, technocratic problem-solving increases with distance from the top layer. Why should we be concerned when allegedly the best experts from industry and government make health decisions? The story told here and elsewhere suggests that there are differing views on the best scientific standards and rules, and these differences affect the safety of products. Devices can perform well but be clinically ineffective. Committees are insulated from the public, meet behind closed doors, decide in secrecy and are not held accountable to any elected body. With the exceptions of draft directives, most decisions on highly scientific and specific issues no longer appear on the agenda of the Council, the Commission or the European Parliament.

Second, a need for consensus-building on scientific advice among the major stakeholders and new institutional dynamics may mask intense political-ideological and interprofessional conflicts over risk issues that were predominant as recently as a few years ago. Yet the public remains concerned about risks to health in most EU countries and is reluctant to accept consensus-based scientific evidence, as shown by the debates in the European Parliament and its committees over the BSE crisis, breast implants, patient consent forms, or similar topics involving decision-making and health risk management.

Third, a focus on scientific decision-making tends to privilege the larger member states, which possess the necessary expertise and scientific capacity (Joerges and Vos 1999; Vos 1999b). This conclusion resonates with observations from the medical device field. Sources close to the regulatory process note that France, Germany and the United Kingdom were allowed to lead the process from 1990 onwards, while the remaining member states basically took a back seat behind the 'big three'. Together with Italy, the 'big three' propose, bargain, and recommend rules for action; prior to enlargement in 2004, they controlled forty votes out of the sixty-two needed for a qualified majority in the Council (Art. 205 of the Treaty of Amsterdam, previously Art. 148 of the Treaty of Maastricht). In the in vitro diagnostics sector the two main players are France and Germany, which usually act jointly on behalf of other countries. A similar distribution of influence by industrial interests and countries can be expected for the remaining committees relevant in this field.

In fact, the distribution of influence and power can be seen in the medical device field from EU-level committees to the global committee structure, the Global Harmonization Task Force (GHTF) for medical devices, which is concerned with global regulatory convergence. The composition of the GHTF and its four sub-committees tends to be dominated by Anglo-Saxon representatives from large multinational corporations on both sides of the Atlantic, despite efforts to rotate the chair between geographic regions. EU-level working groups seem to be dominated by representatives of industries located in the 'big three' countries regardless of whether they represent native European corporations or subsidiaries of US companies. ISO and International Electrical Committee (IEC) standard-setting committees show a similar representative pattern, with national standard-setting bodies playing an important role. Data and preliminary analysis on the origin and participation of international scientific elites suggest a similar pattern; but a systematic assessment is still required (Altenstetter 2001).

The In Vitro Diagnostic Directive and domestic implementation

After having transposed directives, member states are able to organize their own methods and mechanisms for implementation. While past research focused heavily on the AIMD, the MDD and the three crucial stakeholders – national regulators, manufacturers and notified bodies (Altenstetter 2002) – this section will focus on the particularities of the IVDD. For domestic implementation of pre-market controls, national regulators have three policy instruments at their disposal: inspection of manufacturers, evaluations, and post-market controls. Their use depends on resources and capacities, which vary significantly across the fifteen pre-2004 member states. Prior to the IVDD and depending on the country, a 'piecemeal approach' to regulation existed. The oldest and most comprehensive legislation existed in Germany (1978, covering groups of products), France (1982, covering all diagnostic products), Spain (1987, covering HIV and hepatitis tests) and Italy (1991, HIV). Outside the Union, Austria and Switzerland had also implemented regulation (in response to AIDS). According to an industry insider (Suppo 1997; 2000: S4.1), diagnostic companies reacted in 'patchwork fashion' to the 'patchwork nature of regulation'.

The IVDD follows the legal architecture of the AIMD and MDD. However, it contains a number of provisions and complex annexes that make it a highly unusual *new-approach* directive in at least three ways: rules and procedures are quasi-harmonized at the European Union level; registration and notification requirements, which are normally seen as trade barriers, are introduced; and, similarly to pharmaceutical regulation, common technical specifications (CTSs) are established for evaluation, re-evaluation and batch verification. While the IVDD covers heavy equipment and computer laboratory systems and in vitro diagnostic (IVD) products, the following comments apply to in vitro products only. Typically, IVD products are single-use devices; when they fail to perform as intended, they constitute unacceptable health risks and mislead those carrying out analysis and diagnosis. Unlike essential requirements for the AIMDD and the MDD, CTSs make the evaluation of clinical and analytical data mandatory; reliance on performance as intended by the manufacturer under the previous two regulations is considered insufficient. In mid-2002 a consensus on draft CTSs for high-risk devices emerged among the major stakeholders. In the past, the industry and the Commission refused special requirements for IVD products. CTSs were pushed by national regulators led by France with the support of Germany and other countries (*Regulatory Affairs Journal (Devices)*, January–March 2002: 37).

Power-sharing between the European Union and member states leans towards the former in the implementation of the IVDD. In this case, member states are not entirely free to choose methods of implementation, as they are under the MDD and AIMDD. Moreover, the IVDD has produced spillover effects on medical institutions, laboratory medicine, diagnosis and analysis, and free-standing laboratories, thus raising fine legal points probably understood only by a few legal specialists from the United States and Europe. Delays in implementation are normal events and not peculiar to medical devices. The IVDD was adopted in December 1998, eight years after a first draft was discussed in the European Union. It was to be transposed by 7 June 2000, and after December 2003 only CE-marked IVD medical products were to be placed on the market. Yet most countries did not make the deadline, which was postponed until 6 June 2000 (*Regulatory Affairs Journal (Devices)*, February 2000: 45). Table 3.3 illustrates IVDD implementation status as of August 2001.

In vitro diagnostic products were grouped into four categories according to the risks to public health and/or patient treatment:

- general products;
- self-testing items;
- Annex II List A, which includes, among other things, test kits for rubella, toxoplasmosis, phenylketonuria and blood glucose;
- Annex II List B, which includes test kits for HIV, human T-cell lymphotrophic virus (HTLV), hepatitis, and some blood grouping products, including those used to test donated blood.

Data generation, collection, analysis and evaluation of IVD products follow the same four categories. Unlike previous national regulation in a few member states, the IVDD covers not only reagents, but also automatons, robots, computers, etc. The inclusion of entire laboratory systems in the scope of the Directive led to enormous uncertainties among all parties involved for the period from 1999 to 2001. Moreover, when the IVDD was adopted, no one really knew or understood the meaning of the above lists. Legal consequences ensued, depending on whether transposition was 'deliberately' or 'accidentally' out of line with the scope of the Directive (Hodges 1999a). Delays in designating ten notified bodies specifically accredited for handling conformity assessment procedures and quality control of IVD products added to the uncertainty.

IVD products are high-risk products and as such require registration and notification of manufacturers, authorized representatives, distributors, and products. In the United Kingdom, manufacturers must register with the Medical Device Agency (MDA), which in 2002 was merged with the Medicines Control Agency to become the Medicines and Healthcare Products Regulatory Agency (MHRA). In France they register with the French Agency for Health and Product Safety (AFSSAPS), and in Germany with the Federal Institute for Drugs and Medical Devices (BfArM). Registration in other EU countries can also be with a regulatory agency located in the same area as the head office of the company. In the event of problems with IVD products, this agency serves as a lead agency, even though the products may have been distributed in another country. National regulators can, but need not, require registration of products prior to their launch on the market. When they regulate, they must not exceed EU provisions. Manufacturers must obtain a certificate from one

Table 3.3 IVD Directive: status of implementation

EU state	Implemented or due	Registration fees?	Language of registration file
Austria	Yes	Registration fees not enforced	Non-Austrian applications accepted in English
Belgium	No; due by year-end [i.e. end of 2001]	None likely	Non-Belgian applications accepted in English or French on European registration form
Denmark	Yes	No fees	Non-Danish companies can use English on European form
Finland	Yes	No fees	Non-Finnish companies may give Finnish authorities a copy of notification to original competent authority provided it is in English and an EDMA form[a]
France	Yes, but not fully	Annual tax of 0.15% of French sales once sales reach €762,245	Files to be in French with some translation into English
Germany	Due early 2002a	No provision for fees	Details awaited
Greece	No	None expected	For non-Greek companies, English copy of notification made to the relevant competent authority will be accepted
Italy	Yes	No fees	As per directive
Ireland	Yes	No fees	As per directive
Luxembourg	No	None expected	As per directive
Netherlands	No	None due	May not request registration files from non-Dutch companies during transitional period before European data bank set up
Norway	No; due soon	None expected	As per directive
Portugal	Yes	No	As per directive
Sweden	Yes	Detailed fee requirements, payable annually on a scale linked to number of products being registered	Registration procedures only applicable to Swedish companies
UK	Yes	For UK-based manufacturers and authorized representatives, 70 (Z 105) by registration dossier, which may include several products or groups of products. No fees from non-UK-based manufacturers or authorized representatives	For non-UK companies, copy of notification to relevant competent authority will be accepted if in English

Source: *Clinica* August 2001: 37.

Note

a The form was drafted by the European Diagnostics Manufacturers Association, according to *Medimark Europe News*.

of the ten notified bodies specifically accredited for IVD products. Member states have discretion to impose additional restrictions, and have used this opportunity in many of the policy areas listed in Table 3.2. For biotechnology firms, safety reporting regulations are more challenging than for other medical device manufacturers. Regulations differ, depending on the product – drugs, biological entities, devices, or biological products – as well as the country, and on whether reporting refers to clinical investigation (now evaluation) in the pre-market phase or during post-market surveillance (Kingma 1998). All in vitro diagnostics share one experience: the speed of technological innovation tends to outpace the speed of regulation even faster than with other medical devices.

For the recall of products, the IVDD stipulates that where a member state requires medical practitioners, medical institutions or the organizers of external quality assessment schemes to inform the national lead agency (or, in EU legalese, so-called competent authorities) of any incident referred to in the directive's first paragraph, it must take the necessary steps to ensure that the manufacturer of the device concerned or its authorized representative is also informed of the incident (Art. 11(2) of the IVDD). The exact definition of 'manufacturer' (Articles 1, 2f), however, is of real concern to the industry. The IVD industry is extremely complex: not only do companies purchase components from other firms, but sometimes the entire product is made by another company. Regulators in countries that have already developed some form of IVD regulation are well aware of these hurdles to determining accountability for manufacture (Suppo 2000: S4.12).

The IVDD differentiates between 'placing on the market' and 'putting into service'. The latter can have several meanings and, depending on the meaning, invokes the responsibility of different actors. A product can be 'put into service' after installation of any special equipment, upon delivery at the hospital, only at the moment of use, or even when products are put in a catalogue or advertised on the Internet. 'Home-brewed products' were exempt from the IVDD under pressure from lobbying by UK microbiologists, who feared that the products they prepared in laboratories would fall under the scope of the IVDD (Suppo 2000: S4.12). The 'big two' in the IVD field did not object, since the issue posed no threat to their industries. However, in-house manufactured products ranging from home-brewed products to the sterilization of single-use devices for multiple use in hospitals may come under the purview of EU regulation in the future. On 10 May 2001 the European Court of Justice ruled against a Danish hospital whose in-house manufactured product caused medical harm. This ECJ ruling introduced a requirement whereby all such in-house manufactured products may come under the product liability directive as amended (85/374/ECC; *Clinica* June 2001: 962).

Reporting procedures

Since there is no social science information in this field, in order to understand problem-oriented implementation we have to rely on industry sources. If the issues addressed in Table 3.4 are not resolved, they can pose serious health risks to patients and users, particularly in countries that have had no regulation at all. Inconsistencies in terminology and differing interpretations of the reporting requirements by national regulators in each country are reported. The information appears credible and plausible.

National variations across member states

The objective of EU regulation is to secure uniform interpretation, application and implementation in all states of the European Union. Yet there is a paradox. Although member states are more restricted concerning implementation of IVD products than concerning medical devices, uniform reporting of accidents and near-accidents in the European Union has a long way to go (Altenstetter 2003b). The European Diagnostics Manufacturers Association drafted a European form for use; however, national forms were developed instead in Sweden, the United Kingdom, Belgium, Denmark, France, Germany and Spain (Brown 2000). France, Germany and the United Kingdom, which regulated IVD products prior to EU regulation, continue to use their own routines, data banks and forms for reporting accidents and incidents with these unusual products. For example, the British MDA required medical devices used in clinical investigations to be subject to reporting requirements; it thus went beyond the scope of the non-binding EC Vigilance Guidelines. In addition, the

Table 3.4 Experience with reporting of adverse incidents due to IVD products

- The information available, while considerable, is of poor quality.
- Competent authorities (CAs) demand early answers when information is not available or relevant; redundant reporting requirements lead to redundant queries from CAs.
- Some CAs do not hear appeals from manufacturers.
- Independent experts are unavailable in some sectors, and sometimes only available to CAs.
- Some overreaction to problems (e.g. breast implants).
- Directives use inconsistent terminology and exclude important requirements, including the following:

  1 The AIMD has no notification requirement in case of incidents involving clinical trial devices.
  2 The IVDD has no undertaking requirements when Annex V (Type testing) is combined with Annex VIII (Production Quality Assurance).
  3 The EC Vigilance Guidelines have no legal status.

Source: *Regulatory Affairs Journal* (Devices) May 2001: 147.

MDA requires observance of product-specific guidelines for breast implants, heart valves and joint replacements, as well as guidelines for recalls and post-marketing surveillance of hip joints.

The German Ministry of Health has extended long-established practices to require a safety officer in hospitals under hospital legislation and regulation of medical devices and IVD products. A safety officer must be based in Germany to represent a manufacturer, importer or authorized representative. Germany intends to report adverse incidents on German forms, in addition to those included in the non-binding EC Vigilance Guidelines. Similarly, French regulation requires a vigilance correspondent to represent a manufacturer and its authorized representative. AFSSAPS also requires French forms in addition to those recommended for use in the EC Guidelines. AFSSAPS requires reporting, in French, of serious injury or death without delay, contrary to EU regulation, and near-incidents on a quarterly basis.

While it may seem odd to outline these highly technical details of the regulatory process, they are not irrelevant for policy. Instead, they point to important observations about the member states: a strong legacy of past administrative practices; a desire to control path-dependent regulatory mechanisms and processes; a lack of trust across the member states; a desire to educate their own target groups in the health sector; and a preference for their own tools of compliance, enforcement and problem-oriented implementation. These circumstances hint at the difficulty of systematic cross-national research on reporting injuries, death or near-death: data are not comparable, and researchers are faced with complicated methodological and definitional problems (Altenstetter 2003a, b). In the Commission's words, 'statistical data on reported cases are extremely heterogeneous', ranging from comprehensive reporting by France and the United Kingdom, primary reliance on reporting by manufacturers in Germany, to very limited reporting in most other countries, as documented in Table 3.5.[10]

The European regulatory data bank for medical devices, EUDAMED, follows legal and administrative categories for registering incidents, accidents, deaths, and recalls of medical and in vitro devices. In November 2001 the data bank was reviewed by the MDEG. In the Commission's view, EUDAMED is 'not captive' to industry, is 'user-friendly' and reflects 'state of the art' knowledge (Brekelmans and Nonneman 2000). But when the juror serves as jury, the situation is murky. On the other hand, a case for a centralized regulatory data bank at the EU level can be made; its advocates see virtue in streamlining information generation, collection and assessment. In contrast, the 'big three', while not opposed to EUDAMED, see advantages in a decentralized regulatory and information system that they control.

The suggestion that national administrative practices and arrangements are losing ground under the pressures of Europeanization and even

Table 3.5 Vigilance reporting in the member states

Member state	2001			2002		
	CA reports sent	Manufacturer reports received	User reports received	CA reports sent	Manufacturer reports received	User reports received
Austria	None	49	21	2	106	26
Belgium	4	284	15	1	346	12
Denmark	None	96	60	None	144	100
Finland	None	101	52	None	118	51
France	6	697	5,189	8	994	5,083
Germany	104	1,332	480	67	1,335	543
Greece	–	–	–	–	–	–
Ireland	1	54	16	7	114	34
Italy	–	–	–	–	–	–
Luxembourg	None	No data	No data	None	No data	No data
Netherlands	5	328	3	1	400	40
Portugal	5	45	24	None	78	15
Spain	6	127	23	4	119	21
Sweden	2	249	250	2	276	315
UK	34	1,586	5,448	42	2,014	5,000
Norway	No data	No data	No data	1	107	164
Switzerland	4	204	33	7	269	48

Source: Draft HS August 2003. Downloaded on 12 August 2003 from http://www.europa.eu.in/comm/enterprise/medical_devices/ca/vigilance_statistics.pdf.

globalization of medical device regulation may be premature. By examining the items on the GHTF agenda, we can document global and regional convergence of regulatory goals, strategies and ideas about quality, safety and performance standards, and about evaluation in the case of IVD products. On the other hand, Commission data (2003b) and 'grey' literature report on the divergence of regulatory arrangements and procedures across the 'big three', and the twenty-five EU member states (Altenstetter 2005). Rather than diminishing, the importance of the 'regulatory state' is increasing under the cross-pressures of global and regional regulation and domestic healthcare reforms. Instead of regional convergence, national variations will further increase after enlargement in 2004.

The power-sharing arrangements between the EU and member states do legitimize variations in regulatory responses to medical technologies and health risks. In addition, the principle of subsidiarity further encourages not only the coexistence of European and national initiatives but also various responses. Below the national level, the medical device regulatory regime, which consists of four sub-regimes, features many more differences in implementation and outcomes than are already identified in a single country case at the level of macro and meso structures (Altenstetter 2003a).

Concluding comments and lessons

With the passage of the three medical device directives, most European countries have been asked for the first time to control the market access of medical devices, engage in post-market surveillance and establish a vigilance process in the interests of users and patients. Prior to Community regulation, France and Germany operated a statutory regime and the United Kingdom a voluntary regime; each focused on different aspects. For example, in France only a small proportion of healthcare products were subject to regulation in the 1980s. By contrast, Germany's long-established focus on the safety of equipment led to the requirement of a safety officer in hospitals as early as the 1970s, and the United Kingdom's voluntary reporting has been in place for the past forty years or so. The major challenges for all three are to adapt a legacy of prior practices and rules to new ones, to apply and interpret European legislation, and to strengthen medical vigilance and incident reporting while maintaining the health protection standards achieved prior to the Community system. Reliance on a complex mixture of European and national rules and procedures is a fact of public administration and management in these and the remaining member states.

The drafting of the AIMDD in 1990 and the MDD in 1993, the redrafting of the IVDD in 1997–1998 and again in 2002, as well as the drafting of a human tissue and cell products directive since 2002 has produced significant changes, in addition to a number of Commission Decisions. In particular, one can observe a process of differentiation, toughening and reclassification of the highest-risk products, such as breast implants, heart valves, stents and joint replacements. Stakeholders, in particular in the IVD field, have rallied behind higher protection levels in the interest of public health. They have favoured the harmonization of EU rules on the one hand while upholding national preferences on the other. France is submitting all medical devices to evaluation procedures similar to those that apply to pharmaceuticals in order to prove that new products have higher benefit/risk ratios than older ones. If a product or procedure is found not to have an added value when compared to existing procedures and therapies, it will not be included in the national benefits catalogue and reimbursed by public payers. British regulators share similar views. In the past decade both countries have become veterans of using technology assessment to aid decision-making for new breakthrough technologies. A laggard for close to a decade, Germany has now endorsed the view that the litmus test of breakthrough therapies is whether they show higher benefit to risk ratios than established products, therapies and surgical procedures. Though the German enterprise of technology assessment is small and capacities are rather limited, it was aggressively pursued by the minister of health for disease management programmes in time for the federal elections in September 2002. In the future the Commission (2003b) will insist on more harmonized implementation throughout the member states.

In fact, there is a considerable gap between the rhetoric of assessing medical devices to aid decisions on including new therapies and procedures in national benefits catalogues, de-listing ineffective therapies and procedures, and substituting clinically effective and possibly cost-effective therapies and procedures. In all three countries, risk–benefit analysis and technology assessment in healthcare, while presented as objective science, are used for decisions on coverage, reimbursement and price-setting by the British National Health Service and the French and German statutory health insurance programmes. This view may contrast with those of advocates of healthcare technology assessment (HTA) and evidence-based medicine. Yet even advocates of rigorous evaluation as a precondition for market authorization – that is, obtaining the CE mark – admit that the process will always involve problems, perhaps even unsolvable ones. If central findings of technology assessment and recommendations through practice guidelines are relevant for national decision-makers only and do not trickle down to clinical practice and patient care, they may have little more than symbolic value despite being costly. But normative declarations cannot be equated with empirical evidence. Whether a shift from rhetoric to reality has actually occurred needs to be documented.

Most regulators and industry leaders agree that the process and procedure for market access – that is, CE-marking – need improvement, as do post-market surveillance and adverse incident reporting in each member state. National regulators agree on grand goals, but differ on much more:

how to strengthen oversight and enforcement over certification bodies; whether and, if so, to what extent they can rely on product approvals from third countries; and whether reporting requirements should include as large a target audience as possible, including medical institutions, users and patients, or only manufacturers, as is the case in Germany. However, all three agree on stricter harmonized European standards (EN) and international standards (ISO), as well as common technical specifications (CTSs) for the manufacture of IVDs.

The European Commission and the industry dislike unilateral national measures. Member states do not hesitate to engage in their own proactive and reactive strategies when they consider them necessary. By the same token, member states support the development of European rules, provided they leave room for national rules and action. Over the past ten years, industry leaders and policy-makers from the three countries have pushed hard for the establishment of a medical device regulatory regime distinct from the entrenched regulatory regime for pharmaceuticals. Borderline products were the exceptions. With dramatic medical advances such as tissue engineering being made during this period, another layer of reality is catching up with the key actors. However, the fourth directive on human tissues and cell products is expected to offer clarity and end uncertainties. Eventually, the sectoral regulatory regime for medical devices will consist of four sub-regimes, each with distinct requirements and mechanisms. In a decade, the learning curve across all stakeholders has been considerable. There remains a widely shared dilemma: knowledge production and innovations outpace appropriate regulatory responses.

Several lessons emerge from this research on medical device regulation. First, the research speaks of the complexity of the relationship between European law and national law, and between emerging highly specialized European and national case law pertinent to medical devices.

Second, it points to two factors impacting upon national policy autonomy in the health field: autonomy is being eroded by the implications of single-market directives; and, through separate processes, autonomy is expanding at the same time through benchmarking for 'best regulatory practices' across a multi-level committee system that spans the global, transnational and national levels and allegedly includes the world's best experts.

A third lesson is that the pre-eminence of domestic institutions, administrative capacities and national preferences are characteristics of regulatory practices in medical devices.

Fourth, to the extent that European health policy exists at all, it is fundamentally linked to the European regulatory policy rooted in the creation of a single market, which produces many cross-cutting issues and effects on healthcare systems. The regulation of medical devices has involved considerable learning through trial and error, correction and adaptation as well as feedback of experience, and information-sharing and new insights have been put to work over a ten-year period.

A fifth lesson is that regulation linked to market creation does not have to be a race to the bottom. In fact, global and regional regulatory harmonization of medical devices has *not* lowered standards. Rather, the quality, safety and performance standards and the evaluation, re-evaluation and batch verification of IVD products have raised the safety threshold in the European Union and beyond. Finally, despite a growing body of literature on healthcare in the European Union, we still have a shortage of systematic empirical data and information on the effects of the single market and European regulations on healthcare systems. While the OECD data bank has advanced cross-national research in the health sector considerably over the past two decades, it has not facilitated systematic comparative analysis of medical devices and innovations, post-marketing surveillance or medical vigilance systems; nor has the European regulatory database, EUDAMED. We still do not have systematic information on reimbursement, pricing and price-setting, purchasing practices, site planning of heavy medical equipment, the cost of training of highly skilled staff, equipment utilization, or equipment maintenance and servicing over and above what was known in the early 1990s (Banta *et al.* 1994). The conditions under which information between investors, clinical investigators and vendors are transferred are well-kept secrets, as is information on test sites for medical devices and sites funded by medical supplier firms. How healthcare reformers in most European countries can achieve the savings they promise by building bridges between local delivery sites and distributors, vendors and purchasers, in the absence of information, remains a mystery.

Using previous research as a guide has meant that an agenda for future research emerges. In the health sector the *politics of policy-making* framework has been favoured over other approaches to explain national developments in health systems and path-dependent interpretations of policy formulation and adoption. Yet in domestic implementation studies, path-dependent developments and structures are even more significant. 'Path-breaking' reforms that are enacted may be stopped short, delayed, altered or subverted in implementation, and this is true regardless of whether we consider the implementation of transposed EU directives or of domestic legislation. Also, path-dependent explanations in one sub-sector do not explain developments in another sub-sector and are often insensitive to sectoral variations in implementation. For example, who would have predicted that the medical device regime would consist of four directives which, as a minimum, can entail up to four distinct institutional arrangements for implementation in a country?

To understand the effects of Europeanization on healthcare policies, we need to complement the *politics of policy-making* framework with insights from comparative public policy, EU governance and European integration studies. Four research traditions in particular may be helpful in this regard: the national adaptation framework (Héritier *et al.* 2001); the literature that attempts to come to grips with the various facets of Europeanization (Bache 2003); a policy implementation framework that integrates a top-down and a bottom-up perspective and focuses on organizational actors and interdependent multi-organizational systems and networks rather than hierarchies; and sectoral and issue-oriented studies specific to a policy sector. Studies on economically significant sectors should be supplemented by studies on politically sensitive sectors such as pharmaceuticals, medical products and food safety. All four traditions relate to the multi-level, multi-unit and multi-actor nature of governance and networking; single-actor systems with a clear locus of responsibility and accountability do *not* exist. Empirical evidence for the merging of European administrative space and national space (OECD 1998) can only result from a plurality of approaches. Though they are changing, national structures, administrative arrangements and procedures remain firmly in place.

Notes

I want to thank the GSF-Medis Institute and its successor, the Institute of Health Economics and Healthcare Management (IMG), in Munich, Germany, for providing me with uninterrupted research support and a stimulating environment during a ten-year period; the Research Foundation of the City University of New York for approving several research grants between 1994 and 2000; and the Institut d'Études Politiques de Paris and the London School of Economics and Political Science for their support during my sabbatical in 1999–2000.

1 Several additional directives are relevant for the enforcement of the three main directives. The most recent directives are Directive 2003/63/CE amending Directive 2001/83/CE; Directive 2003/32/CE of April 2003 concerning the use of tissues of animal origin; and Directive 2003/12/CE on the up-classification of breast implants. Other relevant directives include the Clinical Trials Directive (2001/20/EC), adopted on 4 April 2001; the so-called Blood Directive (2000/70/EC), adopted on 23 October 2001; and the much earlier Personal Protective Equipment Directive (89/686/EEC), adopted on 21 December 1989.

2 For details, go to http://www.europa.eu.int/rapid/start/cgi/guesten (accessed 12 July 2003).

3 Dr David Jeffreys, Head of Devices Sector, MHRA (UK), speaking about regulatory reform in Europe at the AdvaMed International Conference in Washington, D.C. on 9 September 2003 (http://www.AdvaMed.org, accessed 10 July 2003). The European Parliament adopted a fourth directive on Quality and Safety for Human Tissues and Cells on 16 December 2003. This topic was initially on the agenda of medical device regulation in the early 1990s but could not be resolved as a result of major disagreements between France on the one hand and the Commission and other member states on the other. Human tissues and cells were initially covered by the IVDD adopted in December 1998 but had to be dropped to secure the passage of the IVDD.

4 http://www.europa.eu.int/comm/enterprise/medical_devices/tissue/index.htm (accessed 12 July 2003).

5 Contrary to common understanding, CE does not stand for the French term for 'European Community'; rather, it means 'Conformity with European regulations and directives' (*Conformité Européenne*).

6 The *old approach* (1969–1984) introduced five different methods of harmonization: total harmonization; optimal harmonization; reference to standards; conditional recognition of approval; and mutual recognition of approval.
7 Risk assessment, a risk management process and a risk–benefit analysis are preconditions for market authorization. Risk assessment may be described as 'a scientifically based process comprising four steps: hazard identification, hazard characterization, exposure assessment and risk characterization'.
8 This directive is the subject of a cross-national project on Tissue Engineering and Governance (TERG) operating out of the University of Cardiff and including Alex Faulkner, Julie Kent, Ingrid Geesink and David Fitzpatrick.
9 For a list of the Committee's Opinions, go to http://europa.eu.int/comm. food/fs/sc/scmp/index_en.html.
10 For a record on reports by competent authorities, go to http://www.europa. eu.int/comm/enterprise/medical_devices/ca/notif_report.htm   (accessed   12 August 2003).

References

Adcock, J., Sorrel, S. and Watts, J. (eds) (1998) *Medical Devices Manual*, Haslemere, UK: Euromed Communications.

Altenstetter, C. (1994) 'European Union Responses to AIDS/HIV and Policy Networks in the Pre-Maastricht Era', *Journal of European Public Policy* 1 (3): 413–440.

—— (1998a) 'Collective Action of the Medical Device Industry at the Transnational Level', *Current Politics and Economics of Europe* 8 (1): 39–60.

—— (1998b) 'Implementing EU Regulatory Policy on Medical Devices: The Case of Germany', in D. Chinitz and J. Cohen (eds) *Governments and Health Systems: Implications of Differing Involvements*, Chichester, UK: Wiley, pp. 452–462.

—— (2001) 'Multi-level Implementation Networks: The Case of Medical Devices and Patient Care', presented at panel, 'Policy Networks and Multi-level Decision-Making in Europe', European Community Studies Association (ECSA) Biennial International Conference, 31 May–2 June, Madison, Wis.

—— (2002) 'EU and Member State Regulation of Medical Devices', *International Journal of Technology Assessment in Health Care* 18 (4): 228–248.

—— (2003a) 'Health Safety in France: Public and Private Issues in Health Care Responsibilities at the Crossroads of European Integration', draft book manuscript.

—— (2003b) 'Safety and Quality in Diversity? The Case of Reporting Injuries, Accidents and Death', unpublished manuscript.

—— (2005) 'International Collaboration in Medical Device Regulation: Issues, Problems, and Stakeholders', in M. Mackintosh and M. Koivusalo (eds) *Commercialisation of Health Care: Global and Local Dynamics and Policy Responses*, London: Palgrave (in press).

Bache, I. (2003) 'Europeanization: A Governance Approach', Paper presented at the Eighth EUSA Biennial Conference, Nashville, 27–29 March 2003.

Banta, H. D., Gelband, H., Jönsson, E. and Battista, R. N. (1994) 'Health Care Technology and its Assessment in Eight Countries: Australia, Canada, France, Germany, Netherlands, Sweden, United Kingdom, United States', *Health Policy* 30 (1–3): 1–421.

Bennetts, P. (2001) 'The Lifetime of a Device', *Regulatory Affairs Journal (Devices)* May: 120–123.

Börzel, T. A. and Cichowski, R. A. (2003) *The State of the European Union*, vol. 6. *Law, Politics, and Society*, Oxford: Oxford University Press.

Brekelmans, C. and Nonneman, S. (2000) 'EUDAMED Enterprise Directorate General Unit G4 and Unit R3 13/14/11/2000', Slides (EUCOMED Document no. 012825).

Brown, C. (2000) Presentation at 'Medical Device Regulation' Conference, 9–10 October, London.

Commission of the European Communities (1994) *Guide to the Implementation of Community Harmonization Directives Based on the New and Global Approach*, Brussels and Luxembourg: European Commission.

—— (1999) *Guide to the Implementation of Community Harmonization Directives Based on the New and Global Approach*, rev. 2nd edn, Brussels and Luxembourg: European Commission.

—— (2003a) *Communication from the Commission to the Council and the European Parliament: Enhancing the Implementation of the New Approach Directives*, Brussels, 7 May 2003, http://www.europa.eu.int/eur-lex/prif/en/dpi/unc/dc/2003/com2003_0244.en.doc (accessed 12/8/2003).

—— (2003b) *Communication from the Commission to the Council and the European Parliament on Medical Devices*, http://www.europa/eu.int/eur-lex/prif/en/dpi/cnc/doc/2003com2003_0386.en.doc (accessed 12 August 2003).

Elmore, R. F. (1979) 'Backward Mapping: Implementation Research and Policy Decisions', *Political Science Quarterly* 94: 601–616.

European Commission (2001a) Health and Consumer Protection Directorate-General, Directorate C: Scientific Opinions, C2 – Management of Scientific Committees; Scientific Co-operation and Networks, *Opinion on the State of the Art Concerning Tissue Engineering*, Adopted by the Scientific Committee on Medicinal Products and Medical Devices 1 October 2001.

—— (2001b) Enterprise Directorate-General, *Conformity and Standardisation, New Approach, Industries under New Approach, Pressure Vessels, Medical Devices, Metrology*, Brussels, 22 June 2001. DG ENTR/G/4/HS. Working Group on Natural Latex, draft minutes, Meeting in Brussels, 22 May 2001, no. 013359.

—— (2001c) Draft minutes (013358), Clinical Evaluation Task Force meeting, 7 June 2001, Brussels.

European Confederation of Medical Devices Associations (EUCOMED) (1998) *Annual Report 1997–1998*, Brussels.

—— (2001a) *EUCOMED Position Paper Concerning the Need for Future Regulation of Human Tissue Products*, 29 March.

—— (2001b) *Comments from EUCOMED on Scientific Opinion on the State of the Art of Tissue Engineering Produced by the Scientific Committee on Medicinal Products and Medical Devices on 1 October 2001*, http://europa.eu.int/comm/food/fs/sc/scmp/out37en (accessed 12 July 2003).

—— (2001c) *Comments from EUCOMED–HTP on Opinion on the State of the Art Concerning Tissue Engineering: Scope/Definitions*.

Fouilleux, E., De Maillard, J. and Smith, A. (2001) 'The Role of Council Working Groups in the Production of European Problems and Solutions', presented at Workshop 'Governance by Committee: The Role of Committees in European

Policy-Making and Policy Implementation', European Community Studies Association (ECSA) Biennial International Conference, 31 May–2 June, Madison, Wis.

Goggin, M. L., Bowman, A. O., Lester, J. P. and O'Toole, L. J. Jr (1990) *Implementation Theory and Practice: Toward a Third Generation*, Glenview, Ill.: Scott, Foresman.

Haibach, G., Schaefer, G. F. and Türk, A. (2001) 'Policy Implementation and Comitology Committees: Differentiating between Policy Legislation and Policy Implementation', presented at the workshop 'Governance by Committee: The Role of Committees in European Policy-Making and Policy Implementation', European Community Studies Association (ECSA) Biennial International Conference, 31 May–2 June, Madison, Wis.

Héritier, A., Kerwer, D., Knill, C., Lehmkuhl, D., Teutsch, M. and Douillet, A. (2001) *Differential Europe: The European Union Impact on National Policy-Making*, New York: Rowman & Littlefield.

HIMA-EUCOMED (1999) 'Executive Summary', *Improving Patient Access to Medical Devices and Technologies: Common Understanding on Health Care Funding, Reimbursement and Technology Assessment*.

Hodges, C. (1999a) 'European Regulation of Medical Devices', in J. O'Grady and I. Dodds-Smith (eds) *Medicine, Medical Devices and the Law*, Cambridge: Greenwich Medical Media.

—— (1999b) 'General Product Safety', *Regulatory Affairs Journal (Devices)* August: 228–233.

—— (1999c) 'EC Data Protection Directive', *Regulatory Affairs Journal (Devices)* August: 209–212.

International Journal of Technology Assessment in Health Care (2002) 18 (2): 159–455 (Special Issue devoted to HTA in Europe).

Joerges, C. and Neyer, J. (1997) 'Transforming Strategic Interaction into Deliberative Problem-Solving: European Comitology in the Foodstuffs Sector', *Journal of European Public Policy* 4 (4): 609–625.

Joerges, C. and Vos, E. (eds) (1999) *EU Committees: Social Regulation, Law and Politics*, Oxford: Hart.

Kent, J., Faulkner, A., Geesink, I. and Fitzpatrick, D. (2003) 'Governance of Human Tissue Engineered Products in Europe: The Case for a New Regulatory Body', Paper presented at the conference 'Innovation in Europe: Dynamics, Institutions and Values', Roskilde University, 8–9 May.

Kingma, W. (1998) 'Managing Adverse Events Reports in a Biotech Company', Paper presented at the Fourth RAPS European Conference, 'The Way Forward', 26–29 April, London.

Ladeur, K.-H. (1999) 'Towards a Legal Concept of the Network in European Standard-Setting', in C. Joerges and E. Vos (eds) *EU Committees: Social Regulation, Law and Politics*, Oxford: Hart.

Landfried, C. (1999) 'Regulation of Biotechnology by Polycratic Governance', in C. Joerges and E. Vos (eds) *EU Committees: Social Regulation, Law and Politics*, Oxford: Hart.

Lowi, T. J. (1964) 'American Business and Public Policy, Case Studies and Political Theory', *World Politics* 16: 677–715.

Majone, G. (1996) *Regulating Europe*, London: Routledge.

—— (1997) 'The New European Agencies: Regulation by Information', *Journal of European Public Policy* 4 (2): 262–275.

Matthews, B. (1998a) 'Materials of Animal Origin Used in Medical Devices' (1), *Regulatory Affairs Journal (Devices)* February: 14–24.

—— (1998) 'Materials of Animal Origin Used in Medical Devices' (2), *Regulatory Affairs Journal (Devices)* May 1998: 93–102.

Maurer, A. and Larsson, T. (2001) 'Committees in the EU System: Alternative Approaches to Building Legitimacy in a Multi-level System', Paper presented at the workshop 'Governance by Committee: The Role of Committees in European Policy-Making and Policy Implementation', European Community Studies Association (ECSA) Biennial International Conference, 31 May–2 June 2001, Madison, Wis.

Mendrinou, M. (1996) 'Non-compliance and the European Commission's Role in Integration', *Journal of European Public Policy* 3 (1): 1–22.

Najam, A. (1995) *Learning from the Literature on Implementation: A Synthesis Perspective (WP-95-61)*, Laxenburg, Austria: International Institute for Applied Systems Analysis.

Neuhold, C. and Polster, K. (2001) 'The Role of European Parliament Committees in the EU Policy-Making Process', presented at the workshop 'Governance by Committee: The Role of Committees in European Policy-Making and Policy Implementation', European Community Studies Association (ECSA) Biennial International Conference, 31 May–2 June 2001, Madison, Wis.

Organization for Economic Cooperation and Development (1998) 'Sustainable Institutions for European Union Membership', *SIGMA Papers* 26: 21.

Peterson, J. and Bomberg, E. (1999) *Decision-Making in the European Union*, New York: St. Martin's.

Rhinard, M. (2000) 'Governing in Committees: An Analysis of the Democratic Legitimacy of the European Union Committee System', presented at the International Political Science Association World Congress, 1–5 August 2000, Quebec City.

Sandholtz, W. and Sweet, A. S. (1998) *European Integration and Supranational Governance*, Oxford: Oxford University Press.

Scharpf, F. W. (1978) 'Interorganizational Policy Studies: Issues, Concepts and Perspectives', in K. Hanf and F. W. Scharpf (eds) *Interorganizational Policy-making: Limits to Coordination and Central Control*, London: Sage.

Stone Sweet, A. (2003) 'European Integration and the Legal System', in T. A. Börzel and R. A. Cichowski (eds) *The State of the European Union*, vol. 6, *Law, Politics and Society*, Oxford: Oxford University Press, pp. 18–47.

Suppo, M. (1997) 'The Future of Regulatory Affairs in Europe for the IVD Industry', *Regulatory Affairs Journal (Devices)* November: 260–262.

—— (2000) 'Some Gray Areas of the IVD Directive', in J. Adcock, S. Sorrel and J. Watts (eds) *Medical Devices Manual*, Haslemere, UK: Euromed Communications.

Tallberg, J. and Jönsson, C. (2001) 'Compliance Bargaining in the European Union', Paper presented at European Community Studies Association (ECSA) Biennial International Conference, 31 May–2 June 2001, Madison, Wis.

Thompson, G. (2000) 'Clinical Evaluation and Investigation of Medical Devices in Europe', Presentation, 4 December 2000, London: IBC Conferences.

van Schendelen, M. P. C. M. (1998) *EU Committees as Influential Policymakers*, Aldershot, UK: Ashgate.

Vos, E. (1999a) 'EU Committees: The Evolution of Unforeseen Institutional Actors in European Product Regulation', in C. Joerges and E. Vos, (eds) *EU Committees: Social Regulation, Law and Politics*, Oxford: Hart.

—— (1999b) *Institutional Frameworks of Community Health and Safety Regulation: Committees, Agencies and Private Bodies*, Oxford: Hart.

Wessels, W. (1998) 'Comitology: Fusion into Action; Politico-administrative Trends in the EU System', *Journal of European Public Policy* 5 (2): 209–234.

Yanow, D. (1996) *How Does a Policy Mean? Interpreting Policy and Organizational Actions*, Washington, D.C.: Georgetown University Press.

4 European food safety policies

Between a single market and a
political crisis

Christophe Clergeau

Is health a pretext or a real objective in debate on food safety? The food
issue is above all a matter of economic actors – farmers, consumers, food
processing industries, storage and transport firms, and retailers – all trying
to organize the market to their best advantage. Yet food safety has progressively become a key component of European Union (EU) health
policy, as the evolution of the Treaties attests. The Treaty of Amsterdam
stipulates that the harmonization of national legislations has to aim for a
high level of consumer protection in which available scientific data are
taken into account (Art. 95). Veterinary and phytosanitary issues, which
formerly fell under the Common Agricultural Policy, are now covered by
Art. 152 on public health.

The Union has adopted comprehensive food laws in which the general
principles, standards and procedures of food safety regulation are defined.
European Commission inspectors ensure that this Community law is
observed uniformly throughout the Union. Two separate administrations
are responsible for its implementation. Within the Commission the Directorate-General for Health and Consumer Protection drafts food legislation
and supervises controls. It also has supervisory authority over the European Food Safety Authority (EFSA). This semi-independent agency eval-
uates risks for human, animal and plant health and serves as a forum for
solving conflict between national expert bodies. It thus appears that food
policy has been incorporated into the European Union's health policies
and that the protection of human health is now the major concern guiding
public action in this domain. But how can we explain the fact that it took
four years for products likely to be contaminated by bovine spongiform
encephalopathy (BSE), identified in 1996, to be banned and destroyed
throughout the Union? Why has the controversy over genetically modified
organisms (GMOs), which continues to fuel conflict between the pro-
GMO EU Commission and anti-GMO countries, still not been settled?

The complexity of this relationship between food and health in
Community policies is explained by its history, which can be summed up in
three phases corresponding to three different Community policy orientations. During the first phase, covering the period up to the mad cow crisis

in 1996, food issues were split into two policy subsystems: the Common Agricultural Policy (CAP) subsystem and the foodstuffs subsystem. Foodstuffs were considered to be industrial products among others and were therefore covered by the general rules of the single market. Attempts to unify food policies came up against resistance from the CAP subsystem. The health dimension came into play only from the point of view of product safety and scarcely at all from a nutritional point of view. Food safety was seen as a potential obstacle to the free movement of goods, both within Europe and internationally, before becoming a real public health issue. At that stage the idea behind a food agency was not to guarantee food safety but to improve the Union's administrative capacity to pass regulations and monitor their application.

This subordination of public health issues to economic considerations led up to the mad cow crisis in 1996 and the beginning of the second historical phase. The outcome of this crisis was a set of major EU reforms. The Treaty of Amsterdam granted more importance to the protection of health; scientific committees were reformed and their power enhanced; and all functions of expertise and control concerning food were grouped under a new directorate-general. Yet this unification of food-related matters was partial. Economic legislation and organization were still split between the CAP and the foodstuffs subsystems, and European political actors deliberately limited reforms to emergency measures for dealing with the political crisis triggered by the mad cow crisis.

From 1999, other crises were to pave the way for a new set of reforms, the creation of the Directorate-General for Health and Consumer Protection, and the setting up of EFSA. All the essential tools of Community food policy were grouped together within these two administrations, and European intervention was more forcefully asserted. Yet tension still remains between the two objectives of protecting health and ensuring the smooth functioning of the market. The absence of clear political choices has led to contradictory decisions. This chapter sets out to explore these three phases in the development of European food safety policy, with a view to understanding the limits of its health dimension and the uncertainties concerning its future.

The Common Agricultural Policy and the internal market: food between two separate subsystems

Although it is an obvious category of daily life, food was previously a non-object in Community policy. The anteriority of the CAP regarding unification of the internal market and its specificity gave rise to an autonomous policy sector. Annex II of the Treaty of Rome, with reference to Art. 38, defines a positive list of products that benefit from the measures of the CAP. These correspond to primary agricultural products such as meat or cereals, which in this Chapter I refer to as 'agrifood'. Other products, called foodstuffs as opposed to agrifood, automatically fall under the common regulations applied to goods circulating in the European Economic Community (EEC). Until 1996 this initial distinction induced the development of two distinct policy subsystems characterized by very different legal underpinnings, institutions and public policy styles.

For the actors of the CAP, both DG VI (Agriculture) and the leading agricultural organizations, food was not an issue that warranted attention. It was confused with the objective of developing productivity in order to supply markets with sufficient quantities at the lowest possible cost. Implementation of the CAP led to the development of extensive veterinary and phytosanitary legislation for product safety, but this legislation was considered above all as a component of agricultural productivity.

As regards foodstuffs, with the new approach of harmonizing national legislation and the project of completing the internal market, new public policy principles and tools were developed, and the emphasis put on their universal scope and capacity to regulate all food-related issues. The Food Division of DG III (Industry and the Internal Market), the food industries, European consumer unions and Members of the European Parliament (MEPs) all considered that the separation between agricultural products and foodstuffs was meaningless and had to be removed. In relation to the economic and technical realities of food, this separation was artificial; it was a constant factor of interaction and conflict between agricultural policy and a foodstuffs single market. Understanding this conflict requires a successive examination of the two different subsystems.

Foodstuff safety: invention of a Community policy between single market and scientific expertise

The first attempt at harmonization of national legislation to create a real common market for foodstuffs was a failure. The wish to give each product a Community definition came up against national peculiarities and the rules of unanimous decision-making. It was the Court of Justice of the European Union that ended the deadlock with its Cassis de Dijon ruling. This decision set the principle of mutual recognition by specifying that any product produced legally in an EU country could be sold commercially in another country of the EU without having to comply with the legislation of that country. This principle could be limited only in the name of mandatory requirements such as environmental protection, and protection of consumers' rights and their health. In the early 1980s the Delors Commission revived European construction around completion of the single market and a new approach to harmonization of national legislation. In the area of food it became essential to harmonize legislation on mandatory requirements so that these would no longer be a source of new obstacles to the free movement of foodstuffs. Between 1985 and 1995, public policies on foodstuffs developed in four main directions: control of national technical standards and regulations; revision of legislation relating to products that may be dangerous for human health; enactment of general health rules that the actors had to comply with, although they were free to choose the means for doing so; and fine-tuning of regulatory systems in which scientific expertise and political decision-making were articulated (Smith 1994). The policy to protect consumers and their health, in the name of which most Community public action relating to foodstuffs was taken, was one of the measures accompanying the establishment of a single market initiated by the Commission. But there can be no doubt as to its motivation. At the time, Community intervention in the field of health and consumer protection was primarily aimed not at setting a high standard of protection, but at achieving harmonization, which would deprive member states of the possibility of justifying impediments to trade in the name of mandatory requirements. Health remained subordinate to achievement of the single market goal (Smith 1994).

This orientation generated conflict around the definition of the level of protection specified in the legal documents that set the new standards. Two advocacy coalitions confronted each other (Sabatier and Jenkins-Smith 1999); whereas DG III and the agrifood industry, fully in favour of the single market, tried to limit the level of constraints on the economic actors, the European Parliament, a co-legislator in this field, European consumer unions and the Commission's Consumer Protection Service strove to raise the level of protection. Yet these two coalitions agreed in essence, for both were in favour of European construction and the successful accomplishment of the single market. They shared a similar conception of the principles of food safety regulation, and especially the role of scientific expertise.

Community food safety policy was based on two pillars. The 1993 Directive[1] on the hygiene of foodstuffs stipulated that producers had a general obligation to identify and manage health risks related to their activities. It established microbiological criteria (e.g. regarding listeria and salmonella) and rules of hygiene to comply with, but left producers free to choose the means for doing so. These means had to be defined on the basis of the Hazard Analysis Critical Control Points (HACCP) system, which relates to the critical points in the chain of production. This orientation attests to the will to encourage professionals to take specific steps in this respect. The creation of standards, the core of Community policy, was entrusted to DG III and its Standing Committee on Foodstuffs (StCF). This committee consisted of representatives of the member states and acted as a regulatory body. Its mission was to draft legislation, define managerial methods for the application of Community legislation, and validate national technical standards and regulations on which the Commission had to be notified.

This apparatus and legislation specifically on products associated with a potential health risk were based on scientific information produced by the

Scientific Committee for Food (SCF). The SCF, reformed several times since its inception in 1974, was the Commission's reference in its conception of scientific expertise. Members of the committee were appointed by the Commission for their scientific competence, to ensure their autonomy from any form of political pressure. Their independence regarding economic considerations was guaranteed by compulsory expression of interests. The committee's work, often based on consensus, was confidential, but opinions were often published. The aim was to manage scientific expertise objectively, totally unconstrained by economic, political or any other interests. Gradually the SCF's role was increased, not only by the Community institutions, which recognized the quality of its work and made consultation with it mandatory, but also by the Court of Justice of the European Communities (CJEC), which based its rulings on the committee's opinions (Vos 2000). Thus, the role and influence of the scientific community were progressively enhanced. In an area marked by uncertainty and the complexity of problems, this committee was responsible for producing information on which the definition of standards and the resolution of conflicts between institutions were based. Information and opinions produced by the SCF were the groundwork of the formulation of standards by the StCF. During deliberations organized within the StCF, only arguments based on scientific discourse were considered valid; political and national preferences were secondary. The primary role granted to scientific references facilitated the development of social learning and the emergence of a common culture based on the definition of solutions to problems objectified by expertise (Joerges and Neyer 1997). Yet this role of science did not necessarily imply the predominance of the search for an optimal level of health protection. The object of this regulatory committee's work was above all to set standards to promote the accomplishment of the single market.

The development of this European policy raised two new questions. The first concerned the maintenance of the separation between agrifood and foodstuffs that circulated within the same market and posed fairly similar product safety problems. The second question concerned the Commission's capacity to meet the needs of production of scientific data, formulation of standards, and control of their implementation. The vast majority of actors in the foodstuffs subsystem considered that food policies needed to be grouped together. They argued for the adoption of a framework directive in order to develop a comprehensive approach to the food chain and to extend the regulatory apparatus based on scientific expertise to agricultural products. They furthermore considered that the Commission ought to be more effective. In their opinion, the production of scientific expertise needed to be enhanced so that the numerous new products available could be evaluated and European interests defended at the World Trade Organization (WTO). The Commission's administrative capacity also needed to be strengthened to guarantee the efficiency of the single market and the uniform application of Community legislation throughout all the member states.

The European Parliament had been in the forefront of this struggle since 1989. With the support of consumer unions, it defended the creation of a single administrative structure covering all food products and grouping together the production of scientific expertise, the formulation of regulations, the control of their application, and the management of crises and a rapid alert system. Parliament saw this structure either as a new autonomous directorate within the Commission, or as an independent agency. The main idea was to *improve* the functioning of the single market; more protection for health was scarcely mentioned in the arguments put forward, and when consumer protection *was* mentioned, it primarily concerned economic rights, not health. Despite Parliament's strong commitment, these proposals remained fruitless. The food industry shared the general philosophy but feared too much government intervention, especially controls, that might limit the autonomy of private actors. As for the Commission, it was hesitant. While exploring all possible alternatives, it remained paralysed when faced with internal disagreement, and took no significant initiatives. After giving up the idea of creating a specialized agency, in 1990, the Commission suggested setting up a European network to mobilize the member states' capacities for expertise at the service of the SCF. This was achieved in 1993[2] (Smith 1994; Vos 1999). Clearly, these early debates on the creation of a European food agency, centred on an attempt to rationalize the administrative organization of European policies, were very far removed from the health issues that in 2002 justified the creation of the EFSA.

Agrifood safety: a policy under influence

We shall now turn to the parallel world of agrifood. It is striking to note that, throughout these years leading up to the mad cow crisis, technical objects as similar as agrifood and foodstuffs belonged to such different institutional and normative spheres. Food as a concept was virtually absent from the CAP. For its dominant actors, and especially farmers' unions, the CAP was an autonomous policy at the service of farmers, managed by them. Therefore, food issues had to be subject to the interests of producers. The latter's relationship to food was generally limited to their mission of providing sufficient quantities of products at a moderate price.

Before 1996, food played a decisive part in the CAP subsystem only from the point of view of 'signs of quality'[3] and veterinary and phytosanitary issues. The veterinary and phytosanitary sector managed agrifood safety regulations within the CAP subsystem, constituting a world apart in the agriculture DG and, more generally, the agricultural sphere. Historically, veterinarians have been subordinate to agricultural production in most European countries. Although their hope was to become the doctors of food, they first became technicians of breeding at the service of farmers, technicians whose intervention could increase productivity. This historical background facilitated the development of a dual animal health culture: first, as a service to the development of production, and second, as a component of public health (Hubscher 1999).

The Community veterinary sector was organized around the Standing Veterinary Committee (StVC), which acted as a regulatory committee and could rely on expertise of the Scientific Veterinary Committee (SVC). The distinction between experts and decision-makers was difficult to establish in so far as the vast majority of the members of the SVC and all those of the StVC were veterinarians with the same professional culture. The doctor-veterinarians of the StVC were senior officials but also considered themselves as experts. These two committees seemed to be under far more control by the member states than existing committees in the foodstuffs domain. There was not the same concern to formalize procedures in the functioning of the SVC as in the SCF. Appointment of its members by the Commission simply endorsed the member states' proposals, and the States' representatives on the StVC were generally the heads of national veterinary services. Veterinary issues were considered above all as economic and political issues to be negotiated. We thus witnessed a bureaucratic type of functioning that was predominantly intergovernmental and fairly close to that of the Agriculture Council itself.

Thus, the creation of a single market for agriculture did not have the same effects as in the case of foodstuffs. The harmonization of legislation relating to products had already been achieved in the CAP context. By contrast, the single market entailed the elimination of veterinary border controls between countries and the obligation for national veterinary services to control all production sites. It consequently became essential to develop Community inspection to verify the uniform application of veterinary legislation in the different states. On the eve of the BSE crisis the results in this respect were very poor. Community inspection remained in an embryonic state, isolated in Dublin and deprived of the means to fulfil its mission. This closure regarding any non-economic issue or factor likely to call into question agricultural actors' control on the CAP helps to explain the indifference observed in relation to health issues and the denial of BSE. At the time, the only debate on the subject concerned the boundaries between agricultural policies and foodstuff policies. The two subsystems disputed control of food policies and the symbolic and economic stakes involved. Despite the fact that it ran through all these different policies, the health dimension remained absent. The legal autonomy of the CAP and the institutional power of the agricultural sector enabled it to fight off all attacks, from the project to create a single food agency to the idea of a framework directive for all food legislation.

Developing food safety policies to resolve the 'mad cow' crisis (1996–1998)

When it erupted on 21 March 1996, the BSE issue was not entirely new. It was the confirmation of a possible link between BSE and a new variant of Creutzfeldt–Jakob disease identified in humans that triggered a major shock in the CAP subsystem. Consequent to this crisis, which rapidly turned political, substantial institutional changes were implemented. Yet decisions on the management of health risks remained insufficient. It was only in 2000 that tests on cattle were generalized and bovine products presenting a risk of contamination were effectively banned and destroyed throughout the European Union.

The mad cow crisis: a political as much as a health crisis

From the spring of 1996 the agricultural sector's monopoly over veterinary issues came under severe attack. Other actors were brought into play in the management of the crisis, with the creation of a Multidisciplinary Scientific Committee on BSE and an inter-DG group within the Commission to steer crisis management. New actors harnessed the mad cow issue, especially journalists specializing in health or jurists who proposed reforms. Yet on the whole, management of the crisis followed standard procedures, via regulation of the meat market and embargoes.

From April to June 1996, political treatment of the mad cow crisis focused on its agricultural dimension and on the consequences of the embargo on British beef decided on 27 March 1996. Journalists published articles that seriously implicated decision-making processes at the Commission and the 'manipulation' of scientific expertise, but they received little attention. It was only at the end of June, when the French weekly *Que Choisir* published the 'Castille report',[4] that the debate changed and the controversy shifted on to the political responsibilities of the Commission. The debate of 16 July 1996, in which the Commission, supported by the Council, tried to wash its hands of all responsibility, jolted the European Parliament into action. The absolute priority of the single market was challenged, as were the removal of veterinary controls and the inadequate attention paid to public health. The combat also shifted on to political ground and institutional issues. On 17 July, Parliament decided to create a Commission of Inquiry consisting mainly of MPs of the agricultural and environmental commissions hostile to or critical of the CAP. The Commission of Inquiry's work, which lasted for six months, gradually veered towards an extremely harsh implication of officials at the agriculture DG. This controversy fuelled a full-blown political crisis, culminating in Parliament's threat to censure the Commission.

The final report by M. Ortega[5] strongly condemned the way in which the Commission and the Council managed the BSE crisis, as well as the

United Kingdom's attitude. It recommended profound changes to the regulation of food-related risks at the Commission, and to policy concerning BSE. The CAP and failure of the veterinary system were strongly criticized, while the role of scientific expertise in the legitimization of regulatory decisions was challenged. The facts that expertise was harnessed by national interests within the SVC, that minority opinions were ignored and that decision-makers tended to give precedence to their political preferences over scientific expertise were denounced. Consensus around the principles of the internal market and the way in which European institutions aimed to trade off the objectives of protection of public health against those of free circulation was called into question. Britain threatened to paralyse Community institutions. Parliament warned that it would censure the Commission. It was therefore European construction as a whole that was threatened by a crisis which destabilized its main founders and institutions. 'All in all, it seems that in this time of crisis, "Europe" came apart' (Chambers 1999: 99).

Search for a strategy to end the political crisis

The Commission and Parliament had everything to lose in this crisis that threatened European construction and their legitimacy. Private economic actors also needed the rapid restoration of consumer confidence and a return to normal functioning of markets. Ending the crisis became a priority. The problem to solve was no longer a health crisis but the consequent political crisis. Its resolution involved two steps. The first aimed to reduce the extent of the crisis by imposing an appropriate 'policy narrative' (Radaelli 1999). Initially the debate highlighted two themes: submission of scientific expertise to free-market laws and economic interests, and harmfulness of the CAP and its productivist agricultural model that disregarded risks for consumers. But as the months went by, the crisis narrative came to focus more on the themes defined by the European Parliament. The report by the Commission of Inquiry published in February 1997 formalized a narrower narrative in which the different items were ranked. Aspects related to the CAP were toned down considerably, and the key issue became the harnessing of scientific expertise by economic interests and, to a lesser degree, the lack of democratic legitimacy and the absence of transparency of the Community decision-making system. On the basis of this altered narrative, an approach centred on the definition of a new system of regulation of food-related risks and a modification of inter-institutional balances was adopted.

The second step in the resolution of the crisis was organized on this basis and involved the adoption of a programme of institutional reforms. This programme was planned in line with the different stages of Michel Dobry's theoretical frame related to ending crisis strategies (Dobry 1992). The public policy narrative condemned the veterinary system steered by the member states in which scientific expertise seemed to be subject to political authority. It contributed towards the legitimization of the programme of reforms proposed in the Parliamentary Commission of Inquiry's report. This report was set out around three priorities: grouping together scientific committees and Community inspection in a new institution that was independent of economic interests; amendment of the Treaties to uncouple veterinary and phytosanitary matters from the agricultural sector and to increase Parliament's role in these areas; and, lastly, drafting unified food legislation and a framework directive to combat BSE. The context of crisis and the weight of urgency made this type of upheaval credible and created an obligation to act and to implement change (Keeler 1993).

The health dimension in reforms

Parliament and the Commission formed a real partnership to steer the reform process. The two opponents thus became allies. Parliament secured close control over the implementation of reforms, and its legislative role was extended in the Treaty of Amsterdam. On 18 February 1997, Jacques Santer, then President of the Commission, presented his institution's reform programme to his new partner: the European Parliament.

The elements of the Parliamentary programme incorporated into the Commission's proposals were above all those designed to provide a direct answer to the political crisis. Those changes that had a symbolic impact on fundamental inter-institutional balances were excluded. The will to reform was reflected first in the Treaty of Amsterdam. When the protection of human health was at stake, veterinary and phytosanitary legislation was to be passed on the basis of Art. 152, relating to public health, and no longer on that of Art. 37, concerning agricultural policy. Thus, only veterinary issues, considered secondary by the agricultural sector, were affected by this reform. The member states would be able to take safety measures more easily when they had scientific evidence of the existence of possible danger for human health, even in those areas in which European harmonization had been achieved. Thus, while the reform took into account the need for a solution to the crisis, the member states were able to safeguard their interests and to influence the orientation of the Treaty, which gave no clear signal of an upsurge of Community intervention. The dead end in which calls for a comprehensive approach to food and unification of food legislation found themselves reinforced this analysis. A Green Paper on the general principles of food legislation in the European Union[6] was published in April 1997, but no explicit provision was made for unification of food laws. In the absence of a strong political will, legislative continuity prevailed over changes.

In the final analysis, changes were implemented only in those areas that fell exclusively within the Commission's competences and that proved to be indispensable for finding a way out of the political crisis. The Commission's services were reorganized along two principles: strict separation between risk evaluation and management, and separation between legislation and control. The first principle was inspired by international norms; the second was the product of the crisis. It was in the name of these two principles that the new DG XXIV, 'Consumer Policy and Consumer Health Protection', encompassed all scientific committees and Community inspection services, while legislative units remained localized within the industry and agriculture DGs. In the area of risk expertise, the principles governing the operation of the SCF were simply generalized to all scientific committees and reinforced on a few points. Committee members were no longer to be appointed by the Commission on the basis of proposals by member states, but by the Scientific Steering Committee (a pluridisciplinary committee to supervise the specialized committees). Scientists could sit on only one committee at a time, for a maximum of two consecutive mandates, and were allowed financial compensation for expenses incurred. Procedural rules were specified, and the composition of the committees, the dates of meetings, the agendas, the minutes, the motions carried (including minority ones) and expressions of interest were all publicized.[7] Thus, with the new DG XXIV a new unified Community policy on food safety emerged, based on the two pillars of scientific expertise on the one hand and control and inspection on the other. This new policy constituted the core of the Community response to the BSE crisis. It recycled and generalized an institutional model that had previously been applied only to foodstuffs. At the time that it was presented (February–April 1997), it enjoyed wide consensus. Based on scientific legitimacy, this orientation was designed to bestow new legitimacy on Community policies and to show that Europe and the single market could once again function normally and guarantee the protection of human health.

Back to normal?

By grouping together scientific expertise and Community inspection under DG XXIV, the reform initiated the unification of EU food policy and especially its health section. The reform movement seemed to be concluded. While Parliament wanted to push further by grouping together all competences within a single administrative unit, the Commission replied that the differentiation of distinct institutional sites with scientific opinions and control, on the one hand, and legislation on the other, was the best way of guaranteeing the protection of consumers' health. From the spring of 1997 everyone tried to organize and support the system adopted, even if that meant overlooking certain ambiguities. It was a time of celebrating 'the return to normal' and 'the restoration of trust'. On 4 July 1997 the Commission adopted an inter-services agreement[8] that specified relations and procedures between the different Directorates-General involved in the area of food. This document described administrative mechanisms but never stated how the balance was to be found between the scientific elements guiding the expertise applied at DG XXIV and the economic considerations of the agriculture and industry DGs, which were still in charge of drafting laws. The CJEC enhanced the credibility of reforms by endorsing the embargo on British beef and putting public health on the level of a basic principle of Community law (Smith 1997; Vos 1999).

At the European Parliament and conferences organized by the Commission, everyone, including agricultural officials, was very pleased about the new complementarity between the internal market and consumer concerns. In February 1997 Jacques Santer's proposals were well received and only a few MEPs wanted to take the reforms further. In the following months, Parliament abandoned most of its historical aims, such as the creation of an independent agency. The Commission remained silent as to its future projects, and the Green Paper on food law, published in April 1997, seemed to be a dead letter. Despite a parliamentary debate in March 1998 and specific commitments made by the Commission to swiftly translate it into a legislative programme, nothing had materialized by the spring of 1999. There is nothing exceptional about such delays in Community policy-making, but here they show that once the political crisis had been defused, the Commission no longer saw the reform of European food safety policies as a priority.

In the agricultural field the BSE crisis was followed by no significant change. The Treaty of Amsterdam did not alter the general terms of the CAP, and Parliament and the Commission were unable to impose joint decisions. Within the agriculture DG the functioning of the SVC remained unchanged. In 1997–1998 this directorate successfully opposed unification of food legislation in the framework of the Green Paper, and defended slight adjustments and simplification in veterinary legislation (Smith 1997). During the same period the decisions taken by the Agricultural Council regarding BSE sometimes ran counter to the protection of human health. The most significant element concerned proposals to ban specified risk materials on a list, and the terms proposed by experts at the end of 1996. Throughout 1997 and 1998 the Commission's proposals were rejected by the majority of member states, those that considered themselves unaffected by BSE. They wanted to ensure that their markets would not have to bear the economic brunt of measures that they believed were not warranted as regards human health. The Agricultural Council also delayed the examination and adoption of a framework directive on the combat against BSE, designed to provide a stable legal base for the *ad hoc* measures taken until then.

In fact, the reforms introduced in the aftermath of the BSE crisis were not all that negative for the agricultural sector. The services that left the agriculture DG (expertise and control) were marginal and mainly represented sources of annoyance for the economic actors concerned.

These actors wanted to support reforms in the hope of benefiting from the restoration of consumers' trust without having to deal with a significant loss of autonomy or transformation of public policies. The health dimension was therefore diluted, in a sense, in the search for a strategy to dissolve the crisis, and in the reform process. The limitations to change and the subsiding of pressure from public opinion led to contradictory decisions that did not always take the protection of human health into account.

Institutionalization of a new health policy, 1998–2002

In late 1997 and in 1998 the opposition to real change seemed to have triumphed. Yet the reforms following the BSE crisis had triggered new dynamics, and unsolved issues constituted significant potential factors of change. It is on this basis that we can understand how a new health alert was to allow the adoption, in only a few weeks, of innovations that shortly prior to that had seemed inaccessible. In July 1999 Romano Prodi announced the creation of a European Food Safety Agency. In the autumn he tabled a new food strategy in Parliament, which was to lead to a comprehensive overhaul of food-related laws.

A new configuration of European policies

The 1997 reforms involved a profound reconfiguration of relations between the actors and coalitions concerned. The economic actors in the agrifood sector were destabilized by the BSE crisis and lost control over public policy-making when they lost control of the scientific expertise at the heart of the industry DG's regulatory apparatus. Leadership shifted into the hands of consumer unions, the European Parliament and, above all, the new DG XXIV, 'Consumer Policy and Consumer Health Protection'.

This DG was attributed with every virtue. It defended consumers' rights, protected citizens' health by allowing independent scientific expertise to be heard, controlled the application of Community law, and thus helped to change the attitudes of the member states. It rid itself of existing contradictions and promoted both the internal market and citizens' rights. This was, at least, how its officials perceived their role. The DG's action and image in public opinion were supposed to restore confidence and attract various actors: consumer unions, which had never before been able to rely on such a powerful ally; scientists, for whom it was a tool guaranteeing their autonomy and enhancing their role; and, lastly, industries and even farmers, for whom the public's trust and support were valuable resources. Rid of the problems related to the adoption of legislative measures, the DG saw itself as a pressure group at the service of consumer protection against economic interests. Owing to all these assets, it had a particularly strong identity and dynamic, reinforced by the leadership of EU Commissioner Emma Bonino and by internal trade-offs at the Commission that were almost always in its favour. Its financial and human resources were rapidly increased, thus enabling it to offset its initial administrative handicaps. This was the case, in particular, with the arrival of veterinarians from the agriculture DG. Although they introduced a new professional culture, the dynamic of construction of the DG and the impression of being pioneers in the public health field reinforced its cohesion. For the DG and its partners, support from the European Parliament and the monopoly on scientific expertise were powerful levers of influence. Experts and MEPs became key players in the production of public food safety policies, irrespective of the nature of the products concerned.

How the shortcomings of limited change paved the way for new reforms

This new configuration of European policies nevertheless encountered problems, and the apparatus set up in 1997 remained fragile and unstable. The main cause of difficulty was the fact that the reform was incomplete. The agriculture and industry DGs retained control over legislation, so that in certain cases they were able to prevent scientific data from being taken into account. This was particularly true in the agricultural sector. In 1998, twelve of the then fifteen member states were charged by the Commission in the European Court of Justice for failing to implement the new standards on pressure-cooking of meat and bonemeal for animal feed. There was a difference in the rationale underlying the organization of expertise and controls, on the one hand, and law-making on the other. In the former case, DG XXIV developed an all-encompassing approach to food. When it came to legislation, however, the industry and agriculture DGs carried on working independently, thus maintaining an artificial distinction between foodstuffs and agrifood. This fragmentation of competences was strongly criticized by those who defended the idea of one big agency and a framework directive for all food laws. They denounced the Commission's opposition to change in these respects.

   The second difficulty was related to debate on the role of science in the decision-making process. Many scientific experts considered that the separation between evaluation and risk management was artificial, and called for a direct role in the definition of standards. By contrast, the idea that scientific expertise should be the exclusive base for the definition of standards was challenged by others. Some questioned the illusion of perfect objectivity and impartiality of expertise. Others defended the responsibility of politicians and use of the 'precautionary principle' for taking protective measures that sometimes went further than experts' recommendations. Moreover, during this period the Commission urged international organizations to take legitimate factors other than science into account in order to justify measures hindering the free movement of goods. Clarification therefore seemed indispensable.

The third difficulty stemmed from differences in the political guidelines and the institutional mechanisms at different levels of competence: international, European and national. The separation between Community legislation and inspection, which also concerned risk management, was a unique characteristic of the European Union. It was justified only by the circumstances of the crisis and the will to place the economic DGs under the surveillance of DG XXIV. But this situation ran counter to the principle of separation between evaluation and management of risks prevailing at international level and applied in the member states. The EU was, moreover, lagging behind compared to the reforms in the organization of scientific expertise developed in certain member states. For instance, in 1997–1998 the United Kingdom and France created autonomous food safety agencies, primarily in charge of the production of scientific expertise. This disparity increased the risks of conflict between the Commission and the member states, as the autumn 1999 conflict with France over the issue of raising the embargo on British beef attests.

Finally, the 1997 reform triggered off a process of destabilization of the veterinarians' situation within the agriculture DG, where only officials from the legislative units were left. The veterinary sector was loath to accept its fragmentation among several directorates and its increasing marginalization within the agriculture DG. Hopes for a rehabilitation after the BSE crisis prompted a majority of veterinarians at the Commission to turn their backs on the world of agricultural production and to shift their vocation back to that of being 'food doctors' (Hubscher 1999). This development caused many of them to want to leave the agriculture DG, a move that the heads of the directorate did nothing to oppose. This tendency was reinforced by the consequences of the Treaty of Amsterdam, in terms of which veterinary and phytosanitary issues affecting human health fell under Art. 152 and joint decision-making with the European Parliament. Veterinarians of the agriculture DG found themselves in a legal and political world that differed sharply from that of the CAP. They worked on a daily basis with new actors, notably consumers' unions and elected representatives on the Environment, Health and Consumer Protection Commission of the European Parliament.

All these details and difficulties bear witness to the incomplete nature of the reforms, and constituted so many incentives to initiate new ones. Yet at the beginning of 1999, routine and institutional permanence seemed to prevail. The Commission nevertheless launched new projects on two important fronts: the evaluation report on the expertise system, entrusted to the heads of the scientific committees in May 1999,[9] and preparation of a communication on the precautionary principle, aimed essentially at advocating use of this principle at the WTO (Clergeau 2003). Yet there was nothing to hint that significant new reforms were on their way.

The Prodi Commission and creation of the European agency: a successful conclusion?

The simultaneous occurrence of a political crisis and a health crisis set off the reform process once again in the spring of 1999. The political crisis, independent of any food issues, simmered throughout the winter of 1998–1999 before breaking out in the spring. The Commission was accused of bad management, and some of its members of misappropriation of funds. Under pressure from Parliament and the threat of a censure motion, the Santer Commission resigned on 16 March 1999. The new Commission formed by Romano Prodi thus presented itself before Parliament in a very difficult context. It had to show that it would take Parliament's criticism into account, and was prepared to embark on profound reforms to its functioning. Just when the 'accused' Commissioners were being heard by the parliamentary commissions, the 'dioxin chicken' crisis broke out in Belgium.[10] Failure at an animal feed production plant had caused the entry of PCBs (polychlorinated biphenyl) into the food chain and contaminated a large number of chicken farms in several European countries. This crisis highlighted failings in the Community alert system and shortcomings in legislation relating to animal feed. In the context of change at the Commission, it took on a very particular dimension, underscoring the limits of Community action in an area that was supposed to have been profoundly reformed after the BSE crisis. This new crisis revived the memory of the previous one and its economic and political consequences. For the new Commission, the danger and the obligation to react were therefore strong.

Political mechanisms similar to those characterizing the BSE crisis were reproduced during this new crisis and resulted in the opening up of a new policy window. It was once again in partnership with the European Parliament that the Commission was to propose answers to the crisis. Criticism focused on two issues. The first concerned the insufficiency of the Commission's competences to monitor and manage crises. The second concerned the existence in Community law of legal gaps that threatened the protection of human health and were related to the persistence of two distinct legislative systems for agrifoods and foodstuffs. On 21 July, Romano Prodi announced in Parliament the plan to create an independent agency for food and medicines. The Commission's plans took shape during the summer. On 5 October in Parliament, Romano Prodi and David Byrne, the new Commissioner in charge of health and consumer protection, presented a declaration by the Commission on public health and food safety. Several specific commitments were made: to revive the project to unite food legislation and prepare a White Paper prefiguring legislative proposals; to present a communication by the Commission on the precautionary principle; and to create an autonomous food safety agency without delay. During this debate, many MEPs appealed for a single Directorate-General in charge of food safety.

This programme was pushed through. The White Paper on food safety[11] and the Communication on the precautionary principle[12] were published on 12 January and 2 February 2000 respectively, and the legislative units of DG III and DG VI were attached to the DG for Consumer Policy and Consumer Health Protection, which again changed its name, to 'Health and Consumer Protection', in the spring of 2000 – thus marking a new step in the shift of Community apparatus towards health. Following publication of the White Paper, the Commission tabled a proposal on 8 November 2000 for 'laying down the general principles and requirements of food law, establishing the European Food Safety Authority and laying down procedures in matters of food safety'. After amendments by Parliament and the Council, this regulation was finally adopted in January 2002.[13] After several months of gestation, the new European Food Safety Authority became operational in May 2003.[14]

These new reforms profoundly modified the organization of Community food safety policies. They constituted the conclusion of a long march towards the establishment of a comprehensive approach to food, in which the protection of consumers' health took priority. For the first time, the notion of foodstuffs was defined by Community law and included agricultural products. Unification of food legislation thus became irreversible and was soon embarked on. In order to ensure the coherence of legislation, a single new regulatory body replaced the different specialized committees. The regulations adopted clarified and reinforced the general principles promoted in the framework of the reforms – that is, a high level of protection of health, the precautionary principle, traceability of products, producers' responsibility, etc. These principles created new obligations for producers and gave political decision-makers a reliable legal base for protecting human health, including in the case of an absence of formal scientific proof. The implementation of these guidelines was entrusted to a single Directorate-General at the Commission, independent of the economic sectors concerned: that for Health and Consumer Protection, which thus became one of the most important DGs within the Commission. Constantly reinforced throughout the series of crises and reforms since 1997, it had finally obtained substantial financial, human and legal resources. It was given supervisory authority over EFSA, the creation of which reinforced the quality and independence of the scientific expertise on which decisions were based. The DG could also supervise the drafting of legislation and make use of the Food and Veterinary Office, an aggressive and active inspection service. It was thus equipped to control Community food safety policies.

The creation of EFSA generated stormy debate, especially between the Council, Parliament and the Commission. Initially the Commission tried to make the Authority more its armed wing than a body of scientific expertise. Several of its proposals were also intended to guarantee tight control by the Commission over the Authority's organization and work.

The Council opposed this orientation and tried to take control of the Authority via the presence of a large number of national government representatives on its board. Eventually the European Parliament managed to impose its position. It forced the Authority's competence to be narrowed down to food safety only, and its missions centred around risk evaluation and the production of scientific expertise. Parliament also reinforced the Authority's autonomy *vis-à-vis* the Commission and the member states.

A new public health policy is born?

These were significant reforms, marking a big step forward in the inclusion of health considerations in European policies. Yet can we say that the European Union is equipped with a coherent health policy on food? The construction of a single market and successive health safety crises have indeed spawned a Community food safety policy, but Community public action in the health field remains embryonic and legally limited to support for national policies. Although food quality policy has an important role, owing to Community recognition of quality labels, it remains confined to the agricultural sector and is implemented without any real coordination with the issues of product safety or public health.

The second limit of reforms is related to contradictory principles of action within the same new 'large' DG for Health and Consumer Protection. The Commission still grants primacy to the single market and observes its international commitments, especially WTO rules. It also grants particular importance to innovation and economic development. The new orientation in favour of protection of consumers' health is therefore relative. Between 1997 and 2000 these different principles of action were advocated by the different DGs confronting one another at the Commission. Emma Bonino forcefully defended the public health theme and consumers' rights. Her DG fought for citizens' rights, against the DGs representing economic interests. Today the DG for Health and Consumer Protection has in its hands scientific expertise, control, drafting of legislation, and international negotiations. It is therefore the target of intense lobbying by economic actors, for whom the stakes involved in the definition of technical and health regulations are very high. The directorate is no longer in a position of confrontation or arbitration with the other DGs; it is within the DG for Health and Consumer Protection itself that the confrontation of principles of action and interests takes place, and that a balance needs to be found between consumers' protection and their health, the rules of the single market, technological innovation, and international trade. Hence, this DG's force is not necessarily synonymous with a stronger engagement, in the sense only of a high level of protection of health – as the systematically pro-GMO attitude of Commissioner Byrne and the DG for Health and Consumer Protection attests. Its internal equilibriums, its fields of competence and its daily functioning make it more a food DG whose mission is to contain the demand for technical and health regulations, while producing the most important resource in any market: consumer trust. The refusal to create a European public health authority grouping together all the Commission's scientific committees, and the preference for the creation of an Authority limited to food safety, bear witness to the fact that priority is granted to the assertion of a sectoral food policy, rather than an all-encompassing public health approach. In the future this rationale could once again run counter to the requirements of public health.

Finally, food safety is still an area of competence shared between the European Union and its member states. This situation is a third limit to the development of a real common policy. The powers of the member states have been strengthened rather than weakened by the health crises, since the safeguard clauses in the Treaties, which enable the member states to take unilateral measures, have been extended. The weakness of the Commission's powers in crisis management has strengthened the member states' legitimacy. Even though the Commission plays a dominant role in the production of legislation, most of the implementation and control of that legislation remain in the hands of the member states. History has shown that some of them develop highly protective practices while others refuse to put a stop to risky ones, or choose to develop technological innovations that are not risk free. These divergences always result in stalemate in Community action and show that the member states still enjoy a substantial degree of latitude. Some countries, such as France or the United Kingdom, have been able to develop scientific expertise agencies more quickly than has the Commission. They have wanted to protect that asset and have not wanted the EFSA to be allowed to arbitrate in cases of conflict between divergent scientific expertise in different countries. The Authority can therefore only organize dialogue and confrontation of expertise to try to overcome points of divergence. Thus, the 'Europeanization' of scientific expertise has not been taken to its logical conclusion, and expertise can still be used as a resource for lasting strategies to protect specific national policies in the area of food safety.

In the light of the history of these policies, three elements will be decisive in the future. The first relates to clarification in the implementation of reforms adopted between 2000 and 2002. Use of the precautionary principle and the search for articulation between national and Community scientific expertise will necessarily generate conflict. The political and/or regulatory resolution of such conflict will stabilize the dominant principles of action. The second element concerns trends in international trade rules. Current debate at the WTO and the Commission on the Codex Alimentarius wavers between greater liberalization on the one hand and more protection of consumers' health and rights on the other. Europe is in the front line of this confrontation, the outcome of which will necessarily be imposed on it (Clergeau 2003).

The third element concerns the crises that in the past played a major role in the adoption of reforms. The same thing will happen in the future if institutional complexity and the importance of the interests at play favour the status quo. The capacity to make crises into opportunities for change and acceleration in the implementation of reforms will depend on the state of public opinion in Europe, and on the existence of policy entrepreneurs who rely on a determined coalition of diversified, close-knit actors. What will the situation be now that Europe has been enlarged to twenty-five members?

Notes

1 Directive 93/43 of 14 June 1993.
2 Directive 93/5 relative to scientific cooperation relating to food.
3 Accomplishment of a single market around the notion of 'mutual recognition' implied a risk of excessive uniformity and undermining of the specificity and diversity of agricultural products. Under pressure from France, the pioneer in this respect, the Commission supported the adoption of a Community policy on 'signs of quality'.
4 Notes taken by an official responsible for food issues at the Consumer Protection Services, during a meeting in the early 1990s at which the Commission and the DG for Agriculture allegedly deliberately ordered secrecy on BSE and related health risks.
5 M. Ortega (1997) Report on Alleged Contraventions or Maladministration in the Implementation of Community Law in Relation with BSE. European Parliament, Temporary Committee of Inquiry into BSE, doc. A4-0020/97/A of 7 February 1997.
6 Commission Communication on the General Principle of Food Law in the European Union, COM (1997) 176 of 30 April 1997.
7 Commission Communication on Consumer Health and Food Safety, COM (1997) 183 of 30 April 1997.
8 Inter-services operations manual establishing cooperation procedures between Directorates-General III, V, VI and XXIV, 4 July 1997, http://europa.eu.int/comm/dgs/health-consumer/library/pub/pub01-en.htmltop.
9 Philip, J., Kemper, F. and Pascal, G. (1999) 'A European Food and Public Health Authority: The Future of Scientific Advice in the EU', report to the European Commission.
10 During the same month, June 1999, a second crisis concerning Coca-Cola cans broke out.
11 White Paper on Food Safety, COM (1999) 719.
12 Communication from the Commission on the precautionary principle, doc. COM (2000) 1 of 2 February 2000.
13 Regulation no. 178/2002; OJEC L31, 1 February 2002.
14 www.efsa.eu.int.

References

Chambers, G. R. (1999) 'The BSE Crisis and the European Parliament', in C. Joerges and E. Vos (eds) *EU Committees: Social Regulation, Law and Politics*, Oxford: Hart Publishing, pp. 95–106.

Clergeau, C. (2003) 'Vers une exception alimentaire? La Sécurité des aliments entre globalisation et crises politiques', *Politiques et Management Public* 21 (2): 103–118.

Dobry, M. (1992) *Sociologie des crises politiques*, 2nd edn, Paris, Presses de la FNSP.

Hubscher, R. (1999) *Les Maîtres des bêtes: les vétérinaires dans la société française XVIIIe–XXe siècle*, Paris: Odile Jacob.

Joerges, C. and Neyer, J. (1997) 'Transforming Strategic Interaction into Deliberative Problem-Solving: European Comitology in the Foodstuff Sector', *Journal of European Public Policy* 4 (4): 609–625.

Keeler, J. T. S. (1993) 'Opening the Window for Reform: Mandates, Crisis, and Extraordinary Policy-Making', *Comparative Political Studies* 25 (4): 433–486.

Radaelli, C. (1999), 'Harmful Tax Competition in the EU: Policy Narratives and Advocacy Coalitions', *Journal of Common Market Studies* 37 (4): 661–682.

Sabatier, P. and Jenkins-Smith, H. (1999) 'The Advocacy Coalition Framework: An Assessment', in P. Sabatier (ed.) *Theories of the Policy Process*, Boulder, Colo.: Westview Press, pp. 117–166.

Smith, J. (ed.) (1994) *Safety, Hygiene, Control and Quality of Agri-food Products in Europe*, Brussels: Le Club de Bruxelles.

—— (ed.) (1997) *New European Food Safety Policy to Promote Good Health*, Brussels: Le Club de Bruxelles.

Vos, E. (1999) *Institutional Frameworks of Community Health and Safety Regulation*, Oxford: Hart.

—— (2000) 'EU Food Safety Regulation in the Aftermath of the BSE Crisis', *Journal of Consumer Policy* 23: 227–255.

5   The emergence of EU governance in public health

The case of blood policy and regulation

Anne-Maree Farrell

Introduction

On 27 January 2003 the Council and the European Parliament formally adopted a new Directive setting standards of quality and safety in relation to blood and blood products[1] (the 'Blood Directive'). Since 1989 a series of laws had been passed at European Union (EU) level concerning the marketing and licensing of 'medicinal products' such as fractionated blood products, although this had been done mainly to further the completion of the internal market (Weatherill 1997). The political fallout from HIV contamination of blood supplies in member states was to provide the catalyst for greater EU involvement in blood policy and regulation in the 1990s, culminating in the adoption of the Blood Directive. Unlike earlier EU legislative initiatives in blood-related matters, this Directive establishes a comprehensive EU-wide regulatory framework for the collection, manufacture and supply of blood and blood products for the first time. Member states had until 8 February 2005 in which to implement the terms of the Directive.

Analysing governance in blood policy and regulation

Blood policy and regulation forms part of the European Union's growing competence and influence in public health governance. What do we mean by 'governance' in this respect? The term has been used broadly in the academic literature to refer to changing patterns of governing at both national and supranational levels (Stoker 1998; Pierre 2000). It appears to be used in diverse ways with a view to capturing empirically observed changes in the process of governing at both levels (Rhodes 1996, 2000). Some commentators, such as Kooiman (1993), emphasize changing patterns in the nature of state–society relations in 'governing', whereas others have used the term in order to explain changing patterns in the way in which the state has sought to 'steer' the regulation of markets (Kazancigil 1998). In the context of politics and policy-making at European level, governance is often referred to as 'multi-level', reflecting the complex and diverse range of actors, techniques and tools involved in decision-making at supranational level (Hix 1998; Sbragia 2000; Hooghe and Marks 2001).

For the purposes of this chapter, the term 'governance' is used first and foremost as an analytical framework in which to pose a number of questions about how EU decision-makers have approached policy-making in public health matters, using blood policy and regulation by way of case study. The material used for the case study was based on both primary and secondary sources, including interviews conducted with those involved in the blood policy-making process at EU level. I identify and examine *factors* that are central to understanding the approach of EU policy-makers to 'governing' in this area. Such factors include (i) the use of 'burden-shifting' from member state to EU level in sensitive public health matters, such as blood safety, with a view to enhancing credibility and legitimacy; (ii) the use of regulatory tools as the preferred method by which 'burden-sharing' is to be achieved; (iii) the development of a more complex and diverse policy community than has been seen at member state level, leading to increased politicization; and (iv) the continuing important role of expert advisers in policy formulation. The last part of this chapter analyses the *patterns* of EU governance in blood policy, revealing a tension between the national governments, aware of the political implications of safety for patients, and a European arena striving to balance scientific, commercial and public interests.

Political fallout from HIV contamination of national blood supplies

The main catalyst for the shift to EU policy-making in blood quality and safety was the political fallout from HIV blood contamination scandals in a number of member states.[2] In those member states where political scandals occurred, high levels of HIV infection among recipients of blood and blood products were attributed, first, to a deficient national regulatory system for monitoring blood quality and safety; and second, to inadequate institutional decision-making processes with respect to the assessment of risk and the management of the national blood supply (Feldman and Bayer 1999; Bovens, 't Hart and Peters 2001). In relation to the first aspect, the creation of an EU-wide regulatory framework through the Blood Directive is a welcome development in transnational standard-setting, taken with a view to increasing the overall safety of the Community blood supply.

In relation to the second aspect, however, the emerging evidence suggests that there is a lack of political will at EU level to address the long-standing problems associated with the management of the blood supply, problems that contributed to high levels of HIV blood contamination in a number of member states. Scientific interests seem set to dominate the EU decision-making process as they have done at national level. Despite aspirations in the Blood Directive about working towards Community self-sufficiency through voluntary donation, there is no publicly available evidence that EU policy-makers have a concrete plan of action to achieve this goal. Instead, it seems that lip-service will continue to be paid to the idea of achieving self-sufficiency in blood and blood products through voluntary donation, while in reality widespread importation of commercial blood products sourced from paid donation will continue in many member states. The emerging pattern of EU governance in this policy sector suggests that 'burden-shifting' by member states will produce a mixed result. On the one hand, safety and quality are likely to be increased through the creation of a transnational regulatory framework for blood and blood products. On the other, the failure to deal with the long-standing problems outlined in relation to the management of the blood supply means that EU policy-makers have not taken on board valuable lessons from the fallout from HIV blood contamination at national level. The ultimate losers from such failure are likely to be consumers of blood and blood products, given the likelihood of future viral or other threats to the safety of the Community blood supply.

The role of regulation in blood quality and safety at EU level

It was not until the 1990s that the European Union began to take an increasing interest in public health matters, and particularly in issues relating to the Community blood supply. Prior to this time, policy-making and regulatory activities in relation to blood-related matters were essentially perceived as being part of national health policy (Altenstetter 1992). Any action taken by the European Union on blood-related matters was mainly a by-product of moves towards the completion of the internal market. With the Treaty of Maastricht coming into force in 1993, new policy competences were created in the areas of public health and consumer protection (see Art. 121 EC). The granting of such competences marked a shift in emphasis on the part of the European Union away from exclusively economic concerns in pursuit of the internal market, to a recognition of the need to engage in more socially oriented policy-making and regulation in the interests of its citizens.

At an institutional level, there was also a marked increase in interest in blood quality and safety issues from 1993 onwards. The European Parliament began to take a much greater interest in public health matters generally (Randall 2001), including issues relating to blood quality and safety. Between 1993 and 1996 the European Parliament passed a series of resolutions on issues relating to blood safety and called upon both the Commission and the Council to take action on the matter.[3] In 1994 the Commission published a Communication providing an outline of the direction that the European Union intended to take in blood policy (CEC 1994). Between 1993 and 1998 the Council also passed a series of resolutions and recommendations on blood quality and safety issues, urging the Commission to take concerted action.[4] In the Treaty of Amsterdam a specific policy competence was created in blood quality and safety (see Articles 152(4) (a) EC). In December 2000 the Commission published a legislative proposal for a Directive to establish a comprehensive regulatory framework for the collection and supply of blood and blood products in the European Union (CEC 2000). This proposal was subsequently adopted (with considerable amendment) by Council and Parliament in January 2003.

As mentioned previously in this chapter, the major catalyst for action at EU level in relation to blood quality and safety had been the political fallout from HIV blood contamination scandals in a number of member states. For example, in France *l'affaire du sang contaminé* had resulted in government decision-makers being called to account in a series of civil and criminal trials, and those in charge of the national blood transfusion service had gone to jail (Steffen 1999). In Ireland a long-running tribunal of inquiry into the circumstances leading to HIV contamination of the blood supply had forced the government to accept overall responsibility for what happened (Lindsay 2002). Both inside and outside Europe, high levels of HIV contamination of national blood supplies had resulted in adverse public reaction, and those at the highest levels of government had ultimately been held responsible for failing to protect their citizens from the consequences of HIV blood contamination. In those countries where scandal had erupted as a result of HIV blood contamination, national governments had been forced to agree to significant financial reparation (Leveton, Sox and Stoto 1995; Krever 1997; Feldman and Bayer 1999; Bovens, 't Hart and Peters 2001).

There were both institutional and economic reasons why national government policy-makers had failed to properly address the risk posed by HIV to the blood supply. There had been a failure to ensure that national blood markets were adequately regulated so that the risk of contamination was minimized or eliminated. Some member states operated a dual market in the supply of blood and blood products to their citizens. Although self-sufficient in whole blood used in blood transfusions, they were unable to meet ever-increasing demands for fractionated blood products, which needed to be sourced from thousands of donors. National blood supplies were unable to satisfy such demands through voluntary blood donation alone (Hagen 1993).

As a consequence, national blood transfusion services had a number of options: first, to establish their own publicly funded fractionation facilities in order to produce fractionated blood products; second, to use public funds to enter into commercial arrangements for the importation of fractionated blood products; or finally, to establish public fractionation facilities as well as importing commercially manufactured fractionated blood products. Those member states that elected to enter into commercial arrangements for the importation of fractionated blood products did so despite concerns by those in charge of national blood transfusion services over their safety. These products were manufactured by commercial companies based in the United States as well as Europe, colloquially known as 'fractionators'. They sourced their products mainly from American donors, who were paid to make their donations. By the end of the 1970s Europe was by far the commercial fractionators' biggest customer. Throughout the 1980s and beyond, it would continue to be an expanding and lucrative market (Starr 1998).

As the consequences of HIV contamination episodes were publicly revealed in a number of member states, the absence of coherent policy-making, the lack of financial investment and the extent of long-standing political neglect in relation to the management of national blood supplies were exposed in the media and in the courts. Some member state governments, including those of France and Ireland, became engulfed in political scandals arising out of the contamination episode. They consequently lost credibility (and therefore legitimacy) in the eyes of their citizens for their failure not only to recognize 'blood' as an important social (as opposed to economic) issue, but also to protect their citizens from the risks of HIV contamination of the blood supply (Steffen 2001; Lindsay 2002).

National governments in member states such as France and Ireland sought to restore their legitimacy in the eyes of their citizens in a number of ways. First, they moved to reform national blood policy and institutions; second, they created regulatory regimes to monitor blood quality and safety; and finally, they sought to shift the 'burden' of responsibility for blood quality and safety to European level. The preferred method by which such 'burden-sharing' would be achieved would be through the use of regulatory powers available at EU level. As Majone (1996) has pointed out, the European Union has limited resources through which it can assume control or responsibility for policy matters. While not having the features of what could be recognized as a nation-state, the Union has nevertheless extended its powers by adopting a position as a 'regulatory state' making use of regulations and directives to create legally binding obligations on member states.

As a result of the availability of EU regulatory powers, member states are able to shift the burden of responsibility in a specific policy sector either partially or entirely to European level. At the same time, they are also able to use such powers as a means by which their credibility (and legitimacy) may be enhanced at national level. This was clearly the mechanism adopted by member states in a bid to reclaim credibility in the wake of the political fallout from HIV blood contamination scandals. It also enabled member state governments to impose a series of EU regulations to improve blood quality and safety on national blood transfusion services that were institutionally resistant to change. In this way, member states could lessen the potential for institutional conflict resulting from the imposition of regulations, particularly where such regulations set higher standards than had previously been in place at national level.[5]

Regulatory strategies have traditionally been used by those charged with 'governing' in order to address 'market failure' in the provision of either public or private services (Ogus 1994: 4; Majone 1996: 28). National blood and blood product markets had failed to protect citizens from the risks of HIV transmission in the blood supply. The political fallout from HIV contamination scandals in member states such as France and Ireland revealed that both national and transnational blood markets had operated in the context of a 'laissez-faire' regulatory environment, where such an environment existed at all. State regulatory agencies charged with ensuring the safety of the blood supply failed to address problems and inequalities in national blood markets. While whole blood collected within national boundaries for the purposes of blood transfusion and/or manufacture into blood products was subject to national regulation (if any was in existence), the same could not be said of fractionated blood products manufactured by commercial fractionators. National regulatory agencies as well as blood transfusion services were essentially reliant on commercial fractionators vouchsafing the quality and safety of their products. They were unable, however, to impose regulatory controls on the sourcing and manufacture of such blood products, as these processes took place outside the national jurisdiction (mainly in the United States). The tragedy of HIV blood contamination had made the failure to adequately address dysfunctional national blood markets painfully apparent. A new approach to regulation was needed. Member states saw supranational regulation at EU level as a way to address national market failure, particularly in view of the transnational nature not only of blood markets, but also of viruses such as HIV.

The role of organized interests in the EU blood policy-making process

The Commission made it clear in its December 2000 Communication setting out its proposal for the Blood Directive that it had consulted with a range of organized interests and organizations in the preparation of the proposal.[6] One such group included medical and scientific professionals who ran national blood transfusion services, colloquially known as 'blood-bankers'. As a result of increasing EU involvement in blood policy and regulation by the late 1990s, national blood-bankers had formed themselves into a representative group known as the European Blood Alliance (EBA) in order to ensure that that they were in a position to lobby and be consulted on blood-related matters at European level.

There was also consultation by the Commission with groups involved in the manufacture and supply of fractionated blood products. One such group included the European Plasma Fractionation Association (EPFA), whose membership comprised plasma fractionators that supplied fractionated blood products sourced from voluntary donation on a 'not for profit' basis. Another group comprised international commercial fractionators that supplied fractionated blood products sourced from paid donors on a 'for profit' basis through private contractual arrangements with doctors and/or national blood transfusion services. The Plasma Protein Therapeutics Association (PPTA, formerly known as the European Association of the Plasma Products Industry (EAPPI)) represented commercial fractionators supplying the European market. It was a regional organization with links to the international fractionation industry, and a parent organization based in the United States. Commercial fractionators formed a distinct but integral part of the global pharmaceutical industry, which is highly influential at EU level (Greenwood 1997).

Other groups consulted by the Commission included groups representing both donors and recipients. The International Federation of Blood Donor Organizations (IFBDO) represented national donor organizations at European level. Highly organized and politically influential donor organizations were a particular feature in some member states but not in others. An example of an influential donor organization with a recognized national political identity was to be found in France (Hermitte 1996). In the case of haemophiliacs who used fractionated blood products on a regular basis in the treatment of their condition,[7] the European Haemophilia Consortium (EHC) was founded in the mid-1990s to represent their interests at European level. Many member states already had national haemophilia organizations that had been formed originally to provide support and assistance to haemophiliacs and their families. As a result of high levels of HIV infection among their membership in the 1980s, however, some of these organizations had moved from simply being support groups to assuming a national political identity as they campaigned in both the media and the courts for justice and financial compensation for their members (Feldman and Bayer 1999). This growing politicization had also led to a recognition on their part of the need to organize and lobby at European level, given increasing EU involvement in blood policy and regulation.

All these groups had a particular interest in the changing patterns of governance in blood policy and regulation that had begun to emerge at EU level by the late 1990s. They would battle it out for influence during the course of the negotiations that took place between EU institutions (courtesy of the co-decision procedure) over the terms of the Blood Directive from December 2000 until January 2003, when it was formally adopted by Council and Parliament. The main institutional arena in which this battle for influence would be fought out was the European Parliament, and specifically in the Committee for the Environment, Public Health and

Consumer Protection (known as the ENVI Committee). These groups focused their attention on the ENVI Committee meetings held at regular intervals to consider and recommend amendments to the substantive terms of the Directive which were then referred to Parliament for approval. Members of the Committee were lobbied by these groups in order to ensure that their views were taken into account in Committee meetings and in any amendments. The EBA, the EPFA and the IFBDO wanted member states to work towards self-sufficiency through voluntary unpaid donation and they wanted recognition of this aim in the Directive. The PPTA was opposed to any proposal that made voluntary unpaid donation a requirement in the Directive.[8] The issue of whether or not self-sufficiency could be achieved through voluntary unpaid blood donation within the European Union would prove to be one of the major points of conflict shaping the course of negotiations over the final content of the Directive. In the end, the adopted Directive would describe voluntary unpaid blood donation as simply a 'factor' to be 'encouraged' by member states, as contributing to 'high safety standards for blood and blood components and therefore to the protection of human health'.[9]

The role of experts in EU blood policy and regulation

Prior to EU involvement in blood policy and regulation in the 1990s, policy-making and regulation on blood-related matters had been dominated by blood-bankers who ran national blood transfusion services. At national level they formed the dominant policy community and operated within state bureaucratic decision-making processes. Other organized interests such as commercial fractionators and donor or recipient groups were not part of this policy community. Prior to EU involvement in blood policy, national blood-bankers had been the dominant policy community for many years at European level through their membership of the Committee of Experts in Blood Transfusion and Immunohaematology (SP-HM Committee), which was convened by the Council of Europe. Although decision-making by this policy community was purely advisory and non-binding at the level of the Council of Europe, the decisions that were made were influential in providing guidance to those engaged in the collection, supply and manufacture of blood *and* blood products in Europe.[10] This European 'policy community' fits neatly with what Haas (1992) has described as an 'epistemic community' brought together by their expert knowledge underlined by their commitment to the principles of voluntary unpaid donation and self-sufficiency in blood. At both national and European level, it was a closed policy community on which national government decision-makers relied extensively in the formulation and implementation of blood policy and regulation.

As stated previously, many European blood-bankers shared a commitment to the twin principles of voluntary unpaid blood donation and self-sufficiency in blood and blood products. The voluntary donor was seen as engaging in an altruistic act, based on Titmuss's (1970) idea of the 'gift relationship'. Under the terms of this 'relationship', blood should be given freely and without financial remuneration to the unknown recipient. Thus, blood was not a commodity to be bought and sold in the commercial marketplace. For blood-bankers, achieving self-sufficiency meant that there would be no more need to rely upon continued importation of blood products from commercial sources where the blood used in the manufacture of such products was sourced from paid donors. However, the reality of the day-to-day management of national blood supplies in many member states meant that achieving self-sufficiency in fractionated blood products would remain purely an aspiration. Supply failed to match demand, and governments failed to match political rhetoric with necessary financial investment to fund public research and fractionation facilities in order to bring about self-sufficiency in fractionated blood products. Instead, significant public funds continued to be spent on the importation of such products from commercial fractionators in order to meet increasing demand.[11] Blood-bankers also viewed blood collected from voluntary donors as being likely to have lower rates of infection than that being given by donors who were given a financial incentive to donate their blood. By the end of the 1970s this viewpoint had been raised to the position of a self-evident truth by blood-bankers as successive scientific studies pointed to higher rates of hepatitis infection among paid donors (Starr 1998). In the 1980s, when HIV posed a risk to the blood supply, many blood-bankers clung to the idea that voluntary donation would ensure that recipients of blood and blood products would be protected from the risks posed by the virus.

While retrospective testing was to show that overall HIV infection rates in Europe were lower where blood or blood products had been sourced from voluntary donation as opposed to paid donation, this did not prove to be universally so (see Table 5.1). In countries such as France, for example, where fractionated blood products used by haemophiliacs were sourced predominantly from voluntary donation,[12] HIV infection rates among recipients were the highest in Europe. This was largely attributable to the fact that France had continued to collect blood from prison inmates who, despite being voluntary unpaid donors, had a high rate of HIV infection due to intravenous drug use (Geronimi *et al.* 1992). At the same time, HIV infection rates among haemophiliacs proved to be high in other member states because of significant levels of importation of fractionated blood products manufactured by commercial fractionators and sourced from paid donors.

The political fallout from HIV blood contamination scandals at national level showed that blood-bankers' commitments to the principles of voluntary donation and self-sufficiency needed to be moderated. Commitment to such principles needed to take into account available epidemiological

Table 5.1 HIV infection rates for haemophiliacs in selected member states, 1992

Country	No. tested	No. positive	Percentage
Belgium	291	19	6.5
Denmark[a]	310	89	28.7
Finland	238	2	0.8
France	2,684	1,036	38.6
Germany, F.R.[a]	3,176	1,177	37.1
Greece	881	176	20.0
Ireland[a]	364	113	31.0
Italy[a]	2,957	768	26.0
Luxembourg	20	2	10.0
Netherlands	217	36	16.6
Spain[a]	2,799	1,147	41.0
Sweden	389	98	25.2
United Kingdom[a]	3,545	1,206	34.0

Source: European Centre for the Surveillance of HIV/AIDS, Paris (WHO–EC Collaborating Centre on AIDS. Date: 31 December 1992). The vast majority of haemophiliacs were tested for HIV antibodies in the mid to late 1980s. The figures given above as at 31 December 1992 provide a good indication of overall HIV infection rates for haemophiliacs in the selected member states.

Note
a These countries had high levels of dependency upon importation of commercial blood products during the time HIV posed a risk to blood supply: 1980–1985.

evidence on risks of infection in their voluntary donor population, as well as the impact of a mixed private/public market in blood products on overall infection rates among recipients. The consequences of HIV-contamination of national blood supplies altered the position of blood-bankers as the dominant policy community in blood-related matters. As the extent of HIV contamination became apparent, blood was no longer simply a medical and scientific issue to be managed by such experts. The social significance of blood and the tragic consequences for those infected with HIV contaminated blood meant that 'blood' became a highly politicized issue and a matter of ongoing public concern. This in turn meant that national government decision-makers were forced to assume a dominant role in policy-making with respect to blood-related matters in order to address growing public concern.

Where scandals developed in member states, such as France and Ireland, national governments were forced to accept responsibility for what had happened and to make financial reparation to HIV-infected recipients. Political responsibility was assumed for the institutional failure to address the risks posed by HIV to the blood supply, a failure that was attributed, first, to the narrow frame of reference for decision-making adopted by the dominant policy community of blood-bankers, and second, to inadequate state regulatory control. In the political fallout from HIV blood contamination scandals, however, there appeared to be little public examination of how best to restructure national blood and blood product markets given widespread agreement that continued importation of commercial blood products had contributed significantly to high rates of HIV infection in recipients (Leveton, Sox and Stoto 1995; Krever 1997; Steffen 1999; Lindsay 2002).

The consequences of HIV blood contamination scandals at national level contributed to blood policy-making and regulation becoming highly politicized at EU level. In addition, the process of policy-making at EU level generally contributes to a more politicized environment, as a range of interests and actors are able to seek influence in ways that would not be possible at national level. The politicized nature of EU policy-making was revealed during the course of negotiations on the substantive terms of the recently adopted Blood Directive. Blood-bankers, who had previously formed the dominant policy community at European level through the Council of Europe, were now simply one group among several interests, actors and institutions seeking to influence the blood policy process.

Although blood-bankers were one group among others during the most political phase of the policy process with regard to the Blood Directive, it is clear that they will remain crucial to ensuring the proper implementation of its terms in the future. Article 30 of the Blood Directive provides for the Commission to consult relevant scientific experts in relation to implementing the medical and scientific requirements imposed by the Directive. It is unclear from the Directive, however, what form of consultation of scientific experts will be adopted by the Commission. Initially, the Commission had proposed that a committee of member state representatives be established to ensure implementation and ongoing review of the substantive provisions of the Blood Directive (CEC 2000: para. 9, Explanatory Memorandum). It was also intially suggested that members of the Council of Europe's Committee of Experts on Blood Transfusion and Immunohaematology be nominated to this new EU committee.[13] Given the very recent adoption of the Blood Directive, it remains to be seen what shape scientific advice on blood-related matters will take in the future. It does nevertheless seem that national blood-banking 'experts' may yet again be in a position to reassert their dominance in the blood policy process as the 'politics' involved in the drafting and adoption of the Directive dies down.

Emerging patterns of governance in blood policy and regulation

A number of observations can be made about the evolving structures or patterns of governance at EU level in relation to blood policy and regulation. The increasing EU involvement in this policy sector observed over the past ten years has been brought about mainly as a result of political fallout from HIV blood contamination scandals at member state level. The failure to minimize and/or prevent widespread HIV contamination of blood supplies and the tragic consequences that followed for recipients of blood and blood products have meant that 'burden-shifting' from member state to EU level has become the preferred option for managing the difficult social and political issues raised by blood.

One of the long-term consequences of the fallout from HIV blood contamination scandals at national level has been a recognition of the political nature of policy-making on blood-related matters. Public reaction to the exposure of maladministration of the national blood supply highlighted the continuing social and cultural significance attached to 'blood' as a sign of the importance of social and communal relations in advanced industrial democracies (see Nelkin 1999). Furthermore, it provided a touchstone through which public distrust of those in political authority was revealed. In a bid to reassert legitimacy in the eyes of an increasingly distrustful public, government decision-makers were required to show that the 'public interest' was placed at the centre of policy-making and regulation in matters relating to blood safety. There was a recognition that government policy-makers needed to take account of potential political outcomes in the assessment of risk (see Douglas 1992). From this point on, policy-makers' ultimate point of reference would be that which was politically acceptable over and above what was considered by experts to be scientifically reasonable.

This having been taken on board at member state level in relation to matters of blood safety, the question remains as to whether this approach has become part of the emerging structures of governance in blood policy and regulation at EU level. It is clear that representatives of member states that have suffered from HIV blood contamination scandals have brought this new approach with them to decision-making at EU level (Vogel 2001). What is not so clear is whether this approach is actually translating into practice. Although it is acknowledged at paragraph 23 of the Recital to the Blood Directive that voluntary unpaid blood donation should be encouraged at member state level, as it could contribute to high standards of safety in blood and blood products, it nevertheless failed to be included in the Directive as a *requirement*. Were commercial interests favoured over consumer safety in this instance? Commercial fractionators would have found it difficult to maintain and/or expand their lucrative European market in the supply of blood products if the Blood Directive had specified voluntary donation as a requirement for the sourcing of whole blood and fractionated blood products. In the failure to enshrine voluntary donation as a requirement in the Directive, it could be argued that commercial interests were given priority over the public interest in ensuring high standards of blood safety.

In addition, did some member states wish to avoid any detailed public examination of their failure to achieve self-sufficiency in fractionated blood products through voluntary donation, which would have become a pressing issue if it had been made a requirement in the Blood Directive? Exclusion of this requirement meant that member states avoided having to account for their failure to achieve it to date. Requiring such accountability may have revealed a lack of commitment on the part of several member states to providing the necessary financial investment to bring about self-sufficiency in fractionated blood products. This had resulted in continuing high levels of dependency on the importation of commercially manufactured blood products, which had, in turn, contributed to high rates of HIV infection among those of their citizens who regularly used such products.

The political sensitivity of this situation for some member states is such that the Commission has failed to publish up-to-date data on levels of dependency among member states on continued importation of commercial blood products. The last time data were published on the matter was in a Commission Communication in 1994, and even that was based on information that was collected as far back as 1989 and 1991 by the Council of Europe's Committee of Experts. At the time of the Communication in 1994, it was noted that extracting what few data had been obtained from member states had proved to be difficult (CEC 1994). In summary, emerging patterns of governance in blood policy and regulation at EU level reveal a highly politicized process in which commercial *and* state interests have influenced not only the choice of issues on policy agenda, but also how issues have been dealt with.

Notwithstanding this highly politicized process of policy-making in relation to blood at EU level, it is likely that blood-bankers will continue to have a prominent role in ongoing policy formulation and implementation, mainly because the Blood Directive explicitly states that the Commission will need to consult with relevant scientific experts on blood-related matters. This provides a 'window of opportunity' (Kingdon 1995) for blood-bankers to maintain their dominance in blood policy-making in the long term. It is clear on the face of the Directive that a significant degree of medical and scientific expertise will be required to ensure its effective implementation across member states. Given the limited resources and expertise of the Commission in this policy sector, it is likely that it will be highly dependent on advice received from such experts in informing their approach to the future of blood policy and regulation at EU level.

The role and functions of expert committees operating under the auspices of the Commission, however, have recently come in for a great degree of criticism, particularly in the wake of the Commission's poor handling of the BSE crisis in the late 1990s. Such criticism prompted the Commission to undertake a review of the system for the provision of scientific advice at EU level. In December 1999 a report was published on the future of scientific advice at EU level and it recommended that mechanisms needed to be created to ensure that the system of scientific advice was politically accountable in the public interest, with the authors conceding that several scientific advisory committees had been subjected to pressures that had resulted in a perceived bias towards political and industrial, rather than consumer, interests (CEC 1999).

What the findings of this Report revealed is that the scientific assessment of risk must take account of the public interest where there are risks to public health. Nowhere is this likely to be more important than in the case of EU management of future transnational public health risks, such as those posed by viruses to the Community blood supply. What remains to be seen is whether there is the political will at EU level to bring this about in practice. Concerns remain that 'consultation' with scientific experts in blood policy and regulation will result in a retreat into a narrow scientific and technocratic frame of reference for decision-making, which may fail to address the political nature of the assessment of risks to public health.

Conclusion

This chapter has examined emerging patterns of 'governance' in blood policy and regulation at EU level. The political fallout from HIV blood contamination scandals in a number of member states was the catalyst for increasing EU involvement in the 1990s in policy-making and regulation on blood-related issues. This led to the creation of a specific policy competence in the area in the Treaty of Amsterdam, as well as the adoption of a Directive on blood quality and safety. For the first time, the Directive will create an EU-wide regulatory framework for the collection, manufacture and supply of blood and blood products.

I have also identified a number of factors that are central to this emerging pattern of 'governance' in blood-related matters at EU level. First, member states have sought to engage in 'burden-sharing' with the European Union in the management of blood quality and safety primarily as a legitimating tool in view of the loss of credibility in the wake of HIV blood contamination scandals at national level. Second, the main mechanism by which such 'burden-sharing' has been achieved is through the use of EU regulatory powers, as seen in the adoption of the Blood Directive. Power over implementation and enforcement will be 'shared' between member states and the European Union, while at the same time providing an opportunity for national governments to show their citizens that they are taking decisive action to promote consumer safety in blood and blood products. Third, increasing EU involvement in blood-related matters has led to a greater 'politicization' of the policy-making process, with a number of interests and institutions vying for influence.

The European Parliament has become the key institutional arena in which this battle for influence has been played out to date. It marks a change from policy-making at member state level previously dominated by a closed policy community of blood-bankers involved in the running of blood transfusion services and usually operating within the confines of state bureaucracies without the need to be politically accountable to elected bodies such as parliaments. The politicization of policy-making on blood quality and safety, however, has not led to any public examination of how best to structure the European blood market, or to any questioning of the reasons for continuing high levels of dependency on the importation of commercial blood products in certain member states. It seems that for the foreseeable future, political aspirations of achieving self-sufficiency in fractionated blood products sourced from voluntary blood donation will continue to operate as a legitimating tool for policy-makers without reference to the commercial realities of the Community blood market.

Finally, despite the greater politicization of the policy-making process in blood-related matters at EU level, which saw national blood-bankers become one group among several vying for influence, it seems likely that they will maintain a prominent role in ongoing policy-making, given that consultation with scientific experts is required under the terms of the Blood Directive. A big question mark still remains, however, over how the Commission will approach its consultation with scientific experts and what frame of reference will be used in decision-making processes with respect to assessing risks to the Community blood supply.

While the patterns of governance are becoming clearer in EU blood policy and regulation, and are likely to become more so in the future with the implementation of the Blood Directive, a number of unresolved issues remain. First, the Union needs to define more explicitly how it will balance scientific interests with political concerns when assessing public health risks. Second, member states need to clarify how they intend to achieve the goal of self-sufficiency through voluntary donation. Finally, the European Union has focused on economic matters for most of its history, and only recently has increasing attention been focused on addressing the social concerns of EU citizens. Policy competences in consumer protection and public health are evidence of this new focus. What is not clear in the case of blood policy, however, is whether the Union's traditional commitment to the promotion of economic interests has been properly balanced against the need to take account of 'the public interest' in ensuring consumer safety in blood and blood products. How to ensure that this 'public interest' remains at the centre of the decision-making process in blood policy is likely to be one of the more problematic issues to be resolved in EU public health governance in the future.

Notes

1 Directive 2002/98/EC setting standards of quality and safety for the collection, testing, processing, storage and distribution of human blood and blood components and amending Directive 2001/83/EC *Official Journal of the European Communities* (OJ) L 33, 8.2.03, p. 30.
2 Interview with European blood-banking official (15 August 2001).

3 The European Parliament passed a series of resolutions on blood safety and self-sufficiency through voluntary unpaid donations in the European Community (OJ C 268, 4.10.93; OJ C 329, 6.12.93; OJ C 249, 25.9.1995; OJ C 141, 13.5.1996).

4 *Council Conclusions on 13 December 1993 on self-sufficiency in blood in the European Community* (OJ C 15 18.1.1994); *Council Resolution of 2 June 1995 on blood safety and self-sufficiency in the Community* (OJ C 164, 30.6.1995); *Council Resolution of 11 December 1996 on a strategy towards blood safety and self-sufficiency in the European Community* (OJ C 374, 11.12.96); *Council Recommendation of the 29th of June 1998 on the Suitability of Blood and Plasma Donors and the screening of Donated Blood in the European Community* (OJ C 203, 21.7.1998 (98/463/EC).

5 For example, in evidence recently given to the Public Accounts Committee of the UK Parliament, the Chief Executive of the National Blood Authority admitted that most of the regulations to which the National Blood Service now adheres emanated from the European Union, as there were no nationally agreed guidelines on a range of issues relating to blood quality and safety (see evidence of Mr Martin Gorham, CEO, National Blood Authority on 4 April 2001 (answer to Question 52)): *Report of the Public Accounts Select Committee (UK Parliament – 16th Report) (2001) reviewing the Public Audit Office Report on the National Blood Service*, London: The Stationery Office.

6 Other international bodies consulted included the Council of Europe, the International Red Crescent Society (the Red Cross manages blood transfusion services in many countries) and the World Health Organization (WHO). All such bodies have long-standing interests in matters of blood quality and safety.

7 Haemophilia is a genetic disorder carried by females but affecting only male offspring and results in a deficiency in clotting factor VIII or IX. There are different levels of severity of the condition. It results in spontaneous internal bleeding, mainly into joints and organs. Haemophiliacs often require regular infusions of a blood product that is rich in the clotting factor in which they are deficient. As a result of continual internal bleeding, many severe haemophiliacs can suffer from severe and chronic physical disability.

8 Personal communication by blood-banking official.

9 See paragraph 23 in Preamble and Article 20(1): *Directive 2002/98/EC setting standards of quality and safety for the collection, testing, processing, storage, and distribution of human blood and blood components and amending Directive 2001/83/EC* (OJ L 33, 8.2.03, pp. 32, 36).

10 Interview with European blood-banking official (15 August 2001); interview with commercial fractionator official (30 June 2001).

11 For example, in the United Kingdom successive national governments repeatedly committed themselves to achieving national self-sufficiency in blood and blood products from the mid-1970s onwards. Following long-standing financial neglect, the government eventually committed some financial resources towards the building of a new public fractionation facility, which opened in 1987 (see Berridge 1996). It is not clear, however, that self-sufficiency has ever been achieved (interview with UK public fractionation official, 20 September 2002).

12 While the French HIV blood contamination scandal has been attributed mainly to the use of whole blood and fractionated blood products sourced from French voluntary unpaid donors, Soulier (1992: 39) points to the fact that there was also importation of commercially fractionated blood products sourced from foreign paid donors in the early 1980s when HIV/AIDS was a risk to the blood supply.

13 Interview with European blood-banking official (15 August 2001).

References

Altenstetter, C. (1992) 'Health Policy Regimes and the Single European Market', *Journal of Health Politics, Policy and Law* 17 (4): 813–846.

Berridge, V. (1996) *AIDS in the UK: The Making of Policy 1981–1994*, Oxford: Oxford University Press.

Bovens, M., 't Hart, P. and Peters, B. G. (2001) *Success and Failure in Public Governance: A Comparative Analysis*, Cheltenham: Edward Elgar.

CEC (Commission of the European Communities) (1994) *Commission Communication on Blood Safety and Self-Sufficiency in the Community* (COM (94) 652 (final) 21.12.1994).

—— (1999) *The Future of Scientific Advice*, Paper prepared by Professors W. P. J. James, F. M. Kemper and G. Pascal (EFPHA and FSA: 8 December 1999) (see http://europa.eu.int/comm/food/fs/sc/future_food_en.html).

—— (2000) *Communication from the Commission to the Council, the European Parliament, the Economic and Social Committee of the Regions setting out a Proposal for a Directive of the European Parliament and Council setting standards of quality and safety for the collection, testing, storage, and distribution of human blood and blood components and amending Council Directive 89/381/EEC* (COM (2000) 816 (final) 13.12.2000. 2000/0323 (COD).

Douglas, M. (1992) *Risk and Blame: Essays in Cultural Theory*, London: Routledge.

Feldman, E. and Bayer, R. (eds) (1999) *Blood Feuds: AIDS, Blood and the Politics of Medical Disaster*, New York: Oxford University Press.

Geronimi, J., Henry-Bonnot, P., Feltz, F., Morelle, A., Roquel, T. and Vernerey, M. (1992) 'Les Collectes de sang en milieu pénitentiare', Paris: Joint Report from the Inspection Générale des Services Judiciaires ISGJ RMT 1392 and the Inspection Générale des Affaires Sociales, IGAS, Code Mission SA07 no. 92 119 (November 1992).

Greenwood, J. (1997) *Representing Interest in the European Union*, Basingstoke, UK: Macmillan.

Haas, P. (1992) 'Introduction: Epistemic Communities and International Policy Co-ordination', *International Organisation* 46 (1): 1–33.

Hagen, P. (1993) *Blood Transfusion in Europe: A 'White Paper'*, Strasbourg: Council of Europe.

Hermitte, M.-A. (1996) *Le sang et le droit*, Paris: Éditions du Seuil.

Hix, S. (1998) 'The Study of the European Union II: The "New Governance" Agenda and Its Rival', *Journal of European Public Policy* 5: 38–65.

Hooghe, L. and Marks, G. (2001) *Multi-level Governance and European Integration*, Lanham, Md.: Rowman & Littlefield.

Kazancigil, A. (1998) 'Governance and Science: Market-Like Modes of Managing Society and Producing Knowledge', *International Social Science Journal* 155: 69–79.

Kingdon, J. W. (1995) *Agendas, Alternatives and Public Policies*, 2nd edn, New York: HarperCollins.

Kooiman, J. (1993) 'Social-Political Governance: Introduction', in J. Kooiman (ed.) *Modern Governance: New Government–Society Interactions*, London: Sage, pp. 1–8.

Krever, H. (1997) *Commission of Inquiry on the Blood System in Canada*, Final Report, Ottawa: Canadian Government Publishing.

Leveton, L. B., Sox, H. C. and Stoto, M. A. (eds) (1995) *HIV and the Blood Supply: An Analysis of Crisis Decisionmaking. Committee to Study HIV Transmission through Blood and Blood Products*, Division of Health Promotion and Disease Prevention. Institute of Medicine, Washington, D.C.: National Academy Press.

Lindsay, A. (2002) *Report of the Tribunal of Inquiry into the Infection with HIV and Hepatitis C of Persons with Haemophilia and Related Matters*, Pn 12074, Dublin: Government Stationery Office.

Majone, G. (1996) *Regulating Europe*, London: Routledge.

Nelkin, D. (1999) 'Cultural Perspectives on Blood', in R. Bayer and E. Feldman (eds) *Blood Feuds: AIDS, Blood and the Politics of Medical Disaster*, New York: Oxford University Press, pp. 274–292.

Ogus, A. (1994) *Regulation: Legal Form and Economic Theory*, Oxford: Clarendon Press.

Pierre, J. (2000) 'Introduction: Understanding Governance', in J. Pierre (ed.) *Debating Governance: Authority, Steering and Democracy*, Oxford: Oxford University Press, pp. 1–13.

Randall, E. (2001) *The European Union and Health Policy*, Basingstoke, UK: Palgrave.

Rhodes, R. A. W. (1996) 'The New Governance: Governing without Government', *Political Studies* 44: 652–667.

—— (2000) 'Governance and Public Administration', in J. Pierre (ed.) *Debating Governance: Authority, Steering and Democracy*, Oxford: Oxford University Press, pp. 54–90.

Sbragia, A. (2000) 'The EU as Coxswain: Governance by Steering', in J. Pierre (ed.) *Debating Governance: Authority, Steering and Democracy*, Oxford: Oxford University Press, pp. 219–240.

Soulier, J.-P. (1992) *Transfusion et sida: le droit à la verité*, Paris: Éditions Frison-Roche.

Starr, D. (1998) *Blood: An Epic History of Medicine and Commerce*, New York: Alfred A. Knopf.

Steffen, M. (1999) 'The Nation's Blood: Medicine, Justice and the State', in E. Feldman and R. Bayer (eds) *Blood Feuds: AIDS, Blood and the Politics of Medical Disaster*, New York: Oxford University Press, pp. 95–126.

—— (2001) *Les États face au Sida en Europe*, Trans-Europe series, Grenoble: PUG.

Stoker, G. (1998) 'Governance as Theory: Five Propositions', *International Social Science Journal* 155: 17–28.

Titmuss, R. (1970) *The Gift Relationship: From Human Blood to Social Policy*, London: George Allen and Unwin Ltd.

Vogel, D. (2001) 'The New Politics of the Risk Regulation in Europe', Paper given at Centre for the Analysis of Risk and Regulation (CARR), London School of Economics and Political Science, August 2001.

Weatherill, S. (1997) *EC Consumer Law and Policy*, London: Longman.

6 Towards a European bioethics policy?

Institutional structuring and political responses

François D. Lafond

Europe's involvement in the public health field can be described as protean. Whereas research on the existing social welfare systems and the organization of healthcare in Europe is widespread and continues – rightly so – to occupy many specialists, other emerging issues are not receiving the same attention. Political institutions, under various pressures, are being forced to orient their action to areas that until now seemed marginal. This chapter is devoted to an aspect of health policy currently undergoing profound and rapid change: bioethics. The study is nevertheless limited in two respects: first, as I examine the Europeanization of bioethical issues it is impossible to foresee their long-term evolution; and second, the scope of the present chapter is too narrow to allow a detailed analysis of the values structuring these debates, or of their cultural and national underpinnings.

I present the intervention of political actors at both national and European level in the area of biomedical ethics, with a view to drawing up an institutional and historical inventory of Europeanization in this sector. For member states in search of answers to globalization, the European Union and the Council of Europe are the locus of diffusion and learning about diversity. The example of biomedical ethics can serve to evaluate the Europeanization of very particular sectors, and thus to symbolize painstaking European construction. The first section of the chapter defines and analyses the implications of biomedical ethical issues. In the second section we consider the slow institutionalization within states. This is followed, in the third section, by the legitimate intervention of the Council of Europe, and then the slow and forced involvement of the European Union in the fourth. In the fifth and final section I draw conclusions on the Europeanization of biomedical ethics.

Governance of biomedical ethics: a political topic *par excellence*

Two implicit assumptions illuminate bioethical politics. In the first, the function of regulation and control of social activities by the political authorities, with the different actors concerned and according to the particular deliberative system of each sphere of intervention, remains essential. This regulatory activity is accompanied by governments' objective of maintaining and protecting the social link. To this end, public authorities strive to find the best institutional and legal arrangements possible to limit the shortcomings of markets, to ensure that social cohesion is more than just peaceful coexistence of individuals in a given territory, and to guarantee acceptance of the social project that gives meaning to trends in our societies. On the basis of this logic, the reasons, the level, the forms and the intensity of public authorities' actions, depending on the areas or sectors considered, operate in relation to certain values that enable decision-makers and citizens alike to identify the common project better and to assess its accomplishment. Without reviving debates peculiar to political philosophy, it is clearly this *ranking* of values that poses the most problems in our pluralistic societies. Since a number of values are difficult to reconcile, what are the trade-offs of politics and how does it establish its own ranking? Is this difficult balance that has to be found within states not even trickier at European level? The analysis of the way in which European institutions manage to find, or fail to find, legal balances in relation to these different values can therefore prove to be instructive.

The second assumption is that we are facing a new change in the role of politics and its regulatory dimension. As the fields of intervention change, governance with a strong technical-scientific component is emerging. Until recently, questions concerning scientific activities seemed to be reserved for experts and the decision-makers responsible for solving them. This attitude corresponded to the classical view of science as a vehicle of progress and certainties. But the growing complexity, technicity and hyper-specialization of our societies have muddled this image. We now have to face choices or questions concerning 'techno-scientific' progress (Hottois 1999) and its multiple consequences without having the capacity to evaluate and judge the full range of these consequences and their future developments.

Two elements converge and contribute to the emergence of these 'risk societies' described by Beck (1992). First, the perverse effects or externalities generated by the development of our industrial societies cause new threats to weigh on our environment and our very existence. The globalization of trade, the escalation of competition between nations and firms and, finally, the social consequences of these economic practices are attended by a globalization of risks. The most recent examples – the meat hormone controversy, the 'mad cow' crisis, environmental and climatic issues – are all signs of what is likely to increase with the development of modern industrial societies. Simultaneously – and this is the second element – new risks are asserting themselves with the current scientific revolution, amplifying the impression and nature of uncertainty as to our future. The feats and discoveries in the field of genetics and knowledge on the mechanisms of life afford unknown control over our heredity, our reproduction and hence our own development. Deciphering the human genome, cloning, and research on the embryonic stem cell all prefigure our entry into the 'genetic era' so often announced (Blanc 1986).

These discoveries should allow the development of new medical therapies and even transformations in the practice of medicine. Manipulation of living organisms is also impacting on the performance and quality of agriculture and affording new opportunities for all human activities. This is the reasoning of those who, irrespective of their level of involvement, justify and legitimize this research. Yet some social demands and practices are raising questions as to the logical consequences of such dynamics. Issues concerning biotechnology and bioethics are in this sense a perfect illustration of new dilemmas facing our societies. What some analyse as 'the end of nature' (the boundary between nature and culture is said to be less permeable than before) and 'the end of tradition' (since humans will henceforth determine their own destiny) will consequently impact on political systems and on the adoption of collective decisions that governments will make on behalf of society, whether legitimately or not.

It appears that, by defining what the collective considers as risks and the protection it intends to provide for its members, our societies are setting both limits and certainties: limits in the sense that they are seen as determining the practices believed to be socially acceptable, and are thus forced to forecast the future, to anticipate various social demands and potential dangers that could be new sources of discrimination, injustices or even stigmatization (Nelkin and Lindee 1995); and certainties in so far as, by identifying and specifying the protection that societies wish to provide, and defining everyone's responsibilities, we are supposed to have the possibility of reconsidering the collective link, the social contract, as was the case during the emergence of industrial society, with the construction of the social welfare state and its social security systems. The implementation of this governance of risks takes place without existing tools such as planning and forecasting being as malleable and operational as in other fields of political intervention. The recent success of the 'precautionary principle' is a perfect example of this. How ought one to act in a context of uncertainty, especially when the consequences seem to be irreversible?

These political interventions are undertaken in an international environment undergoing profound transformation. For the past fifty years, one of the main political and institutional innovations has been taking place in Europe, with the pooling of national sovereignties. It is in the framework of this European integration that the changes described above can be observed in their finest details, and fruitful analyses proposed. Their heuristic and comparative value enables us to illuminate both the political implications of bioethics and the process of Europeanization in this socially, politically and economically sensitive area.

Gradual institutionalization within states

Without being applicable to all the phenomena concerned by 'scientific governance' in our risk societies, the example of bioethics is sufficiently rich and complex to enable us to understand how biomedical innovations have been addressed, first socially and then politically, in Europe. Qualifying and describing with precision what we mean by biomedical ethics or 'bioethics' has – like the birth of any discipline – been a major issue that has generated an abundant literature (Potter 1971; Engelhardt 1986; Sève 1994; Doucet 1996). Consider, like Hottois and Parizeau (1993: 24), that 'bioethics refers to a generally pluridisciplinary set of research, discourse and practices aimed at clarifying or solving questions of ethical significance raised by the advancement and application of biomedical technosciences'. Three types of mastery with numerous consequences are within reach: the mastery of reproduction; the mastery of heredity; and the mastery of the nervous system. Faced with these new bioethical problems, how does society organize itself? In what way, with what tools and what political discourse has politics become involved? How has it legitimized its action in innovative domains? How have many hitherto distinct categories been disrupted: public action–private life, thing–person, life–death, discovery– invention?

Analysis of the biomedical field and its relations with society and the authorities cannot start with the intervention of political authority only, since that would amount to overestimating its effective role by minimizing the importance of the other social actors' responsibility. To also maintain a dynamic image as close as possible to reality, it is necessary to consider biomedical phenomena in an historical perspective.

Professional self-regulation

The first phase of bioethical politics was a period of self-regulation of the professions concerned. The history of the Second World War is at the origin of issues concerning the protection of individuals as regards scientific experiments and the construction of the notion of consent. It was to guarantee patients a minimum of protection that non-binding international declarations (by international medical associations) recommended that states take adequate measures to avoid any abuse or instrumentalization of the human being (Fagot-Largeault 1985). These professional statements were the first impulse behind the beginnings of institutionalization at the hospital level, along with a reassertion of the need to protect individuals. Local committees emerged in most Western countries, charged with the task of verifying research protocols and ensuring that the consent of people undergoing experiments had been obtained. However, this trend was neither systematic nor really organized. Most of the time it was simply a matter of collegial decision-making and avoiding the sometimes painful isolation of those who have to decide for others (generally members of the medical profession). Self-regulation also took place at a second level, in response to genetic tinkering in the mid-1970s. The actors concerned were no longer only doctors and their professional unions, but also geneticians who were themselves – somewhat theatrically, according to certain participants at the Asilomar Conference – surprised by their own ability to manipulate living organisms and by the potential risks for humans and their environment. After a short moratorium, some practical precautions were defined, but without research being hindered in any significant way (Kourilsky 1990). Finally, self-regulation also involved a third category of actors: biologists. With the development of biomedical science and the goal of relieving the suffering of sterile couples, assisted reproduction techniques left the field of experimentation in the early 1980s. The absence of a normative framework did not systematically mean the complete absence of rules. In France it was practitioners and especially the national federation of sperm conservation centres (Fédération nationale des Centres d'étude de conservation des œfs et du sperme humains, CECOS) that from the outset drew up their own strict set of rules to avoid any negative reaction by government authorities.

The combined appearance of three phenomena related to biomedical progress – that is, experimentation, genetic engineering and assisted procreation – involving different professions, took place in a way that was almost self-referential, without the intervention of the public authorities. But the various ethical and professional norms started showing signs of cracking under the strain of an increasing number of private requests, lawsuits and various fears revealed and amplified by fascinated media. Members of the medical and scientific professions were some of those who called for the intervention of political representatives, considering them to be the only legitimate actors to make choices seen as irreversible. The biomedical field thus confirms what has been observed in other areas: scientists' ability, often overlooked, to get their problems and interests on to the political agenda, and to influence political choices (Ingram, Milward and Laird 1992).

Simultaneous national processes

Similar institutionalization

The entry of biomedical issues on to the political scene corresponds to a second, longer phase in the construction of issues, a phase that materialized in pluridisciplinary institutionalization. Access to the government agenda is always a subject of struggle between the actors concerned, and biomedical ethics was no exception to this rule. Despite the demands of some, others considered that politics had nothing to do with these issues. From their point of view, the fact of putting problems specific to biomedical ethics on to the government agenda was no guarantee of their resolution; it only meant that decision-makers had identified and recognized a need for action. Depending on their resources and interests, on their institutional situation and on the representation of the social order that they conveyed, the actors introduced an important cultural and cognitive dimension into each decision (Gusfield 1981; Jobert and Muller 1987). Institutionalization enabled the different players to continue the construction of the arguments and rhetoric supporting their points of view. Faced with increasingly autonomous social subsystems and with civil services organized functionally, in which different sectoral rationales coexisted, dialogue and the diffusion of information could prove difficult between actors of different cultures. The large numbers involved and their weak collective representativeness were also a reason for this process of institutionalization, apart from existing institutional structures. At the same time, the institutionalization of the biomedical field corresponded to the political authorities' need constantly to obtain precise expertise on swiftly evolving and potentially highly controversial issues. The beginning of the institutionalization phase in France can be pinpointed to 1983, with the creation of the national ethics consultative committee (Comité consultatif national d'éthique). This was the first permanent national committee with a plural composition, despite initial and ongoing criticisms. Its mission was to inform the political authorities on all developments in the life sciences.

Since then, this French ethics committee has become familiar to many European countries: Belgium, Denmark, Finland, Italy, Luxembourg, Portugal, the United Kingdom and Sweden, to mention only those in the European Union.[1] Political decision-makers rarely have the time to reflect on an issue and to find solutions when faced with a shortcoming or dissatisfaction (Rose 1991). They therefore seek solutions that have already been tried before or elsewhere. After the phase of seeking and identifying possible solutions, a government chooses to construct its own response by copying the same model, imitating and adjusting, combining elements from two situations, combining various elements from different countries, or drawing inspiration from other models. The French model has thus served as a reference for other European countries that have borrowed the idea of a permanent and pluridisciplinary national institution.

This institutionalization took place concomitantly with the establishment of temporary commissions or expert missions mandated to prepare reports on the technical feasibility of legislative or regulatory intervention. In all countries the move from bioethics to bio-law was gradual, for normative intervention triggered extensive resistance (Neirinck 1994). Ethics commissions were seen as allowing for preparation of decisions by identifying problems and favouring the emergence of possible alternatives, leaving the choice of the moment to the political authorities (Kingdon 1995). They were thus to be:

- a place of emergence and recording of problems: claims and requests were to be sent to them directly or via the public authorities;

- a place of discussion, of clarification of ideas, of confrontation between concepts, of construction of possible alternatives;
- a place of expertise for politics: government authorities were to be supplied with opinions, advice or technical recommendations;
- a place of amplification and diffusion in society of ethical problems, of raising awareness about biomedical sciences by way of meetings, public hearings and publications.

Disparate national legislation

The third step in the politicization of biomedical ethics was the temporary crystallization of norms, when standards were eventually produced by governments. In all countries, intervention by legislators in the biomedical field triggered numerous comments on its relevance and the form it should take. Although similarities can be identified in the processes of increasing awareness of problems and their implications, in the elaboration of institutional answers and in the virtual simultaneity of the drafting of laws in the late 1980s, the answers provided by the various member states differed substantially on the main points. Biomedical policies diverged in the area of medically assisted procreation, especially as regards modes of access, control of practices in private- and public-sector institutions, the use of supernumerary embryos, and attitudes towards embryonic stem cells. The same applied to research on analysis of the human genome and particularly possibilities for gene therapy, therapeutic and reproductive cloning, predictive medicine, use of genetic testing and the protection of data, as well as the patentability of body parts.

The creation in the United Kingdom of a new legal category, the 'pre-embryo' (from conception up to the fourteenth day), for instance, constituted a stumbling block in Europe from the outset, with consequences in other countries. A total ban on research on embryos in Germany (1990 law) and authorization for studies only in very precise conditions in France, without the integrity of the embryo being affected – which is not very clear, especially since French legislation from 1994 has carefully avoided defining the embryo (Feuillet-Le Mintier 1996) – while research on the 'pre-embryo' is authorized in the United Kingdom (in terms of the Human Fertilization and Embryology Act of 1990) and in Spain (in terms of the 1988 law), naturally raises questions on the consequences of such diversity in Europe. 'Procreative tourism' is encouraged for those who have the means, while some researchers are forced to leave their countries if they wish to practise research described as promising. Recent controversies around research on embryonic stem cells concern the same divisive issue – that is, the status of the embryo in different countries. The example of Italy is interesting, for it is the only country that has not legislated on the issue, precisely because of the extreme tension in its political community.[2] Jurisprudence has been left to deal casuistically with choices that have profound societal consequences. Other divergences exist between European countries – for example, the definition of the population that may have access to medically assisted procreation; health control and the state's financing of these techniques; use of genetic testing, especially by firms or insurance companies; possible use of xenotransplantations;[3] and possibilities of undertaking genetic therapies or not. How can this diversity of national situations be reconciled with European integration and the functioning of institutions, whether in its more integrated form, the European Union, or its more extended form, the Council of Europe?

Legitimate intervention of the Council of Europe

The status of the Council of Europe and its experience in human rights, with the European Convention on Human Rights of 1950, have favoured its engagement in what are often called 'third-generation human rights'. The Council was quick to show an interest in biomedical ethics, thus distinguishing itself from the European Community. Formally, this was not the first time it had taken an interest in the consequences of medical progress.[4] Bioethical issues had found their way on to the agenda largely as an outcome of the Parliamentary Assembly's self-referral of issues. The Parliamentary Assembly of the Council of Europe was behind the intervention of supranational organizations in the area of biomedical policies, which gave it the role of a 'political entrepreneur' (Kingdon 1995). Following the Asilomar Conference in the United States, it initiated debate in 1978 on the risks of possible genetic manipulation. This initial step was finalized by a parliamentary recommendation in 1982 relative to genetic engineering, extended by a recommendation of the Committee of Ministers in 1984 concerning notification on work involving recombinant DNA. The document pointed out problems related to genetic therapy, the storage of genetic data on individuals, and security in laboratories where experiments or industrial applications involved micro-organisms.

From 1980 the Parliamentary Assembly tried to prevent possible risks involved in artificial insemination, which at that stage was still a new technique in the process of being operationalized. This proposed recommendation, which was not adopted, appealed to member states of the Council of Europe to introduce regulations on artificial insemination, especially to limit access to married couples, for organizing the technical procedures, reaffirming the principles of informed written consent, gratuity of sperm donations and anonymity of donors, and penalizing any use of a eugenic nature. Debate on the subject in the early 1980s prefigured contradictory arguments in all countries during the drafting and debating of these laws. Moreover, the idea of incorporating specific provisions into the European Convention of Human Rights, in order to guard against certain risks that genetics might involve from the point of view of human rights, emerged and evolved into a wish to draft a European Convention of Human Rights and Medicine (Gerin 1987).

Since then, questions relating to the biomedical field have remained one of the recurrent topics on the Parliamentary Assembly's agenda. The Assembly maintains a keen interest in biomedical trends, as attested in 1986 by Recommendation 1046 relating to the use of human embryos and fetuses for diagnostic, therapeutic, scientific, industrial and commercial purposes, in 1989 by Recommendation 1100 on the use of human embryos and fetuses in scientific research, in 1994 by Recommendation 1240 relating to the protection and patentability of products of human origin, in 2000 by Recommendation 1468 relating to biotechnologies, and in 2001 by Recommendation 1512 on protection of the genome.

While the Parliamentary Assembly tried, through biomedical policy, to play a part distinguishing it from the European Communities, the secretariat of the Council of Europe and the member states, in the Committee of Ministers, responded positively to this approach by creating structures to institute permanent dialogue between the different experts and national officials. In 1983 the Committee of Ministers created the CAHGE (Ad Hoc Committee of Experts on Genetic Engineering), with a three-year mandate to study genetic engineering, in particular. The idea was, if possible, to define a common policy of member states and, if desirable, to devise a legal tool. The CAHGE had above all to address problems of security relating to the manipulation of human genes, as well as manipulation of embryos in the case of in vitro fertilization. Once its mandate had expired, the CAHBI (Ad Hoc Committee of Experts on the Progress of Biomedical Science) took over at the beginning of 1986 with a far broader mandate: to study all problems concerning the law, ethics and human rights posed by advances in biomedical science. Its objective was identical: the determination, if possible, of a common policy in the member states and appropriate legal instruments. To fulfil its role, the CAHBI formed specific working groups: DNA analyses for penal charges; genetic tests and screening; protection of genetic information; etc. But because by definition an *ad hoc* committee has a limited life, and the amplification of biomedical problems was confirmed, the CAHBI was replaced by the CDBI (Steering Committee on Bioethics), the Steering Committee on Bioethics, from November 1992. The terms of the CDBI's mandate were identical to those of the CAHBI. This new transformation reflected the perpetuation of the Council of Europe's treatment of biomedical policies – an institutionalization similar to that observed in the member states.

The CDBI is composed of about sixty national experts and representatives who meet two or three times a year. Apart from representatives of the member states, observers are allowed to attend on behalf of some countries – for example, the United States, Australia, Canada, Japan and the Vatican – and international organizations – for example, the European Union, the OECD, UNESCO (United Nations Educational, Scientific and Cultural Organization), the WHO and the European Science Foundation. The Committee constitutes and mandates restricted working groups on topics requiring more in-depth reflection. In keeping with its initial mandate, it has drawn up the European Convention on Human Rights and Biomedicine, signed at Oviedo on 4 April 1997 by twenty-two of the forty member states of the Council of Europe. This Convention came into force on 1 December 1999 because six countries initially ratified it: Denmark, Spain, Greece, San Marino, Slovakia and Slovenia.[5] As the first international legal instrument in the field of genetics, this document is of particular interest in the light of the conditions in which it was drafted and its formulation of answers to biomedical questions. It bans any discrimination against a person for his or her genetic heritage, allows the use of predictive tests for medical reasons only, authorizes selection of the unborn child's sex to avoid a serious hereditary disease, bans the production of embryos for research purposes, and defines the notion of informed consent. It is generally considered to be 'liberal', largely influenced by the minimalist British and Spanish legislation. Article 15 of this convention allows the possibility, unless banned by a country's national law, of authorizing in vitro research 'only on embryos no older than 14 days'. This explains why more restrictive countries such as Germany, Austria, Belgium and Ireland refused to sign it. The United Kingdom also refused to sign, but for reasons of principle rather than disagreement on the content.

The Council of Europe had wanted it to be a framework document to which additional protocols could subsequently be added. In fact, most of the issues had been a subject of stormy debate between the member states within the CDBI, represented by their national experts, and agreement was impossible. Five additional protocols were required to complete the convention, on subjects ranging from the status of the embryo and possible authorized research, to the terms of transplantations of organs and tissues of human origin, the conditions in which biomedical research had to be practised and the implications of discoveries on human genetics. The drafting of these legal instruments, which were binding only on the states that agreed to them, took place in specific task forces. The idea was to introduce flexibility into a purely intergovernmental system. In other words, since unanimity and the veto system weighed so heavily on procedures, only with the segmentation of issues was there any hope of finalizing these documents (Immergut 1992).

The first protocol to be drafted was the one banning human cloning. Signed by nineteen states and open to ratification since January 1998, this protocol, consisting of eight articles, prohibits 'any intervention aimed at creating a human being that is genetically identical to a living or dead human being'. It clearly benefited from the concerted voices raised in 1997 after the birth of the ewe Dolly in Scotland. As a declamatory announcement of a general principle, it remained silent on the actual conditions under which this type of objective could be achieved and on possible controls. Since then, reflection has been refined and a distinction has been made between reproductive cloning, which is to be formally prohibited, and the cloning of cells (since then known as therapeutic cloning!), which could prove to be a tremendous vehicle of knowledge (Atlan *et al.* 1999).

Nevertheless, this protocol, ratified by thirteen states, is the only one to have come into force.[6] Yet whether we consider the additional protocol relating to the transplantation of organs and tissues of human origin, which was open to signature in January 2002 but which has still not obtained the five ratifications needed to come into force, or the protocol relative to biomedical research, which has still to receive approval by the Committee of Ministers, the sluggishness and inertia of the Council of Europe are obvious. With its means and decision-making process, the Council can come up with a document satisfying all the member states only if it adopts the minimalist position, or if it maintains certain ambiguities on essential points (McLean and Elliston 1995). Even though the intergovernmental procedure of the consensus required can be a factor of richness in preparations and discussions, it is not a guarantee of effective decision-making.

The Council of Europe facilitated the emergence of a network of actors and experts by organizing symposiums and thus promoting the circulation of ideas and the construction of problematiques. These transnational 'epistemic communities' of actors working on the basis of particular expertise helped to identify the nature of problems and to make the context in which ideas were interpreted more familiar, by grouping together scientific data and orienting politicians' intervention in precise scientific frameworks, thus facilitating the emergence of a coherent system of thinking (Adler and Haas 1992). But in the area of biomedical ethics, we note the presence of different communities struggling to each have their own point of view and system of references accepted. In this respect the international conferences organized by the Council of Europe in 1989, 1993, 1996[7] and 1999 (Conseil de l'Europe 1990c, 1994, 2000) revealed existing contradictions while simultaneously favouring the diffusion of information and collective learning on the issues at stake and the stumbling blocks involved, through transdisciplinary and transnational dialogue.

This type of involvement by the Council of Europe in biomedical science was possible only because the member states gave it the necessary mandates. The European Ministerial Conference on Human Rights in March 1985 in Vienna has very often been cited as a founding event in the Council's engagement in the bioethical domain (Conseil de l'Europe 1988). Following the speech delivered by then French Minister of Justice, Robert Badinter, which attracted a great deal of attention, the conference adopted a resolution on 'human rights and scientific progress in the areas of biology, medicine and biochemistry'. In this resolution the Committee of Ministers was recommended to take adequate measures to intensify the Council of Europe's activity, to find common principles, and to promote efforts to make it a point of European convergence for work performed at national level – a place of interaction and discussion and, where relevant, 'of common actions at international level'. From the time of the June 1985 informal meeting between European Ministers of Justice in Edinburgh, the ministers addressed ethical and legal problems raised by scientific developments in the areas of artificial human procreation and the manipulation of human embryos. Noting the importance of the questions raised and the inappropriateness of strictly national regulations, the ministers agreed to highlight the importance of advancing 'towards policies and regulations that are harmonized at European level' (Conseil de l'Europe 1985).

Finally, it was during the June 1990 meeting of the Ministers of Justice in Istanbul that the Secretary-General of the Council of Europe presented a report proposing the drafting of a new European treaty for the protection of the human person in relation to biomedical science. Taking up an idea already expressed, especially by the Parliamentary Assembly, Catherine Lalumière considered that the Council of Europe had to 'find common solutions to new challenges' (Conseil de l'Europe 1990a). The conference adopted Resolution no. 3 relating to bioethics, asking the Committee of Ministers to entrust the CAHBI with this mission and to give it the means to draft a Framework Convention 'stating common general norms for the protection of the human being in the context of the development of biomedical sciences', while leaving it free to determine the topics addressed (Conseil de l'Europe 1990b).

The European Union: slow and forced involvement

In the absence of competences clearly established by the Treaties, the European Union's intervention was marginal, reactive and gradual. First, bioethics transcended traditional sectoral structures, which complicated action by the Community. The functional organization of the Commission (research, health, consumer protection, etc.) did not allow biomedical ethics and its implications to be grasped in their full complexity. Second, these areas were recognized as possible objects of Community intervention at a late stage. It was only in 1987 that a section devoted to 'technological research and development' was included in the Treaties. The Treaty of Maastricht then effectively reinforced research policy (Articles 130 onwards, which later became 163 onwards) and interventions in the area of public health (Art. 129, which became 152) as well as consumer protection (Art. 129A, which became 153). These were subsequently further reinforced by the Treaty of Amsterdam. Finally, relations between the European Community and human rights, largely contingent on the mechanisms established in the framework of the European Convention of Human Rights, have evolved since the adoption of the Fundamental Human Rights Charter in December 2000. The European Union has acquired an additional dimension in the area of biomedical ethics, since eight articles of the Charter can be directly referred to with regard to biomedical ethics. The most obvious is of course Article 3, relating to the 'right to the integrity of the person', which specifies first and foremost that 'any person has a right to his/her physical and mental integrity'. In particular, it is the second paragraph that constitutes an innovation and that, once incorporated into the *acquis communautaire*, will be subject to legal interpretation.[8] As in the case of the Council of Europe, the European Parliament was the key political player within the Communities. It was following rumours concerning certain 'trafficking in fetuses', and possible uses of fetuses in the context of a total absence of legislation, that the European Parliament added the consequences of the development of genetics to its agenda. From 1984 a proposed resolution on the abusive use of living embryos was referred to the different parliamentary commissions for their opinions. This proposal was followed by a large number of spontaneous initiatives by MEPs concerning regulation of artificial insemination, the use of substances from human fetuses, the advancement of biology, ethical issues, genetic manipulations, etc. The parliamentary legal commission tried to take into account all the questions raised and to determine, with the adoption of the reports by Messrs Rothley (1988) and Casini (1989), what it should undertake. The two resolutions passed in March 1989 were the outcome of five years of preparation, debates and hearings within different parliamentary commissions, until the European Parliament's position was set. Their content was complementary. The first, requested by the Legal and Citizens' Rights Committee, was about ethical and legal problems concerning genetic manipulation. The second, requested by the same committee, was on artificial insemination in vivo and in vitro. The Rothley Report was a warning about genetic research methods and the need for normative intervention in order to draw up a precise legal framework. The document also expressed Parliament's first reaction to research concerning analysis of the human genome.[9] The Casini Report expressed the same cautious attitude regarding artificial insemination. It noted that these techniques should not create embryos that were 'superfluous, destined to death or improper use'.

It was on the occasion of the adoption of the specific research programme 'Analysis of the Human Genome' (1989–1991) that the European Parliament fully used its new competence relative to research, contained in the Single European Act (European Commission 1990). The cooperative procedure enabled it to obtain substantial amendments to this research programme, initially designed by the services of the Commission. The rationale justifying Community intervention was primarily of an incentive nature, aimed at catalysing the efforts of European research centres and laboratories in a 'pre-competitive' perspective. This notion was the vague but convenient basis on which the Commission's intervention in the research domain was legitimized and most of its programmes designed (Jourdain 1995). In addition to an amendment to the title of the programme and references contained in the project that might suggest that certain eugenic abuses were not firmly condemned (Hermitte 1993), the European Parliament obtained a commitment that part of the funding would be for ethical, social and legal aspects of the analysis of the human genome (Baert *et al.* 1995). Since then, and in line with the US model, all community research programmes have devoted a small share of their budgets to studies on the ethical, social and legal consequences of research on the human genome (European Commission 1998).

The European Parliament has thus been a prime mover behind public reflection on the evolution and consequences of biomedical ethics. Two recent episodes attest to its wish to play that part. The first was the creation in 2001 of a temporary commission on genetics and the other new technologies of modern medicine. Its mission was to reflect on the ethical, social, legal and economic aspects of the development of modern medicine and to provide the European Parliament with detailed analyses in order 'to take authentic political decisions and to set out specific guidelines'. After a year's work and ten hearings, the Commission drew up a very rich proposal. In particular, it asked Europe to intervene far more forcefully in promoting public debate, and for a restrictive legal framework to be drawn up. The MEPs on this commission felt that the European Union had to ensure that the practice of genetic testing was harmonized, to regulate the use of personal genetic data, to standardize the patentability of procedures and products derived from biological material, to ban reproductive cloning, etc. The plenary session debate showed the extent to which biomedical ethics could be a source of controversy. The resolution was finally refused by a large majority: some found it too liberal, others too restrictive (Parlement européen 2001). The second example is drawn from the negotiations that dragged on in the institutional triangle (Commission, European Parliament and Council of Ministers) on the occasion of the adoption of the Sixth Framework Programme for research and development (2003–2006). For nearly two years, the adoption of the entire Community research programme (an amount of €16 billion) seemed likely to flounder on the issue of the financing of embryonic stem cells. Certain states (notably Italy, Germany, Austria, Ireland and Portugal) were opposed to the Commission funding and thus promoting research banned in their own countries. Many debates involving member states, the Commission and the European Parliament therefore placed biomedical ethics at the heart of European construction. In reality the solution found was only temporary (European Commission 2003).

While the European Parliament played a motivating role, the Commission also adjusted to the situation. As early as July 1988 it had set up a working group initially called the 'Predictive Medicine Working Party' and then, from January 1989, known as the 'Study Group on Ethical, Social and Legal Aspects of the human genome analysis programme' (ESLA). This group, composed essentially of scientists and national experts appointed by their respective states, had the mission of helping the Commission in putting together this new programme. Once the programme had been agreed, the group's mission was to advise the Commission, to promote public debate on the ethical, social and legal aspects of the analysis of the human genome, to evaluate applications for funding, with the Commission's services, and to make recommendations on future initiatives by the Commission (Working Group 1991).

In March 1990 an informal meeting of the Ministers of Research of the then twelve member states and representatives of the Commission was organized by the German government in Kronberg. The aim was to compare points of view and discuss 'ethical principles of research on embryos and the human genome, as well as possibilities of application of the results of this research'. The outcome of this meeting was an inventory of points of agreement between different countries, without any legal implications. The ministers also announced the creation of two working groups. The first was ESLA, mentioned above, which was simply given official recognition. The other was a working group on research on the human embryo (HER), whose mission was to observe developments in legislation and practices in the field of research on the human embryo in the member states, and to identify those areas where consensus was possible, and the means to reinforce it. This group of twelve scientists published a report presenting the state of legislation concerning the embryo in Europe (DG XII 1995). It was subsequently replaced by another group in charge of protecting human embryos and fetuses (HEF), in December 1994. While the first HER depended on the member states, the new one, composed of twenty-two scientists chosen by the Directorate-General of Research on the basis of their competences, was set up to provide advice and expertise to the Commission. This new group's first task involved the evaluation of research projects submitted to the Commission as part of an application for funds in the framework of the second BIOMED programme, and the evaluation of articles relating to research on embryos contained in the European Convention of Human Rights and Biomedicine.

The successive specific research programmes 'Biomedicine and Health – BIOMED 1' (1990–1994) and 'Biomedicine and Health – BIOMED 2' (1994–1998) corresponded to a far broader public health orientation. The development of research coordination took place as much in the areas of prevention, care and health systems (use of drugs, administration of medicines, industrial medicine, biomedical technologies) as in those of health problems, diseases with a strong socio-economic impact (AIDS, cancer, cardiovascular diseases, neurological diseases and problems posed by ageing) and analysis of the human genome. Research on biomedical ethics is only the fourth component of this programme, which has funded the production of expertise for the Commission and facilitated the emergence of awareness of the different aspects of biomedical ethics.

Within the European Commission the treatment of biomedical ethics involved the former Directorate-General XII (Science, Research and Development) and was partly institutionalized over time, in the form of a unit within that directorate. More importantly, in order to respond to concerns often repeated by the European Parliament, the Commission, then presided over by Jacques Delors, created a group of advisers in 1991 for biotechnology ethics. Considering that public opinion was hesitant as regards biotechnologies, the idea was that ethical questions ought to be taken into account in all

Community programmes and the Commission advised on sensitive ethical issues. The third mandate of the Advisory Group and its renewal (1998–2000) were marked by the extension of its competence and an increase in the number of its members from nine to twelve.

The new European Group for Ethics (EGE) in science and new technologies can self-refer issues or can have issues referred to it by the Commission, the European Parliament or the Council of the European Union. To date, its competence and opinions have gone beyond biomedical ethics alone. The group has also studied areas as varied as the ethical implications of the use of performance improvement devices in agriculture and fishing (1993), products derived from human blood or plasma (1993), and issues raised by the Commission's proposal for a Council directive on legal protection of biotechnological inventions (1993). The EGE group has put forward ethical opinions on gene therapy (1993), the labelling of foods derived from modern biotechnology (1995), prenatal diagnosis (1996), genetic modification of animals (1996), the patentability of inventions concerning elements of human origin (1996), cloning techniques (1997), human tissue banks (1998), research involving the use of human embryos in the context of the Fifth Framework Programme for Research (1998), the use of personal health data in the information society (1999), doping in sport (1999), research on human stem cells and their use (2000), the patentability of inventions involving human stem cells (2002), clinical research in developing countries (2003) and genetic testing in the industrial context (2003).

Recognition of the EGE by heads of state and government is set out in Annex 4 of the conclusions of the European Council in Amsterdam (June 1997). It was in the declaration on human cloning that they reaffirmed their wish to monitor the issue of 'bioethics' as a whole, noting that the member states wished to take all necessary measures to ban human cloning. The European Council also acknowledged the opinion of the Group of Advisers on Cloning (29 May 1997) and asked the Council of Ministers and European Commission to make use of the group's expertise to ensure that human cloning was excluded 'when the different community policies are defined, particularly as regards research and intellectual property, considering that protection of the human being and respect for his/her integrity are fundamental principles'. The Council urged 'the European Union and the member States to contribute actively to this reflection in the framework of their respective competences'.

The way in which European institutions are caught up in issues concerning bioethics can be seen in the fact that the directive relative to patenting of biotechnological inventions, tabled in 1988 and finally adopted in 1998, is still an object of rejection and strong antagonism in Parliament and among several member states. Conflicts primarily concern the patentability of human products. They once again highlight the thorny problem of harmonization of European legislation on patents in general. The aim of this directive was to boost the competitiveness of European industry in the biotechnological field by providing firms with a legal framework to enable them to protect their inventions. To this end, the directive was intended to harmonize and clarify legislation on the patentability of living organisms in the different member states. As regards the joint decision-making procedure, a plenary session of the European Parliament had already rejected the common project of the Committee of conciliation on biotechnologies in 1995, forcing the Commission to redraft the directive and to present a new proposal. The fear of introducing the body and elements of it 'as such' into the economic sphere of patentability was largely responsible for this difficulty. National transpositions of Directive 98/44/CE relating to legal protection of biotechnological inventions were supposed to be effective before 30 July 2000 but were not implemented, causing the Commission to institute legal proceedings against eight member states. The technical nature of the issue is evident, but should not stop this document from being seen as a sensitive and symbolic revealer of tricky biomedical issues (Landfried 1997).

The question is technical mainly because the directive uses subtle legal classifications. On the subject of genes, gene sequences, molecules or cells, the distinction between discovery (non-patentability) and invention (patentability) becomes far trickier than usual. Furthermore, the directive concerns the right to industrial property in areas that are highly competitive. Finally, the question of patentability is culturally and politically sensitive because public opinion is increasingly concerned about issues related to blood and to the advances that analysis of the human genome will clearly lead to. As more knowledge on genes and their functions is acquired, we can conceive that in a number of years monogenic, plurigenic and plurifactoral (depending on the environment) diseases will be treated by gene therapies or drugs directly derived from genetic research. These therapies cannot be found and tested if laboratories are unable to protect discoveries requiring many years of research and considerable investments. At the same time, non-governmental organizations (Greenpeace, Friends of the Earth, etc.) are particularly vigilant in this domain and capable of mobilizing the media, for patentability of living organisms is an emblematic issue in the emerging genetic era. Above all, criticism of this Community directive is based on a critical argument as to European construction itself: the European Union cannot be content to create a single market and limit itself to promoting business and industry when considerations on public health, the environment and the protection of human rights are also at stake.

A process of Europeanization of bioethics?

From this national and European overview, can we deduce that a European bioethics policy exists? There is no clear answer. Our examination and comparison of the situation at national and European level shows that there is a European framework of actors, institutions and documents concerned with biomedical ethics. Despite their different statuses and modes of functioning, the Council of Europe and the European Union are engaged in a similar process of institutionalization and construction of problems, and have initiated the formulation of political answers to the challenges created by the biomedical sciences. We are thus witnessing a process of Europeanization of politics concerning bioethics.

This Europeanization of biomedical ethics is nevertheless still fragmented and disparate. The current initial phase does not defy traditional theories of analysis of European construction represented by the two poles of intergovernmentalism and neo-functionalism. Biomedical policies trigger two types of reaction by the actors themselves: the reassertion of their wish to leave it up to national political authorities to construct their own norms, in the name of subsidiarity; or, by contrast, the call for extensive supranational intervention to harmonize the diversity of national legislations.

For the advocates of the first approach, biomedical policies are far too closely tied to the religious culture, history and founding values of a country to be governed by supranational ethics. The ambivalent attitude of the European Commission in this respect is interesting. Its legal capacity to act in the areas of health and research does not enable it to act directly and autonomously. Only actions of encouragement or complementarity are possible, to support those of the member states. Intervention is legitimate only if the establishment and functioning of the internal market are affected. In that case, and within certain jurisprudential limits, Community actions can be envisaged.

According to those who support the second approach, the risks related to too much diversity of applicable rules can favour the appearance of perverse effects. Moreover, some consider that the search for European harmonization is part and parcel of European integration, despite existing objective and understandable difficulties. They focus on the need to strengthen protection of human rights in direct relation to the risks involved in the development of biomedical science and a future 'predictive medicine'. From this point of view, the idea is not only to remedy distortions related to the existence of different national legislations, but also to envisage European construction as a project of civilization. In this perspective it is necessary to move on from negative European integration to positive integration (Scharpf 1996, 1999). This could apply to the biomedical ethics challenge, thus promoting a vast European public debate in the various national arenas (Habermas 2000).

We have seen that at both national and European level, biomedical policies have started to emerge simultaneously on different agendas. The first response by national and European authorities led to a protean institutionalization at all levels and within each decision-making structure, with a view to perpetuating dialogue. European institutions facilitated the creation of epistemic communities to further their knowledge of biomedical issues and to ensure the widest possible diffusion of that knowledge. In a second phase, laws were passed at national level. Today, although biomedical policies still lie within the ambit of the member states, European organizations also have to take a stand on emerging biomedical ethical issues. The European Convention on Human Rights and Biomedicine as an early initiative is noteworthy. Although it was wanted, drafted and signed by more than half the member states of the Council of Europe, it has not prevented the persistence of a wide diversity of national situations, since each state has the possibility of maintaining stricter rules. Moreover, as for any other international convention, a state can stipulate reservations when ratifying it. The drafting of this European document, like the persistent challenges to the directive on legal protection of biotechnological inventions or the differences between states as regards cloning, confirms the fact that the existence of divergence within each country is naturally found at European level. The processes of construction of problems and institutionalization are very similar. But unlike in nation-states, without precise delegation of competences and a suitable majority decision-making process that is legitimately accepted, *no* binding European legal decision can currently be conceived of in the field of biomedical ethics. This sector thus confirms the findings of other recent analyses, that the main difficulty of our European institutions lies in the capacity to manage 'legitimate diversity' (Scharpf 2002). While it is neither possible nor desirable to reach moral consensus in our liberal societies (Charlesworth 1993), it is nevertheless clear that European political expectations are progressing, progress being made necessary by the irremediable consequences of certain unavoidable choices. This is the process that we are witnessing. The concepts of 'responsibility towards future generations', 'the precautionary principle' or 'the heuristics of fear' (Jonas 1992), for example, have become elements of intense reflection, within both individual states and European organizations. In addition to scientific uncertainty, already present in problems related to the environment and resulting scientific controversies, the choices that need to be made in the field of biomedical policies cannot easily be undone. Faced with these prospects, it is hardly possible – as with economic regulation or redistribution – to adjust them subsequently to the economic, social or political climate, or to the scale of priorities that change with political majorities – in short, to situations that improve or deteriorate.

To conclude, we note that European structures, at the service of states, seem also to be places of diffusion and learning about diversity, where the beginnings of substantial answers to the internationalization of the challenges of our modernity are being elaborated, albeit partially, piecemeal and with a wide range of tools. The pluralism of normative answers is not about to disappear. In fact, we are even likely to be heading for the appearance of situations in which 'clauses of the State's consciousness of bioethics' are established, leading to a closure of 'moral borders', with each state promoting norms on the basis of its roots, its history and its own value scales (Mémeteau 1996).

There is nevertheless no doubt that the Europeanization of biomedical ethics is still in its infancy and that bioethics will remain at the heart of politics and at the core of European integration for a long time to come.

Notes

1 After there had been many *ad hoc* commissions, US President Bill Clinton created a permanent and pluridisciplinary consultative ethics commission in October 1995, the National Bioethics Advisory Commission.
2 In Italy a ministerial decree of 1985 grants the public health service the possibility of practising approved insemination (on couples), while the private sector is free from any intervention or control.
3 'A xenotransplantation is considered to be any operation involving the transplantation or administration on a human receiver of living cells, tissues or organs of animal origin, or of human fluids, cells, tissues or organs that have had ex vivo contact with cells, tissues or organs of animal origin' (Council of Europe, 2003 (my translation from the French)).
4 Following the concern expressed by the Committee of Ministers of the Council of Europe, an expert committee drew up a resolution on the harmonization of member states' legislation concerning removal, grafting and transplantation of substances of human origin: Resolution (78) 29 adopted by the Committee of Ministers on 11 May 1978.
5 In mid-August 2003 the Convention came into force in sixteen states, including Bulgaria, Cyprus, Spain, Estonia, Georgia, Hungary, Lithuania, Moldova, Portugal, the Czech Republic and Romania.
6 Cyprus, the Czech Republic, Estonia, Georgia, Greece, Hungary, Lithuania, Moldova, Portugal, Romania, Slovakia, Slovenia and Spain.
7 The theme of the third symposium was 'Medical assistance for procreation, and protection of the human embryo' (Strasbourg, 15–18 December 1996).
8 '2. In the context of medicine and biology, the following must be respected: free and informed consent by the person concerned, as defined by the law, the prohibition of eugenic practices, especially those aimed at the selection of persons, the prohibition of use of the human body or parts thereof, as such, as a source of profit, and the prohibition of reproductive cloning of human beings' (my translation from the French).
9 It concerned the proposed decision by the Council on the adoption of a specific research programme in the health field, 'Médecine prédictive: analyse du Génome Humain' (1989–1991), presented on 20 July 1988, the process of which was interrupted for a few months after the first reading in the European Parliament.

References

Adler, E. and Haas, P. M. (1992) 'Conclusion: Epistemic Communities, World Order, and the Creation of a Reflective Program', *International Organization* 46 (1): 367–390.

Atlan, H., Augé, M., Delmas-Marty, M., Droit, R.-P. and Fresco, N. (1999) *Le Clonage humain*, Paris: Éditions Seuil.

Baert, A.-E., Baig, S. S., Bardoux, C., Fracchia, G. N., Hallen, M., Le Dour, O., Razquin, M. C., Thévenin, A., Vanvossel, A. and Vidal, M. (eds) (1995) *European Union: Biomedical and Health Research, the BIOMED I Programme*, Amsterdam: IOS Press.

Beck, U. (1992) *Risk Society: Towards a New Modernity*, London: Sage.

Blanc, M. (1986) *L'Ère de la génétique*, Paris: La Découverte.

Casini, C. (1989) *Rapport fait au nom de la commission juridique et des droits des citoyens sur la fécondation artificielle 'in vivo' et 'in vitro'*, Parlement européen (Doc A2-0372/88), 30 January 1989.

Charlesworth, M. (1993) *Bioethics in a Liberal Society*, Cambridge: Cambridge University Press.

Conseil de l'Europe (1985) Direction de la presse et de l'information, *Pour information*, 20 June 1985 [B (85) 29].

—— (1988) 'Direction des droits de l'homme', *Conférence ministérielle européenne sur les droits de l'homme (Vienne, 19–20 mars 1985), Actes de la conférence*, Strasbourg: Division des publications.

—— (1990a) Service de la communication, 16 May 1990 [I (90) 38].

—— (1990b) 17ème Conférence des ministres européens de la Justice (Istanbul, 5–7 June 1990), *Conclusions et résolutions de la conférence*, Strasbourg, 1990, pp. 9–11, 26. [MJU-17 (90) Concl.].

—— (1990c) *L'Europe et la bioéthique*, Actes du 1er symposium (Strasbourg, 5–7 December 1989), Strasbourg.

—— (1994) *Éthique et génétique humaine*, Actes du 2ème symposium (Strasbourg, 30 November–2 December 1993), Strasbourg.

—— (2000) *Conférence internationale sur les questions éthiques soulevées par l'application de la biotechnologie*, Actes d'Oviedo, 16–19 May 1999, vol. 1.

DG XII (1995) *EC Working Group on Human Embryos and Research: Research on Bioethics*, Luxembourg: Office for Official Publications of the European Communities.

Doucet, H. (1996) *Au pays de la bioéthique. L'Éthique biomédicale aux États-Unis*, Geneva: Labor et Fides.

Engelhardt, H. T. (1986) *The Foundations of Bioethics*, Oxford: Oxford University Press.

European Commission (1990) Programme spécifique de recherche adopté le 29 juin 1990, *JOCE* no. L 196, 26 July 1990.

—— (1998) *Ethical, Legal and Social Aspects of the Life Sciences and Technologies Programmes of Framework Programme IV*, Catalogue of Contracts, Luxembourg: Oopec, 1999.

—— (2003) 'A propos du financement communautaire de la recherche sur les cellules souches', press release, 9 July 2003, IP/03/969.

Fagot-Largeault, A. (1985) *L'Homme bioéthique. Pour une déontologie de la recherche sur le vivant*, Paris: Maloine.

Feuillet-Le Mintier, B. (ed.) (1996) *L'Embryon humain. Approche multidisciplinaire*, Paris: Economica.

Gerin, G. (1987) 'Introduzione', in C. Gerin (ed.) *Modificazioni genetiche e diritti dell'uomo*, Padua: Cedam.

Gusfield, J. R. (1981) *The Culture of Public Problems: Drinking–Driving and the Symbolic Order*, Chicago: University of Chicago Press.

Habermas, J. (2000) *Après l'État-nation. Une nouvelle constellation politique*, Paris: Fayard.

Hermitte, M.-A. (1993) 'Le Séquençage du génome humain: liberté de la recherche et démarche démocratique', in F. Furkel and H. Jung (eds) *Bioéthique et droits de l'homme*, Cologne: Carl Heymanns Verlag, pp. 41–65.

Hottois, G. (1999) *Essais de philosophie bioéthique et biopolitique*, Paris: Vrin.

Hottois, G. and Parizeau, M.-H. (1993) *Les Mots de la bioéthique*, Brussels: De Boeck Université.

Immergut, E. (1992) *Health Politics: Interests and Institutions in Western Europe*, New York: Cambridge University Press.

Ingram, H., Milward, H. B. and Laird, W. (1992) 'Scientists and Agenda Setting: Advocacy and Global Warming', in M. Waterstone (ed.) *Risk and Society: The Interaction of Science, Technology and Public Policy*, Dordrecht: Kluwer.

Jobert, B. and Muller, P. (1987) *L'Etat en action. Politiques et corporatismes*, Paris: PUF.

Jonas, H. (1992) *Le Principe responsabilité. Une éthique pour la civilisation technologique*, Paris: Cerf.

Jourdain, L. (1995) *Recherche scientifique et construction européenne. Enjeux et usages nationaux d'une politique communautaire*, Paris: L'Harmattan.

Kingdon, J. (1995) *Agendas, Alternatives, and Public Policies*, 2nd edn, Boston: Little, Brown.

Kourilsky, P. (1990) *Les Artisans de l'hérédité*, Paris: Odile Jacob.

Landfried, C. (1997) 'Beyond Technocratic Governance: The Case of Biotechnology', *European Law Journal* 3: 255–272.

McLean, S. A. M. and Elliston, S. (1995) 'Bioethics, the Council of Europe and the Draft Convention', *European Journal of Health Law* 2: 5–13.

Mémeteau, G. (1996) 'La Clause de conscience de l'État en bioéthique', in G. Huber and C. Byk (eds) *La Bioéthique au pluriel. L'Homme et le risque biomédical*, Montrouge, France: John Libbey Text, pp. 45–54.

Neirinck, C. (1994) *De la bioéthique au bio-droit*, Paris: LGDJ.

Nelkin, D. and Lindee, S. (1995) *The DNA Mystique: The Gene as a Cultural Icon*, New York: Freeman.

Parlement européen (2001) *Rapport sur les incidences éthiques, juridiques, économiques et sociales de la génétique humaine*, Commission temporaire sur la génétique humaine et les autres technologies nouvelles de la médecine moderne, Rapporteur M. Fiori, 8 November 2001. (Final A5-0391/2001).

Potter, V. R. (1971) *Bioethics, Bridge to the Future*, Englewood Cliffs, N.J.: Prentice-Hall.

Rose, R. (1991) 'What Is Lesson-Drawing?', *Journal of Public Policy* 11: 3–30.

Rothley, W. (1988) *Rapport fait au nom de la Commission juridique et des droits des citoyens, sur les problèmes éthiques et juridiques de la manipulation génétique*, Parlement européen (Doc. A2-327/88), 19 December 1988.

Scharpf, F. (1996) 'Negative and Positive Integration in the Political Economy of European Welfare States', in G. Marks, F. Sharpf, P. Schmitter and W. Streeck (eds) *Governance in the European Union*, London: Sage.

—— (1999) *Governing in Europe: Effective and Democratic*, Oxford: Oxford University Press.

—— (2002) 'Legitimate Diversity: The New Challenge of European Integration', *Cahiers européens de Sciences-Po*, no. 1.

Sève, L. (1994) *Pour une critique de la raison bioéthique*, Paris: Odile Jacob.

Working Group on the ethical, social and legal aspects of human genome analysis (WG-ESLA), Report of 31 December 1991.

7 Europeanization of drug policies

From objective convergence to mutual agreement

Henri Bergeron

How can the relative alignment of drug policies in Europe over the past decade be interpreted? How can we explain the fact that public policies have converged on such a controversial subject traditionally governed entirely by individual nation-states, and for which Europe as a community has barely any competence?

Anyone who is familiar with the recent history of the categories that are supposed to define drug issues knows that until the 1990s, problems relative to illicit drugs were expressed primarily in moral terms (decline, decadence, threat to public order, etc.), and that the public authorities' responses were organized around prohibition, eradication and, in many countries, abstinence. The drug problem was defined in terms of violation of the law or mental alienation and self-destruction, rather than in terms of health risks or social consequences for the individual and the community.

As many studies show, two major phenomena were to change the way in which this problem was perceived. The first was the sudden massive increase in drug consumption from the early 1980s (in Europe), attended by a diversification of forms of use; between the citizen (who was abstinent) and the 'sick person' (the drug addict), a new category of occasional or regular users emerged, many of whom were by no means addicted. The second was the appearance of AIDS, which triggered a medicalization of the approach to the illicit drug problem in European countries, especially in countries that had virtually no tradition or active policy concerning public health, such as France, but also Italy, Spain and Belgium (Cattacin, Lucas and Vetter, 1996; Cattacin, Panchaux and Tattini, 1997). In fact, that was the point at which, around the mid-1980s – the early 1980s for some and the early 1990s for others – drugs (and, more specifically, drug use) became a public health issue.

Within a decade, which marked the end of a hundred-year period initiated with the invention of the phrase 'drug addiction' in the 1880s (Yvorel 1992), the perception of drugs changed substantially. Considered for a long time only as a moral and public order issue that called for 'tighter control of youth' and for normative prohibitions and coercion, it increasingly came to be treated as a public health problem necessitating epidemiological surveillance, prevention, care and risk reduction. Concomitantly with these epidemiological and symbolic transformations, public drug policies in Europe also changed. These policies became more balanced, granting more funds and priorities to public health objectives and prevention than before. Today one can reasonably say that, in the fifteen 'old' member states at least, there may be a convergence of national policies characterized only ten years ago by profound differences.

It is tempting to see this convergence as the direct consequence of the above-mentioned epidemiological transformations (mass drug consumption and development of AIDS). But by doing so, political scientists and sociologists often overlook the fact that changes in the nature and/or the extent of problems officially dealt with by public policies rarely induce appropriate and automatic adjustments of the public action concerned. In order to provide a more complete explanation, it is often necessary to consider social and political interventions that fall between public problems and public policies. The political scientist or sociologist should clearly see that the observed convergence – (relative) alignment of different national policies on a subject as controversial as drugs – is a priori by no means spontaneous or natural. The aim of this chapter is to contribute to the explanation of this relative policy convergence (in the second section) and analyse the role of certain European institutional actors in this process.

National policies in Europe: a gradual convergence

During the 1980s and 1990s, in a context of a rapid increase in drug use in Europe and above all the sudden appearance of AIDS, there seemed to be a gradual convergence[1] – with attendant debates and resistance – of European drug policies, which had formerly been characterized by their diversity. This can be considered a remarkable historical event (if it did indeed happen), for public policies in this domain had been defined for decades on the basis of a rationale that was essentially national, marked by the social, institutional and cultural characteristics of each of the member states (Cattacin, Lucas and Vetter 1996; Steffen 2001). Today the member states' national policies are showing such a marked and unexpected tendency to converge that some observers are already postulating the existence of a European model and culture in the management of drug use and the struggle against drug trafficking, money laundering, etc.

Convergence of 'supply reduction' policies[2]

There thus seems to be convergence on the so-called supply reduction part of drug policy, and on the legal status of drug use, or possession of drugs for personal use.[3] Note that this convergence has a symbolic value: while everyone agreed on the need and validity of the struggle against dealers, drug traffic, money laundering, etc., the European countries were divided only ten years ago as to the types of measure (ranging from administrative measures to penal sanctions, including jail sentences) that needed to be taken regarding use or possession for personal use. Recent research, especially by the European Monitoring Centre for Drugs and Drug Addiction (EMCDDA), attests to a somewhat different situation today.

First, several countries have amended their laws so that the use of illicit drugs or their possession in small quantities for personal use, although formally prohibited, does not give rise to jail sentences, and so that therapeutic solutions are given priority where relevant. The law was thus amended or new laws passed in Spain and Italy in the early 1990s, more recently in Portugal (2001), Luxembourg (2001, only for cannabis) and Belgium (2003, for cannabis); less directly in Austria (1998)[4] and Germany (1998 – if the infringement is considered a 'minor' offence) and probably soon in the United Kingdom.[5] Other countries have chosen to frame public action by means of orders or circulars (or other legal instruments), as the Netherlands has been doing for a long time. Denmark (1992 for cannabis), Germany (1994) and France (1999) decided to use such legal instruments to favour therapeutic solutions and, when appropriate, avoid custody measures for people who were simply users.

Second, in many EU countries (EMCDDA 2002a) police and legal practices also tend now to suspend or drop legal proceedings for use of illicit drugs (or possession for personal use), especially cannabis. Here again, therapeutic and/or social measures seem to be favoured in many European countries, but these preliminary conclusions need to be supported by further research.

Thus, irrespective of the legal solution opted for, and apart from the remaining deep-rooted differences in national systems, there does seem to be a tendency in Europe to consider use of illicit drugs, or possession for personal use, a 'minor' offence, in so far as jail sentences seem to be avoided and therapeutic measures given preference. Finally, the public health perspective that has progressively come to prevail in modern definitions of drug problems, and that implies a ranking of risks in relation to different uses of different drugs, has certainly contributed to the 'de-singularization' of national 'supply reduction' policies, or at least some of them – that is, those concerning the highly symbolic incrimination of use and possession for personal use.

Convergence of 'demand reduction' policies

The most remarkable trends have certainly been in 'demand reduction', a term commonly used in specialized circles. This change has taken place essentially in the areas of health and social policies, which have undergone profound change since the mid-1980s, especially with the sudden appearance of AIDS. Although we cannot talk of uniformity, we are witnessing a tendency towards convergence, at least in most member states. This convergence of European public policies seems to be expressed primarily in two trends.

The first concerns the implementation, in most countries of the European Union (EU), of policies largely inspired by the 'harm and risk reduction' theory or paradigm, a management model of drug use based in the Netherlands. The principles, priorities, tools and practices of this model have 'swept across' Europe as a set of 'appropriate' norms and cognitive and professional solutions (in the sense of the US neo-institutionalists) to the management of health and social problems that the different national experts now agree to define in a relatively comparable way (Bergeron 1999; Grange 2004).

Many European countries have thus, apparently, given up the idea of setting eradication and abstinence as priority objectives. The use of drugs, whether licit or not, appears now to be conceived of as a massive, lasting phenomenon in contemporary modern societies. From this new perspective, the drug problem seems no longer to be seen as a fad, a fad that the authorities in the 1960s and 1970s thought could be stamped out. It now also seems necessary to reduce the risks of use – that is, to reduce the prevalence of risky behaviours, as well as the risks and harm associated with risk – and to manage both individual risks, such as desocialization, and risks for the community, such as transmission of infectious diseases. Consequently, pragmatic and practical responses have developed, such as the distribution of syringes, methadone – or similar – substitution programmes,[6] primary care for drug addicts, etc. All these measures were previously excluded from the legitimate arsenal of many policies in European countries.

These changes were echoed by those concerning the representation of one of the main targets of these policies, the drug addict, who had become 'the drug-user'. The latter expression is the reflection of a position that, according to Coester, Laborde and Thévenin, opposed

> an ascetic conception of freedom seen as progress towards self-control, a struggle against psychological and social alienation that the community had the duty to encourage ..., to a liberal individualistic conception that leaves it up to each individual to judge their own behaviour within the limits of respect for others' freedom.
>
> (1994: 7)

In this perspective, drug-users had become individuals capable of reasoning,[7] of participating in the prevention of risks, in the management of damage and, more generally, in the policies catering for them. This is a considerable change: the new approach has meant the inclusion of drug addicts and other users as legitimate actors in the shaping and implementation of public policies, at least potentially, and in political and professional discourse and projects.

Of course, the level of this convergence is not the same in all countries. Distribution of syringes, for example, has been developed in some countries and not as much in others. Even within the same country, significant sectoral and/or regional differences sometimes exist. For instance, methadone may be readily available in specialized care centres and far less so, or not at all, in prison.

The second trend, far more recent and certainly far less prevalent in Europe than the one already mentioned, stems from the will, at least in the health field, to conceive of the use of illicit drugs, psychotropic medicines, alcohol and tobacco as all having the potential to lead to risky usage and even addiction. In the opinion of a part of the scientific community and many European experts and professionals, the concepts of alcoholism, drug addiction and nicotine addiction have to be discarded, or subsumed under the generic term 'addiction'. Although these profound changes cannot be described in detail in this chapter (cf. Bergeron 2003), it is important to note here that, with this trend, the different 'products' are losing some of their symbolic substance, their social significance, as they fit into a generic category in which most of the vocabulary is health related. Alcohol and hashish, for example, become psychoactive substances that act on common neurological paths yet give rise to different social and health risks (Roques 1999). The various products seem to be released from their social and cultural dimensions and to impose themselves in their 'medical transparency'.

The historical trajectory reported here is that of a gradual medicalization in Europe of the definition of drug-related problems and, consecutively, the responses of European states as they attempt to solve them. Throughout this period (1985–2000) there was a shift, as A. Ehrenberg put it, from a 'drug addiction–prohibition' association to an 'addictive practices–risks' association – in other words, from a phenomenon grasped primarily in its moral dimensions, necessitating exceptional policies, to a 'normal' health problem that needs to be treated as such. The European states have, moreover, adopted strategies and action plans similar to those in other public policy domains (EMCDDA 2002b). The managerial discourse and culture dominating the civil service as a whole is spreading to specialized drug policies. Precise and quantifiable objectives are now set and systematic evaluations planned.

The European level: information, coordination expertise and flexible constraints

How can this convergence be explained? What role can be granted to Europe or to the European level in this process of convergence of national policies? Are we witnessing a regular process of Europeanization of policies?

The European Union and the drugs issue

Before I try to answer this thorny question, it would be useful to examine the subject of European competence in this area. We soon find an answer: Community *acquis* in the area of drugs is recent, since the drug scourge was not incorporated into the Treaties until the Treaty of Maastricht (Martel 2003). We might add that it is a limited *acquis*, for in fact the Community's first initiatives are above all political (not judicial).[8] As Céline Martel notes in her history of the inclusion of drugs on the European agenda, 'the awareness of the dangers of drugs appeared on the European agenda at the same time as the spread of the AIDS virus in the late eighties'.

> From 1986, the European Parliament became the relay for these concerns and adopted four resolutions[9] in which it highlights the need for the Member States to act together against this scourge. In 1990, following an initiative by the French State President François Mitterrand, the European Council set up a European Committee to Combat Drugs (CELAD), which adopted the first European Plan to Combat Drugs[10] in 1990, amended in 1992.[11]
>
> (Martel 2003)

With the Treaty of Maastricht, drugs finally entered into the Treaties. But its entry was low-key, in a sense, for the European Union has only limited and fragmented competence in this respect. Drugs are mentioned in a variety of legal documents, scattered throughout the three pillars of the Treaty of Maastricht.

The first pillar, the 'Community Pillar', contains a public health article stipulating that the Community has to promote public health, prevent human diseases and reduce sources of danger to health. These actions should involve the promotion of research on the causes of diseases and their transmission and modes of prevention, as well as information on health and education. It is also stipulated that the Community must complete the action of member states to reduce the harmful effects of drug use on health, including through information and prevention. But on all these subjects, by virtue of the principles of subsidiarity and proportionality, the Community does little more than encouraging cooperation between member states and, if necessary, supporting their action in the above-mentioned areas. There is also a section on 'international cooperation' in this pillar, aimed at combating money laundering, and a 'development' section that provides for the introduction of 'drug' clauses into development agreements with third countries. The second pillar, 'Common

Foreign and Security Policy', states the need to take into account the struggle against drugs, but as yet no instruments have been adopted in this pillar specifically concerning the issue. Finally, the third pillar, 'Justice and Home Affairs', contains a section on 'Combating trafficking'. It is interesting to note that, historically, it was the struggle against trafficking that introduced the European Community into the field of drugs, before any public health concern.

Thus, there are no single, federating 'drug' articles in the Treaties. Nor is there an EU drug policy. Consequently, at European level drug issues are dealt with in a fragmented, compartmentalized way only, without any deeply organized coherence. Action in this respect is primarily the sum of initiatives inscribed in other policies or programmes, even if specific coordination structures, strategies and action plans exist.

When they are constraining, the legal instruments adopted directly on this subject are most often limited[12] to the control of precursors and drugs[13] and to cooperation between member states in the struggle against trafficking (especially administrative cooperation) and money-laundering. On the other subjects, the member states refuse to become involved in bitter negotiations[14] on an issue that, all in all, is not one of the most economic and socially important, even though it is politically sensitive (a negative priority?). But most of the time the instruments adopted are not constraining. They consist essentially of recommendations, resolutions or motions adopted by the Council of the European Union and/or the European Parliament in the areas of promotion of research, education, prevention[15] and information. All the other instruments of the first pillar are not applicable here because they are bound by the subsidiarity principle in the public health field.

Coordination of the issue within European institutions is itself an extremely complex undertaking. First, at the Commission many directorates deal with the drug question separately, despite many efforts by the Drug Coordination Unit in the Directorate-General 'Justice and Home Affairs'. In the Council of the European Union the Horizontal Working Party on Drugs also tries to achieve a comprehensive view of the issue, but other working groups of the Council focus on certain aspects of the problem, e.g. the Working Party on Frontiers, the Multidisciplinary Group on Organized Crime, the Working Party on Public Health and the Police Cooperation Working Party, as well as those working on specific geographic areas (especially Asia and Latin America).

This relative compartmentalization of action, due to the absence of a single regulatory and coordinating pole, is a formidable challenge owing to the transverse nature of the drug phenomenon, with its extremely varied causes and consequences. Moreover, a large proportion of the member states have policy coordination structures at national level. The complexity of the European drug issue has increased substantially with inclusion in 2004 of ten new member states, many of which are situated on the supply routes of the products in question. Drugs have no borders, and some specialists claim that Europe's competence in the matter is no match for the challenges it is now facing.

Yet despite limited competence and relatively little political interest, the European level is progressively going to acquire tools and instruments. Apart from EU strategies and action plans, the Joint Action on synthetic drugs, etc., Europe has given birth to a Monitoring Centre, the technical nature of which scarcely conceals the political effects of its activity.

The European Monitoring Centre for Drugs and Drug Addiction (EMCDDA)

The Monitoring Centre was created in 1993 in the dual context of medicalization of national policies and an absence of any specific and unifying European legal basis concerning the struggle against drugs. In fact, it was founded on the basis of Article 235 of the Treaty of Maastricht,[16] which does not directly target public health or drugs. This article is a flexibility clause that enables the Union to act in areas where it has no specific competence. The EMCDDA was created in the general climate of the triumph of 'epidemiological reason'. From the outset it was primarily devoted to epidemiological surveillance, with the mission of evaluating the extent and nature of the phenomenon, providing objective, reliable and comparable information on what was happening in all the member states (and Norway), seeking to prevent the appearance of new drugs and the development of their use, and so on. It also has to inform the member states and European institutions concerning the prevalence and patterns of drug use in the general population, and of problem drug use in particular, including the demand for drug treatment, the number of drug-related deaths and mortality among drug-users, the prevalence and incidence of drug-related infectious diseases, etc.

The EMCDDA has a management board responsible for managing the Centre and a scientific committee whose mission is to advise and support the Centre's scientific programme. To support its monitoring function, the EMCDDA has organized a network of national focal points in each of the member states, which send it information on the situation in the different countries. To ensure that the information received is comparable, the EMCDDA has developed methods for standardizing collection.

Soon the EMCDDA was no longer satisfied merely with epidemiological information and also made an effort to supply data, analyses and syntheses on the responses and policies deployed throughout Europe: prevention programmes and treatment, drug user coverage, etc. The founders and managers of the EMCDDA believe that all information should help to ensure that European drug policies are grounded less in emotions and more in reason, on the basis of a deliberately objective and comparative assessment of national situations. But the Monitoring Centre makes no political recommendations; it is not a political decision-making organ as such but an instrument at the service of political decision-making. Hence, under no circumstances is it substituted for the decision-making organs of the Union and its member states.

At this stage the paradoxical conclusion to which this short presentation leads is striking: on the one hand, the hypothesis of a gradual convergence of national policies; on the other, persistent weakness of European competence in the field. How can we explain the birth of a form of European control on drugs when there is barely any community competence except in a subsidiary manner in the framework of Article 152 on public health?

Comparison in action

It is still too early to put forward authoritative explanations based on conclusive research findings. New studies have to be undertaken to reveal the mechanisms underlying this relative convergence of European policies.[17] Yet a number of hypotheses can already be put forward. As noted earlier, AIDS has certainly functioned as a principle of reality, prompting European politicians to see the epidemiological dimension of drug abuse and the need to treat it as a health issue. The shock of AIDS to health systems that were unequally armed to deal with this type of epidemic certainly helped to make political decision-makers in Europe particularly sensitive to the need not to take any new risks – a fear that the promoters of these new approaches played on to ensure their triumph.

Yet we must be wary of an interpretation that is over-positivist and postulates the existence of a mechanical link between problems, their definition and their political management. Steffen (2001, 2004) clearly shows this in the case of AIDS: first, the epidemiological data constructed very different national realities, and second, the respective national policies do not systematically respond to these different realities – hence the obvious conclusion showing the relative autonomy of politics and policies in relation to the realities they are supposed to deal with.

It is therefore important not to overlook other phenomena and mechanisms if we wish to illuminate this paradox. In particular, European public policy networks have certainly contributed towards the now fairly common definition of problems and the orientation of national public policies. Relations between national coordinators, networks of professional actors at European level, networks of experts, especially those of 'harm and risk reduction' followed more recently by those, less clinician and more academic, of European addictology, are all social configurations that have worked, and are still working, towards the convergence of national policies. The European Monitoring Centre may also be involved in this process, without necessarily being its only medium.

The Monitoring Centre, by diffusing national research and knowledge, by organizing many workshops between experts from the different

European countries, by producing manuals on 'best practice' as regards treatment, prevention and evaluation, and, above all, by constructing 'harmonized indicators'[18] at European level for evaluating the different situations with the same tools, has certainly contributed towards the 'standardization' of ways of perceiving the issue. This cognitive process naturally contributes directly towards the convergence of measures designed to deal with these situations. By drawing up evidence-based inventories of responses, laws and policies, the Monitoring Centre has, wittingly or not, promoted the convergence of policies. By allowing more systematic comparisons between the different policies of the member states, it has helped to ensure that each state, in a synoptic perspective, compares itself to the others. From a typically political point of view, it favours the importation and transfer of policies between states. The EMCDDA will thus have contributed not only to the diffusion but also to the institutionalization of certain solutions that have gradually been 'imposed as legitimate' – as the neo-institutionalist sociologists put it – in the sub-field of European drug policies.

In other words, and somewhat obviously, a Monitoring Centre is not purely the technical tool that it claims to be. Comparison, in the European political dynamic, is an activity that is certainly above all cognitive, but is also performative. It triggers action. These conclusions are consistent with those of Majone (1996), for whom information in Europe acts as a 'flexible constraint for change'. The convergence of a large proportion of national drug policies can hardly be explained by political consensus leading to legislated harmonization, or by the impulse of the European Court of Justice, as was the case in other domains (e.g. the Cassis de Dijon ruling). Nor, finally, can it be explained by pressure from powerful economic actors. More probably it is the result of the sharing of knowledge and expertise.

It will be necessary to verify and qualify this hypothesis and, above all, to add in-depth reflection on the role of soft laws (Grange 2004) in the explanation of this convergence in the war against drugs. But it seems that this subject is particularly interesting for anyone who wants to observe the ways in which certain models of policies or solutions diffuse throughout the European states, and the role that transnational institutions and actors play in similar processes of appropriation and translation.

What Europeanization?

What does the case of the struggle against drugs and drug addiction suggest in terms of the Europeanization process? The image of a Europe that is pacified and harmonized on the drug issue is false, or at least premature. The member states are still very concerned about maintaining a monopoly over their action, and certain topics such as rooms for sterile injections or the controlled distribution of heroin still generate stormy political and technical debate. Yet no conscientious observer can deny that whereas ten or fifteen years ago there were as many drug policies as European states, today that is certainly no longer the case. An agreement – at least, an objective – has been reached on a minimum common base of health, social and legal measures.

Although the EMCDDA's work cannot be seen as the real cause of changes to national drug policies in the 1990s, it has certainly worked towards the convergence of national policies by contributing to the diffusion of a specific model for managing drug-related problems. Thus, without being the mainspring of change, this instrument at the service of national policies and European institutions has certainly helped to pave the way towards a specific type of change. My conclusion here is consistent with that of Lamping in the present volume (Chapter 1), in so far as the absence of a legal base does not mean that the impact of European integration on national policies should be neglected.

This role of 'indicating the way' is likely to be asserted even more with enlargement, which aims for the inclusion of countries that have not – or not yet – all devised and developed policies against drug addiction and the risks it involves. Some of the new member states of the Union are only now discovering drug- and addiction-related problems and sometimes feel unequipped to deal with their extent and complexity. They are therefore keen to find and adopt models that may not be ready-to-use but at least are considered legitimate by the European family that they have just joined.

Can we say that the drug policy case is an example of the Europeanization process, in the strict sense of the term? If we take the usual definition of the term, 'convergence of ways of doing things by imitating practices of institutions of the Union' (Gaxie and Laborier 2003: 204), it seems that this is not so, as Aline Grange (2004) shows. In fact, a large part of this so-called European model was first developed in certain member states, primarily in national policy networks, and finally found a strategic vehicle for its diffusion in certain European institutions – but by no means all of them. The resulting picture of Europeanization is somewhat different; less top-down and more bottom-up. It is one that more clearly reflects the complexity and dynamic of reciprocal structuring processes between the national and European levels.

In the case of the drug sector, we finally conclude with a paradoxical situation in which national policies are tending to converge concretely in the areas of demand and supply reduction, without the legal foundations of the Union taking these trends fully into account. The proposed constitution recently drafted by the Convention, in which the competence of the Union on drug-related issues remains limited and scattered, bears witness to this fact. This prompts me to raise the following question: is the role of the Union not precisely to promote mutual recognition of the convergent aspects of national policies and to develop them, while leaving the member states with the prerogative of managing that which still divides them profoundly? In a sense, this amounts to promoting a shift from the spontaneous to the well thought out.

Notes

This article relates mainly to the 'old' member states.

1 This is still a hypothesis that needs to be supported by further research before it can be seen as conclusive.

2 This part owes much to the synthetic and comparative work of Danilo Ballotta and Brendan Hughes of the European Monitoring Centre for Drugs and Drug Addiction (EMCDDA) and the (as yet) unpublished study 'Usages de stupéfiants et approches legislatives en Europe', Lisbon, EMCDDA, July 2003.

3 In certain member states of the European Union (e.g. France, Finland, Greece, Luxembourg (excluding cannabis) and Sweden), the use of drugs is illegal. Some other countries have chosen to directly prohibit not their use as such, but rather preparatory acts preceding use and, in particular, possession.

4 In Austria the new law on narcotics (1998) includes the possibility of suspending legal proceedings in case of arrest for possession of a small quantity of narcotics for personal use.

5 In 2002 the UK government announced its intention to reclassify (via statutory measures) cannabis from Class B to Class C. This would grant the police a discretionary power to prosecute, since they could 'settle for' merely confiscating the substance and giving the offender a warning, provided there were no aggravating circumstances. This reclassification was scheduled for 2004.

6 So-called 'low-threshold' methadone programmes have also been introduced to enable addicts to receive substitution without having to comply with a set of conditions such as a commitment to future abstinence. In other words, this type of low-threshold substitution programme enables addicts to benefit from these products for reasons other than caring for their addiction as such. As a result, this possibility was long challenged – understandably so.

7 A number of studies in the humanities have tried to show that drug-users, including drug addicts, are not devoid of rationality, contrary to what common-sense ideas often suggest.

8 Résolution du Conseil sur une action concertée visant à résoudre le problème de la drogue, JOCE no. C 283 du 10/11/1986, p. 80. Résolution du Conseil et des ministres de la santé des États membres, réunis au sein du Conseil du 16 mai 1989 concernant un réseau européen de données sanitaires en matière de toxicomanie, JOCE no. C 185 du 22/07/1989, p. 1. Conclusions du Conseil et des ministres de la santé des États membres, réunis au sein du Conseil du 16 mai 1989 concernant la fiabilité des analyses des liquides corporels pour déceler l'usage de drogues illicites, JOCE no. C 185 du 22/07/1989, p. 1. Conclusions du Conseil et des ministres de la santé des États membres, réunis au sein du Conseil du 16 mai 1989 concernant la prévention du SIDA chez les consommateurs de drogue par voie parentérale, JOCE no. C 185 du 22/07/1989, p. 3.

9 Résolutions du Parlement européen sur la lutte contre la drogue: JOCE no. C 85 du 08/04/1980, p. 15; JOCE no. C 149 du 14/06/1982, p. 121; JOCE no. C 262 du 14/10/1985, p. 119; JOCE no. C 283 du 10/11/1986, p. 79.

10 These programmes served as a basis for the subsequent two action plans: plan d'action de l'Union européenne en matière de lutte contre la drogue 1994–1999 (COM (1994) 234 final du 23 juin 1994) et Plan d'action de l'Union européenne en matière de lutte contre la drogue 2000–2004 (COM (1999) 239 final du 26 mai 1999).

11 Programme européen de lutte contre la drogue. CELAD 126. REV 1.

10234/1/90, le 10/12/1990. et Projet de rapport du Comité européen de lutte anti-drogue, CELAD 126 10589/92, le 03/12/1992.

12 With the exception of the regulation that created the EMCDDA, as we are about to see.

13 Many of the restrictive instruments adopted concern the precursors (first pillar, 'DomesTic Market and Common Commercial Policy') and new synthesized drugs (third pillar). The precursors were chemical products used in industry in the manufacture of drugs (whether synthetic or not). The use of these products can also be diverted, which means that their trade has to be controlled.

14 In July 2003 the Commission's proposal of a Framework Decision (third pillar) aimed at the establishment of minimum rules concerning drug traffic had still not been adopted despite continuing negotiations for over two years (the proposal was submitted in May 2001).

15 With the exception of the December 1996 Decision by the European Parliament and the Council for a community action programme concerning the prevention of drug abuse.

16 Article 235 TCE of the Treaty of Maastricht (308 in the Treaty of Amsterdam) authorizes the Council, provided it rules unanimously, following a proposal by the Commission, and after consulting the European Parliament, to take all necessary measures to achieve one of the objectives of the Community not provided for by the Treaty.

17 Aline Grange's current PhD work on 'How Europe is expanding its sphere of competence: the case of drugs' is promising in this respect. She was scheduled to defend her thesis in early 2004 at the European University Institute of Florence.

18 Harmonized indicators are indicators of prevalence on uses and problems related to use, the definition and methodology of which are common to all member states. This makes it possible to collect comparable information on the situation in the different member states.

References

Bergeron, H. (1999) *L'État et la toxicomanie. Histoire d'une singularité française*, 'Sociologies' series, Paris, PUF.

—— (2003) *Dispositifs spécialisés 'alcool' et 'toxicomanie', santé publique et nouvelle politique publique des addictions*, 'Rapport de recherches' series, Paris: OFDT.

Cattacin, S., Lucas, B. and Vetter, S. (1996) *Modèles de politique en matière de drogue. Une comparaison de six réalités européennes*, 'Logiques Politiques' series, Paris: L'Harmattan.

Cattacin, S., Panchaux, C. and Tattini, V. (1997) 'La Gestion néo-conservatrice: l'Espagne, l'Italie, la Belgique, la France', in *Les Politiques de lutte contre le VIH/SIDA en Europe de l'Ouest*, Paris: L'Harmattan, pp. 127–141.

Coester, D., Laborde, M. A. and Thévenin, M. (1994) *Analyse d'une décision: l'extension des programmes de traitement des toxicomanes par la méthadone*, Mémoire pour la conférence de Mme Legendre, Paris: IEP.

European Monitoring Centre for Drugs and Drug Addiction (EMCDDA) (2002a) *Prosecution of drug users in Europe: varying pathways to similar objectives*, The EMCDDA Insights series, no. 5, Luxembourg: Office of the Official Publications of the European Communities.

—— (2002b) *Strategies and Coordination in the Field of Drugs in the European Union: A Descriptive Review*, EMCDDA, November.

Gaxie, D. and Laborier, P. (2003) 'Les Obstacles à l'évaluation de l'action publique et quelques pistes pour tenter de les surmonter', in P. Favre, J. Hayward and Y. Schemeil (eds) *Être gouverné. Études en l'honneur de J. Leca*, Paris: Presses de Sciences Po, pp. 201–224.

Grange, A. (2004) 'Comment l'Europe étend sa sphère de compétence: le cas de la drogue', Political Science PhD, European University Institute of Florence.

Majone, G. (1996) *La Communauté européenne: un État régulateur*, 'Clefs/Politique' series, Paris: Montchrestien.

Martel, C. (2003) 'Éléments de réflexion sur l'enjeu de l'adhésion de la Turquie à l'Union européenne. Aspects de lutte contre le phénomène des drogues', in C. Flaesch-Mougin and J. Lebullenger (eds) *Les Défis de l'adhésion de la Turquie à l'Union européenne*, 'Regards d'Europe' series, Brussels: Éditions Bruylant.

Roques, B. (1999) *La Dangerosité des drogues*, 'La Documentation française' series, Paris: Odile Jacob.

Steffen, M. (2001) *Les États face au Sida en Europe*, 'Transeurope' series, Grenoble: PUG.

—— (2004) 'AIDS and Health-Policy Responses in European Welfare States', *Journal of European Social Policy* 14 (2): 165–181.

Yvorel, J. J. (1992) *Les Poisons de l'esprit. Drogues et drogués au XIXe siècle*, Paris: Quai Voltaire.

Conclusion

The new politics of European health policy: moving beyond the nation-state

Wolfram Lamping and Monika Steffen

The challenge of this book has been to contribute to a better theoretical and empirical understanding of European health policy, a topic that remains under-researched in the study of European integration and, more generally, in political science. The book focuses on a *dilemma*: how do European Union-driven objectives affect policies placed under exclusively national competence? Because of its particular nature and position, the health sector is one of the most instructive cases for examining the intriguing relationship between national and European competence. It provides a fertile example allowing us to track down the manifold, complex and often surprising impacts of European integration on national policies. The initial questions seemed simple: does the Union level produce European health policies and, if so, how? Does European integration affect domestic health policies and politics and, if so, how? The chapters of this book show the growing impact of 'Europe' on national as well as international health policies. They document a complex process of health policy integration that accelerated during the 1990s and gathered even more speed in the first years of the twenty-first century. The process, however, is variable and in certain cases even appears to be contradictory. Basically, it mirrors the artificial, traditional cleavage in the health policy sector between public health on the one hand and medical healthcare on the other.[1] Furthermore, many variations have been observed in Europe's impact on health policies and in the diverse responses and non-responses to European pressure, all of which need explanation.

Explaining a contradictory picture

Until now, different and contradictory assessments have prevailed concerning the role of the European Union (EU) and the impact of its economic and political integration process on health policies. The content of this book aims to provide clarification and to draw conclusions concerning what seems inextricably complex and confused. The contradictory picture is partly related to the existence of both national and European competence over different domains of the health policy field. Furthermore, as stressed in the Introduction, it is linked to different conceptualizations of health policy and of Europe and Europeanization. Contradictory statements also arise from Europe's somewhat nebulous role in health policy and the fact that EU intervention may take many different forms.

The role of the EU is not that of a service provider. Service provision, on which studies in comparative health policy usually focus, is left to national authorities operating under various institutional set-ups, mainly Bismarckian health insurance and Beveridgian national health systems. In the field of health policies, the role of the Union is mainly a regulatory one, in the sense of Majone (1996); it has the competence and capacity to regulate the activities of other policy actors. The European Union frames the information base of policy-making in the health sector and influences policy agendas and power balances between policy actors at European as well as national level. A clear example is the changing position of the organized medical profession, which enjoys far less influence in the European health policy arena than in the national arena. The Europeanization of health policies includes a clear move away from medical issues and problem-framing, towards consumer and trade interests and conflicts. In this open and more diversified policy area operate not only interest groups and lobbyists, but also expert networks for public health and health technology assessment. The rapidly growing information infrastructures, although unable to compel any actor or country to follow EU guidelines, draw up and diffuse problem definitions, contextual elements, technical solutions and policy alternatives – which explains the 'waves of similar health policy initiatives on the national health policy agendas' (Lehto 2000: 3–4).

EU intervention can take different forms, in general and in the various health policy areas. The Union may intervene as an intergovernmental organization (depending on interest bargaining and compromises with governments); as an international bureaucracy pursuing organizational self-interest (as documented for the Commission in the context of social policies (Niemann 1998: 429); or as an 'international network state' (Castells 1999) (where scientific knowledge and expert advice constitute a major part of supranational decision-making). Furthermore, even though the EU's health mandate has meanwhile been fleshed out, governance structures at EU level are in considerable flux, as illustrated by the internal relocation of health policy from the 'Social Affairs' Directorate to 'Health and Consumer Protection'. In fact, the development of European health policy still depends to a large extent on the strength of political pressure, which explains the importance of 'crises' in the process, and the unequal EU commitments in the various domains of health policy and health-related policies. Neither escalating health expenditures nor tobacco or alcohol consumption have obtained a degree of attention and engagement from the Union comparable to that of the impact-loaded HIV blood and BSE crises, although the former issues have more far-reaching repercussions in terms of financial burdens and potential risks.

All in all, EU health policies demand a different understanding from national health policy arenas. Likewise, health policy itself requires a different understanding from the Europeanization of other policies because of the health sector's inherent characteristics: it is governed by social policies as well as market policies; it forms part of well-established European welfare states struggling to maintain their tricky position between national and global economies; and it is a service sector where provision and benefits cannot be modulated or cut down in the same way as financial allocations.

This book analyses the various ways in which health policies became Europeanized, and points to the variations observed in this process. It maps out a developing European health policy arena with a multi-faceted integration process that proceeds by regulation and/or political compromise in the public health and medicinal product sectors, and by case law and legal compliance in the medical care sector. Both the public health and the medicinal product arenas comprise heterogeneous policy fields, several of which are discussed in this book. Both are marked by different levels of integration, depending on the political sensitivity of the area and on the particular constellation of interests prevailing in the member states. Both involve numerous, widely diverse actors and are therefore characterized by a high level of interest intermediation and intensive lobbying. Not surprisingly, the attractiveness and importance of supranational institutions, as a target for the intermediation of interests and information, is increasing as the European Union acquires more competences in these policy fields. As the chapter by Permanand and Mossialos (Chapter 2) demonstrates, the pharmaceutical sector, a key sector in all health policy systems at national as well as international level, is characterized by a high level of basic interest congruence, particularly between the Commission and the European pharmaceutical associations, at least as long as the creation of the single market is the exclusive policy aim. By contrast, the European healthcare arena is still evolving on almost exclusively national lines, at least at first view. Since the European Union has very few genuine, formal competences in this sector, national ministries and the Council of Ministers are formally still the key players, although, as Lamping (Chapter 1) shows, the European Court of Justice (ECJ) has become an important and effective new policy-maker.

European actors and processes

The analyses presented in this book clearly show that, rather than a direct, Treaty-based impact, it has been the indirect impact resulting from other Community provisions – in particular the single market regime – that explains the multiple facets of European health policy integration. Even though health systems and health policy as such remain formally excluded from Community competence, the *compatibility* of health systems with the potentially deregulating European 'four freedoms' and the competition regime, on the one hand, and the EU's fragmented regulatory competency legitimized by the single market agenda, on the other, have triggered far-reaching processes of adjustment to internal market requirements and have thus fostered European policies, including in the health sector.

The term 'Europeanization' denotes a stretchable concept. Above all, it is an empirical and sectoral phenomenon that requires in-depth analyses – the only way to make the concept operational. Featherstone and Radaelli[2] have insisted on the institutional aspects of Europeanization. In this perspective, changes may result from direct institution-building at EU level or (cross-) national processes of adjusting domestic institutional settings to European integration. The chapters of this book add a *politics* perspective, and suggest a conceptualization of Europeanization as the result of bi-directional, mutual processes of interaction, influencing and norm diffusion. The findings presented here allow three distinct sources of change and pressure for Europeanization to be identified, all of which represent fertile agendas for further research:

The first is *Europeanization by market integration and compliance* – either as spillover processes from the 'four freedoms' and competition within the single European market (SEM) (negative integration; Chapter 1 by Lamping) or in terms of EU-level regulation of market access and functioning (positive integration; Chapter 2 by Permanand and Mossialos, and Chapter 3 by Altenstetter). Two developments – momentous ECJ rulings following courageous actions by individuals to assert their (social) rights as European citizens, and the ongoing process of technically regulating and standardizing healthcare provision at EU level – have lastingly impinged on member states' social policy sovereignty, including the market-related national social security politics. In these areas the Commission and the ECJ, armed with SEM law and strengthened by high expectations on the part of citizens, have gone far in constraining domestic policy choices. The environment in which national health politics will take place in the future has already undergone important changes.

The second is *Europeanization by crises* – which can be understood as a discontinuous and accidental but extremely powerful process leading to competence accumulation at Community level, under the pressure of 'urgency'. While the Commission has demonstrated immense creativity and considerable strategic competences in this process, member states have agreed – for convenience in certain circumstances – to shift responsibility for politically sensitive and demanding policies to the Community level (see Chapters 4, 5 and 6 by Clergeau, Farrell and Lafond respectively). It was mainly severe threats to public health, such as outbreaks of communicable diseases like AIDS or BSE, that induced the Commission to promote cooperation among member states and progressively to institutionalize systems for the surveillance and control of diseases and other collective health threats at EU level. The creation or consolidation of networks and agencies, such as the Communicable Diseases Network set up in 1999 and the new European Centre for Disease Prevention and Control, demonstrates the step-by-step transformation of the institutional landscape of European public health and healthcare policies.

Finally, there is *Europeanization by policy diffusion and discourses* – a phenomenon that is difficult to measure and whose precise effects on a given policy cannot easily be proved. Bergeron, in his contribution on the Europeanization of drug policies (Chapter 7), shows how EU member states' national policies are gradually converging, owing to the Community's stepwise extension of activities – despite its having virtually no competence in this policy field – and as a result of bottom-up effects influencing the European agenda. The chapter demonstrates – *inter alia* – the Commission's ability to turn a nationally sensitive policy item into a European issue. The Commission initiates EU-level policy discussion and discourses between all policy-making parties and policy implementers: professionals, experts, public administrations and governments from all member states. It establishes health policy networks and builds supporting coalitions, institutionalizes health knowledge and, finally, produces comparative assessments of national policy performances. The EU level thus not only fosters new ideas and their intellectual dissemination, but also directly promotes better practices, learning from other member states, new frames for collective debate, and the reshaping of national governments' preferences and perspectives. This aspect of Europeanization – that is, the accumulation of expertise and comparative assessment at EU level – is crucial for the understanding of health policy integration; it involves independent and pro-EU health policy experts, it pools high-level expertise, and it institutionalizes sectoral forums. Such processes have proved to be effective vehicles in gradually introducing a European dimension into national policy discourses and in transnationalizing the policy debates, which in fact means denationalizing politics and policies.

The Commission's offensive cultivation of cooperation with the European health policy epistemic communities and the building up of 'intellectual alliances' play a decisive role in reshaping governments' preferences and perspectives. In this respect, George and Bache (2001: 24–25) have emphasized that epistemic communities are likely to exercise a particularly strong influence over policy when policy-makers face 'uncertainty' about future developments. This is the case in many of the issues related to health policy (Steffen 2004). Moreover, the systematic collection and provision of data,[3] the exchange of knowledge via European forums and committees, and the subsequent diffusion of ideas as well as policy alternatives can have major repercussions for national problem perceptions and problem-solving strategies – and even put considerable pressure on member state governments, as several chapters in this book suggest. In particular, this holds true for the open method of coordination (OMC), discussed by Lamping, the aim of which is to initiate both a competition of 'better practices' and a process-driven convergence of national policies and institutions. Member governments have found themselves in a considerably altered and constantly changing context. While at a formal level they are still powerful gatekeepers in the healthcare arena, *in practice* the policy agenda is increasingly set elsewhere, and pressure groups are becoming aware of the fact that their interests can 'no longer be adequately served at national level alone' (Lindberg 1963: 101). The health sector provides numerous examples of this incremental process of shifting 'loyalties, expectations and political activities toward a new centre' (Haas 1958: 16).

The various chapters of this book have pointed out that – apart from the ECJ's role in effectively clearing all hurdles, and its position as *de facto* master of the EU Treaty – the history of health policy integration is to a large extent the history of the Commission. Despite being an internally divided actor, especially when it comes to the health arena, it has developed an ambitious set of health policy goals of its own making, which it persistently pursues. The Commission, a highly politicized actor providing political leadership *par excellence*, is under constant pressure to legitimize its existence via the production of new initiatives and regulations. Cumulating the capacity of both 'initiator and lobbyist' (Springer 1992: 62), the Commission has become a master of 'soft' governance and strategic variability. This process and its characteristics are most clearly visible in health politics. As several authors of this book show, discussing the European polity without taking the Commission's ambitious, self-interested and variable role into account would mean misunderstanding the very dynamics of European integration. In other words, the Commission's ability to govern effectively despite not having strong formal competence – as observed in health policy – and thus to push outward the frontiers of Community social policy is truly remarkable and warrants further investigation.

Learning from health policy integration

'Health' is a vague, cross-cutting and inherently 'borderless' policy field. How does it relate to 'Europe' and to European integration? It is the impreciseness and eclectic manner in which the Treaty deals with 'health' that is directly addressed when Mossialos *et al.* (2001: 3) state that 'much of the relevant European law has emerged from rulings that have either arisen from considerations in other sectors or by addressing only the issues in a single case, leaving major issues of applicability unresolved'.[4] A wide range of Community legislation and activity has not only intended but also unintended impacts on member states' health systems, precisely because large parts of the European legislation impacting on the health sector have been developed in the general context of completing the internal market, in order to ensure the free movement of persons, goods, services and capital within the Community.[5] Most European health policy should therefore be understood as an *intersection* between health policy and other policy fields in which the European Union has genuine competence. The result has been, and still is, a confusing mosaic rather than a coherent and consistent European health policy concept.

Yet the 'Europe of health' is taking shape, even though its contours still seem bewildering. Core areas of health systems and health regulation have inevitably become subject to an *incremental* process of Europeanization and institutional harmonization, although 'Europe' often takes a devious route, sometimes even haphazardly. The contributions in this book demonstrate an ongoing integration process that, despite the obstacles, follows its own path and its own logic. It affords European actors, especially the Commission, both plausible justifications and ample opportunities for fostering further integration. Health policy thus provides an interesting example of a successful, multi-causal process of denationalizing a policy field with traditionally strong national embeddedness, despite the final destination still being uncertain. European health policy has often been perceived as deriving only from the common market project, as a necessary complement for its advancement and subordinated to economic objectives. The empirical research data and results provided in this book question this narrow perception and suggest that health policy is becoming a value in its own right with its own legitimacy, potentially equivalent to economic imperatives. As health protection constitutes a key element in the relationship of trust between citizens and governments, health policy is likely to move towards the centre of the future integration agenda, as a 'driving force of the European project' (Kleinman 2002: 225).

Irrespective of how the Union develops in years to come, the supranational and national levels are already interwoven and interdependent in many ways. In this context, a European health policy regime is likely to develop as an *issue-specific* policy arena with shared and separated responsibilities and competences between member states and Community institutions. Health policy should therefore be discussed in terms of an addition: the national health policy regimes *plus* the European level. The restructuring and reshaping of European health policy is not, and has little chance in the near future of becoming, a process of 'twenty-five into one'; rather, it is a 'twenty-five plus one' figure. Though European regulation and member-state social law necessarily interact closely, the distribution of power and responsibilities between the two levels varies according to the precise policy areas. In some cases the two levels are still completely distinct. The chapters of this book show examples of integration taking place in diverse areas, at different paces, through multi-dimensional and multi-level processes. They describe the coexistence of areas where harmonization has been fairly successful and effective, and those where divergent national interests have so far prevented further Europeanization.

In the light of Michael Moran's analysis of the 'health care state' (1999) and his distinction between 'governing consumption', 'governing doctors' and 'governing technology', several chapters of this book concern the European governance of technology. Yet the authors of those chapters, like most of the others, focus too on what could be conceptualized as 'governing public health risks': the safety of food, blood, and medical as well as medicinal products, and risks related to drug abuse and to future developments in biotechnologies. All the chapters provide detailed insight into the gradual and differential emergence of *sectoral* regulatory systems *integrating market and risk regulation*, and into the obstacles facing more ambitious and comprehensive European strategies. Farrell's contribution in particular (Chapter 5) shows the difficulty of reconciling industrial and consumer interests, and the tension in EU policy-making between the structure of scientific advice and accountability to public interest. These public health areas, in which the European Union has incrementally developed a policy mandate for positive integration, have prompted researchers to actively investigate the range of new subjects. By contrast, neither the rights of consumers of healthcare (patients and members of health insurance systems) nor the governance of health professionals and provider institutions have so far attracted similar policy and research attention from a European perspective, despite the fact that the ECJ rulings have emphatically illustrated the obligation of governments to respect EU law when regulating their health systems. Meanwhile, the regulatory competence for social security is a divided one; while member states still have the *specific* competence to regulate their social security systems, the European Union holds a *general* policy mandate to ensure national compatibility with the single market and competition law. These different examples document the global and successful, though fragmented and uneven, progress of European policy development. The health policy sector is certainly not a unique example of this type of European integration process, but is probably the case in which it is most obvious, and therefore the most accessible for observation and understanding.

All national health systems are henceforth confronted with a new twofold limit to their autonomy. The European Union defines new entry and exit rules – patient mobility, transferability of entitlements, borderless European healthcare market, etc. – to which they have to adjust their institutions. At the same time, the European internal market and competition regime imposes its rules on national health policy-makers in the form of cartel law, liberalization of legal privileges, European Union-wide possibilities for health service providers to work and invest, development and extension of transnational contracting, possibilities to exploit price differentials within Europe, etc. The impact of European integration on national healthcare and the ways in which governments adjust their institutionalized healthcare governance to it – in terms of regulation of access, funding, membership entitlements, administrative and management practices, cost containment and their participation in the OMC, etc. – are still largely unknown. The opportunities and perils of integration for consumers, providers and purchasers raise challenging questions for scholars of European integration and for European health and social policy actors alike.

Theoretical as well as political debates are developing on the mechanisms and explanations, and the cases, causes and consequences of health policy integration. On the cognitive level, all contributions presented in this volume demonstrate that Europeanization is 'open to different epistemologies' (Featherstone and Radaelli 2003: 332). Many different approaches, conceptual tools and theoretical constructions have been used by the authors, such as comparative politics and public policy analysis, interest intermediation and negotiation theories, multi-level governance concepts, the cognitive dimension of policy-making, discourse analysis, institutionalist approaches, concepts of regulation, and policy diffusion, transfer and convergence. The understanding of the Europeanization process in the cross-cutting health policy sector thus contributes to the progress of theory. In particular, the shift – discerned mainly by Altenstetter but present also in most other chapters – away from European (public) health policy-making, in a top-down perspective, to the domestic implementation and effects of European integration, in a bottom-up perspective – seems a fertile one for future theoretical developments. The content of this book, focusing on a particularly instructive policy sector, complements the general literature on EU-level politics and institution-building.

Future prospects and agendas

Clearly, more research is required on the relationship between European integration and health policy developments, in terms of case studies as well as comparative studies, particularly as the health policy topic exemplifies a far broader issue. The subjects addressed here concern not only what is commonly called 'social Europe', but also, on a more general level, how the European political union interacts with the European welfare state. Since the latter represents the main feature of 'statehood' for the citizen – at least for the older member – the subject is of key importance for the successful development of the European Union. The political agenda for Europeanization and integration thus also indicates a research agenda.

Three directions can be suggested for future research. The first should focus on developments *inside* healthcare systems. Since national healthcare systems, at least in their institutional cores, will remain diverse, the impact of 'Europe' and its economic constraints on national systems and policies will continue to differ. Hurst (1996) argued that European health systems consist of comparable 'building blocks', pursue fairly similar policy objectives and grant comparable rights. They certainly all play a similar tune, but they play it on very different instruments. The question is: to what extent do the instruments or even the musicians need to be changed when new music is to be played? What is the effect of so-called market- and competition-oriented Europeanization on the internal functioning of health systems embedded in national welfare states? What are the consequences in terms of (equal) access to care for patients, in terms of cost-effective management, and in terms of power changes? What are the threats but also the opportunities – for example, for improving internal efficacy? As the contradictory strains on health systems grow – cost containment on the one hand, public demands for more and better care on the other – member state governments need policy alternatives and emulation. They are in search of new policy recipes, but the internationally available ones are seldom adaptable to the national contexts in Europe. Most of them originate from outside the European Union, mainly from the United States (Drache and Sullivan 1999; Ranade 1998). European governments and reformers have to struggle their way through institutional path dependency, powerful veto-players and internationally advertised but unwarranted solutions, with the risk of copying untested and sometimes even bad solutions (Guillén and Cabiedes 2003). New research should not only compare the official content of healthcare reforms, but also engage in the comparative assessment of the effective implementation and outcomes of such reforms, set in context with the European welfare state and the Union commitments.

A second direction should focus on the particular implications of EU enlargement for health policy integration, for two reasons. First, from the point of view of politics, enlargement to twenty-five members complicates existing problems of European decision-making procedures and may produce what Vobruba (2003) calls 'the enlargement crisis'. Second, from the point of view of health policy integration, eastward enlargement will not only increase the existing problem of institutional heterogeneity, but also confront Europe with an even more salient issue: the disproportionate distribution of wealth and economic opportunities within the European Union, reflected in access to healthcare. Against this background, enlargement towards Eastern Europe will probably lead to more restrictive frameworks for future common health policy development in the Union. Attempts to harmonize provision standards among member states will probably be confronted with the largely rejected prospect of nothing more than 'the level of the lowest common denominator – today somewhere between Germany and Greece, tomorrow reflecting the even more extreme conditions of enlargement to the East' (Danner 1999: 66). Conversely, the adjustment of the new accession and candidate countries to European integration and the adoption of the existing EU health policy regime will inevitably lead to a second transition in these countries. It will confront them with new and far-reaching requirements, including requirements that affect their service delivery systems, even though the latter remain under national competence. Health policy in the context of EU enlargement constitutes a promising and challenging research field that will shed light on many intricate and politically salient issues.

The third direction is linked to the fact that the health sector constitutes a core example of social and public services in general. All these services are confronted with the effects of market integration and liberalization, and the EU-induced policy to turn to the market for what were previously exclusively perceived as public goods and public services. In all member states the public service sectors were explicitly exempted from market competition and granted special legal status. Yet the ECJ and the Commission, extremely powerful actors of negative market integration, impinge on long-established national institutions when, for example, they enforce competition on public services and public utilities, despite the fact that these were defined as non-market sectors for normative reasons. The result is growing legal and political uncertainty as to the distinction between economic activity and social policy regulation. The effort to clarify and to draw more general conclusions on the legal criteria and exceptions for organizations, institutions and areas classified as non-economic remains an ongoing process. Since the beginning of the new century, the Union has taken several concrete steps to 'strengthen the equilibrium, coherence, coordination, and synchronization between the social and economic dimensions in the Lisbon Strategy framework'.[6] It has taken measures that can be classified as policies aimed at correcting the outcomes of market integration and at ensuring that national social policies are not eroded by the creation of the internal market (anti-liberalization policies). The Commission actually perceives these 'services of general interest' as 'necessary to sustain allegiance to the Union' (Commission 2000: 23). It conceded that in some cases there is a 'tension between the economic objectives of EU internal market regulations and the social objectives of the health sector' (Commission 2001: 4). New research should shed light on the general problems of public services adapting to the market and to an 'efficiency'-dominated European environment. The health sector offers a fertile case for understanding similar problems in other social service sectors, such as care for the elderly and the educational sector, with an equally deep national embeddedness, formally exclusive national competence, and a comparable level of priority in respect of the political and social challenge.

European health policy integration is a piecemeal process of incremental integration, 'step-by-step and by small degrees' (Lindblom 1959: 81). It is marked by caution and reserve rather than by big ideas and heroic struggle. Dictated by necessity, the careful progress is also wise: European health policy is condemned to advance on a narrow pass between market objectives and risk management, and between two equally important political necessities of making health systems economically sustainable on the one hand and attractive to demanding EU citizens on the other. The protagonists of a deeper social policy integration may regret the slowness and limited range of this development, ignoring the fact that incremental politics are always marked by continuity on the path taken. One should therefore measure the extent to which member states have agreed to yield sovereign rights and public policy competence, not on the scale of common market achievements, but in terms of the obstacles that had to be and have been overcome. The Europeanization of health policies needs to be understood as an incomplete, unsystematic and sometimes accidental process of policy harmonization and adaptation. It offers an example of effective and inspired 'muddling through', rather than of a consistent and clear-cut strategy producing intended results. It is the European Union's custom to invent itself as it goes along. Its policies are subject to 'continual mutation' (Wincott 1996: 170); its shape and purpose are evolving. In this respect, the 'borderless' health policy sector is no exception; it participates in and actively fuels the process, as witnessed in this book.

Notes

1 The reader may regret not to find a comparative chapter on the changing organization of healthcare and the impact of national reforms, in terms of access for patients, power balances and governance structures. However, this part of health policy, in a European perspective, would be too complex for a single chapter. It is the subject of a further book project stemming from the 2001 Grenoble ECPR workshop.
2 Europeanization 'connects different levels of analysis and types of actors, thereby posing complex ontological issues, and it displays asymmetries across institutional settings and policy processes' (Featherstone and Randaelli 2003: 331).
3 Via research projects, the EUROSTAT Working Group on Public Health Statistics, the 'EUCOMP' project, and similar networks in operation at European level.
4 On this particular question, see also Mossialos and McKee (2002).
5 The Commission itself concludes that most initiatives 'have been undertaken as part of policy frameworks in other areas and not on the basis of the Community public health competence in Article 152 of the Treaty' (Commission 2001: 19); and that 'it is a remarkable feature of the health sector that core aspects of health policy ... are not yet regarded as an integral part of the Communities' health agenda' (Commission 2001: 21).
6 Presidency Conclusion, Barcelona European Council, 15 and 16 March 2002 (SN 100/1/02 REV 1, p. 44).

References

Castells, M. (1999) *The End of the Millennium*, Oxford: Blackwell.
Commission of the European Communities (2000) *Social Policy Agenda*, Brussels.
—— (2001) *The Internal Market and Health Services*, Report of the High Level Committee on Health, Brussels.
Danner, G. (1999) 'Torn between National Interests and Community Requirements: The Position of European Health Policy', in B.-M. Bellach and H. Stein (eds) *The New Public Health Policy of the European Union. Past Experience, Present Needs, Future Perspectives*, Munich: Urban und Vogel, pp. 65–71.

Drache, D. and Sullivan, T. (eds) (1999) *Health Reform: Public Success, Private Failure*, London: Routledge.

Featherstone, K. and Radaelli, C. M. (2003) 'A Conversant Research Agenda', in K. Featherstone and C. M. Radaelli (eds) *The Politics of Europeanization*, Oxford: Oxford University Press, pp. 331–341.

George, S. and Bache, I. (2001) *Politics in the European Union*, Oxford: Oxford University Press.

Guillén, A. and Cabiedes, L. (2001) 'Reforming Pharmaceutical Policies in the European Union: A Penguin Effect?', *International Journal of Health Services*, 33 (1): 1–28.

Haas, E. (1958) *The Uniting of Europe: Political, Social and Economic Forces*, Stanford, Calif.: Stanford University Press.

Hurst, J. (1996) 'The NHS Reforms in an International Context', in A. J. Culyer and Adam Wagstaff (eds) *Reforming Health Care Systems: Experiments with the NHS*, Cheltenham: Edward Elgar, pp. 15–34.

Kleinman, M. (2002) *A European Welfare State? European Union Social Policy in Context*, Basingstoke, UK: Palgrave Macmillan.

Lehto, J. (2000) 'Approaches to the Europeanization of Health Policy', Paper presented at the IPSA Conference (International Political Science Association, 1–5 August), Quebec, Research Committee no. 25: Comparative Health Policy. Panel 2 organized by M. Steffen.

Lindberg, L. (1963) *The Political Dynamics of European Integration*, Stanford, Calif.: Stanford University Press.

Lindblom, C. E. (1959) 'The Science of "Muddling Through"', *Public Administration Review* 2: 79–88.

Majone, G. (ed.) (1996) *Regulating Europe*, London: Routledge.

Moran, M. (1999) *Governing the Health Care State: A Comparative Study of the United Kingdom, the United States and Germany*, Manchester: Manchester University Press.

Mossialos, E. and McKee, M. (2002) *EU Law and the Social Character of Health Care*, Brussels: Peter Lang.

Mossialos, E., McKee, M., Palm, W. *et al.* (2001) 'The Influence of EU Law on the Social Character of Healthcare Systems in the European Union', Report submitted to the Belgian Presidency of the European Union, 19 November 2001.

Niemann, A. (1998) 'The PHARE Programme and the Concept of Spillover: Neofunctionalism in the Making', *Journal of European Public Policy* 5 (3): 428–446.

Ranade, W. (ed.) (1998) *Markets and Health Care: A Comparative Analysis*, Harlow, UK: Longman.

Springer, B. (1992) *The Social Dimension of 1992: Europe Faces a New EC*, New York: Praeger.

Steffen, M. (2004) 'AIDS and Health Policy Responses in European Welfare States', *Journal of European Social Policy*, 14 (2): 159–175.

Vobruba, G. (2003) 'The Enlargement Crisis of the European Union: Limits on the Dialectics of Integration and Expansion', *Journal of European Social Policy* 13 (1): 35–62.

Wincott, D. (1996) 'The Court of Justice and the European Policy Process', in J. Richardson (ed.) *European Union: Power and Policy-Making*, London: Routledge, pp. 170–184.

Index

www.ingramcontent.com/pod-product-compliance
Ingram Content Group UK Ltd.
Pitfield, Milton Keynes, MK11 3LW, UK
UKHW020353010325
455677UK00021B/438